CRITICAL INSIGHTS

All the Pretty Horses

CRITICAL INSIGHTS

All the Pretty Horses

Editors
Laura Nicosia, PhD
Montclair State University
James F. Nicosia, PhD
Montclair State University

SALEM PRESS
A Division of EBSCO Information Services, Inc.
Ipswich, Massachusetts

GREY HOUSE PUBLISHING

Cover photo: delectus, via iStock.

Critical Insights: All the Pretty Horses, published by Grey House Publishing, Inc., Amenia, NY, under exclusive license from EBSCO Information Services, Inc.

∞ The paper used in these volumes conforms to the American National Standard for Permanence of Paper for Printed Library Materials, Z39.48 1992 (R2009).

Publisher's Cataloging-in-Publication Data
(Prepared by Parlew Associates, LLC)

Names: Nicosia, Laura, editor. | Nicosia, James F., editor.
Title: Critical insights : all the pretty horses / Laura Nicosia and James F. Nicosia, editors.
Description: Ipswich, MA : Salem Press, a division of EBSCO Information Services, Inc. ; Amenia, NY : Grey House Publishing, 2023. | Series: Critical insights. | Includes bibliographic references and index.
Identifiers: ISBN 9781637004364 (hardback)
Subjects: LCSH: McCarthy, Cormac, -- 1933-1923 – Biography. | McCarthy, Cormac, -- 1933-1923 – All the Pretty Horses -- Criticism and interpretation. | Western stories – Criticism and interpretation. | BISAC: LITERARY CRITICISM / American / Regional. | LITERARY CRITICISM / Modern / 20th Century. | LITERARY CRITICISM / Reference.
Classification: LCC PS3563.C337 A4 2023 | DDC 813.54--dc23

First Printing

PRINTED IN THE UNITED STATES OF AMERICA

Contents

Critical Contexts

Critical Readings

Resources

About This Volume

Laura Nicosia and James F. Nicosia

It can be argued that Cormac McCarthy was a polarizing figure in American literature. The greater part of his corpus, including his 1992 novel *All the Pretty Horses* (*ATPH*), met with, usually, critical success and legions of literary fans. Others rejected his modernist tendencies and economical style inherited by such canonical literary figures as William Faulkner, Ernest Hemingway, and, to a lesser degree, Flannery O'Connor and even Mark Twain. Early reviewers called him a "man's novelist," and that certainly continued with *ATPH.* Such critics overlooked the subtle evolution of American literature exhibited in his stark but recognizable prose, preferring a more substantial postmodern ethic that rejected all things literary. McCarthy nonetheless continued to write from a place of strong stylistic foundation, opponents be damned, and his bleak 2006 novel, *The Road*, silenced most critics with its relentless desolation. Its receipt of the Pulitzer Prize made McCarthy, long admired by serious readers and critics, finally, ubiquitous. The twentieth century's most powerful critic, Harold Bloom, had long since anointed him one of the most important writers of the late-twentieth century, but his now widespread appeal (including, for better or worse, the popularization of *The Road* in movie form), cemented his place in the pantheon of American literature. His earlier corpus now had to be (re)considered. Though earlier works like *Blood Meridian* and *Suttree* had received greater general praise, *All the Pretty Horses* captured wider attention from readers and critics and achieved its status as perhaps his most readable volume.

This scholarly collection brings to light a wide range of insights into the novel that thrust McCarthy into the spotlight as one of the greatest living writers of the late twentieth-to-early twenty-first century. One of Salem's most popular series, *Critical Insights* distills the best of both class and literary criticism of the world's most studied literature. As such, this volume aims to be broad in its discussions and discourse, as well as accessible to the thoughtful reader. The essays within this collection thus attempt to provide an all—embracing critical analysis of one of the most popular and well-respected works by one of the most highly acclaimed writers of the last 40 years.

This volume features 14 in-depth, yet accessible, essays that provide readers and researchers with several avenues into the complex and elusive work that is McCarthy's *All the Pretty Horses.* It begins with two essays on the historical context and the critical reception of the novel; each of which addresses the influence of the time period, explores the influence of the text *upon* and *within* the canon, and plumbs specific details that have captured audiences at its publication, through to today's readership.

After these first four essays, the collection follows with a comparative essay, as well as an essay that utilizes a focused critical lens to provide a focused, in-depth reading of *ATPH.* The heart of the collection then includes ten readings of a wide-ranging nature that serve to whet the reader's appetite for the diversity of methodologies to read McCarthy's novel more lucidly, more thoughtfully, more informedly. The concluding sections are valuable resources for researchers, including a chronology of McCarthy's life and a comprehensive bibliography (both compiled by Montclair State University graduate assistant, Alyssa Roberts) and index. *Critical Insights* provides authoritative insights and analysis suitable for students and teachers alike. Students come away with an enriched sense of the many ways the themes can be studied, appreciated, written, and talked about, making these important connections themselves with easy-to-use guidance.

Reading McCarthy, Reading Reception

This volume begins with "*All the Pretty Horses*: McCarthy's Breakthrough into the American Canon," a brief charting of McCarthy's ascension to canonical status that came with the publication of *All the Pretty Horses.* As a bestseller, it certainly demanded attention, but along with that success also came a broader critical respect for what McCarthy had been doing all along. The novel garnered both the National Book Award and the National Book Critics Circle Award, bringing it widespread attention as both a popular and critical success. As the first of what would become the *Border Trilogy*, the novel, we contend, "famously transcends the canonical definitions of westerns or cowboy literature and in the process forges a new type of western that may or may not have any descendants."

J. Gavin Paul's comprehensive biography collects about as much as we know on McCarthy and sheds a beam of light on the life of a rather reclusive literary figure (he rarely granted interviews), and his interview with Oprah Winfrey in 2007 was one of very few opportunities readers had of hearing him share insight in his own words. As for that, the six-minute interview was not extraordinarily eye-opening or forthcoming. New Criticism is the lens of readers who believe a work can and should be evaluated entirely for what is contained within it; it reveals everything to the reader by itself and requires no external texts or considerations like authorial intention or biography to augment it. McCarthy seems to be a proponent of this approach, allowing his work to speak for itself without explanation on his part. Even when pressed by Winfrey, his own responses, while delightfully honest, revealed merely what thoughtful readers had already gleaned; the novel was likely a love letter to his son. The result is a biography and life that collects information in a thoughtful way (despite the purported autobiographical elements said to be present in *Suttree,* for example), and allows readers to engage with the novels without interference from extratextual elements. Paul lucidly concludes in his biography that one might find the best insight into McCarthy's life by attending to his final two novels, *The Passenger* and *Stella Maris,* "given their extensive gestation period and the fact that their story crisscrosses (amongst many other places) Knoxville, Chicago, New Orleans, Paris, London, Ibiza, Texas, Mexico, and even Providence, Rhode Island, where McCarthy was born, they might very well be thought of as his life's work."

Melinda Knight's masterful essay on the historical context of *All the Pretty Horses* painstakingly maps the novel's importance in context with the evolving world around it. She establishes a strong foundation for readership in acknowledging the title as having come from a traditional lullaby known as "Hush Hush-a-bye." She further recognizes that that lullaby's theme—"the promise of what will occur if children go to sleep without resisting authority by crying" is central to understanding the novel itself, as she contests: "the protagonist John Grady Cole captures the wish fulfillment of the lullaby in a scene toward the end." On his return journey to Texas, he encounters a group of children near the border who want to know more about him, and he "told them how he had come from another country, two young horsemen riding their horse, and they had met with a third who had no money or food to eat nor scarcely clothes to cover himself and that he had come to ride with them and share with them all they had" (243). John Grady tells the children everything that happened, and they debate what he could do now—"find a wise man" or "perhaps a curandera [female folk healer]" or "pray to God" (244). Although horses do figure prominently in the novel, they serve primarily as plot devices, to move the plot along, rather than as the primary subject. What the lullaby signifies, then, is the promise of a reward, which in the case of John Grady is never fulfilled. Understanding the historical context of the novel requires an analysis of two competing narratives: the frontier myth in American culture and the events of the Mexican Revolution. All of this Knight accomplishes in the first few paragraphs of her essay, and continues with a consistent metacognitive analysis of details, both primary and secondary (her critical sources are exemplary and thoughtfully selected). Knight's essay, then, is more than a charting of historical facts, and in fact, is as lucid a reading of the novel as any other critic's undertakings.

Amy Leshinsky charts the novel's evolving reception in her essay, "*All the Pretty Horses* Alters the Reception and Prestige of McCarthy." Indeed, as she remarks, "little attention had been paid to Cormac McCarthy's earlier works," although a handful of critics and literary-minded readers had recognized his talent from the start. Those early readers contend that it was only a matter of time before McCarthy was more widely recognized, and *All the Pretty Horses* in 1992 did capture popular attention. As a winner of the National

Book Award and National Book Critics Circle Award, suddenly McCarthy's name was no longer reserved for literary journals (though, ironically, many of those, like *Kirkus,* failed to appreciate the work) and instead popular magazines and newspapers were reviewing *All the Pretty Horses*. Actor/producer Brad Pitt signed on to read the audiobook version for Random House, Columbia Pictures bid for film rights, and McCarthy became, if not a household name, at least a name known to the reading public. Leshinsky deftly navigates the transition McCarthy makes from respected literary outsider to canonical writer, largely because of the work he does in this novel, and the complete *Border Trilogy* as a whole.

The Western Tradition and Ecology

Aaron A. Cloyd's "Wilderness 2.0: Redefining and Rewilding Wilderness in Cormac McCarthy's *All the Pretty Horses*," represents an exemplar of a critical-lens analysis. Cloyd begins with a recognition that the novel is a work deeply engaged with "redefining and rewilding wilderness." He goes on to explore how setting and linguistic aspects undergird three processes whereby the novel contests traditional definitions of wilderness and works toward constructing new frames of understanding such spaces. First, what is ordinarily considered extrinsic to wilderness—human culture—is brought into contact with that taken as intrinsic to wilderness—nature. McCarthy's wilderness, Cloyd notes, is a site simultaneously informed by customary "substance" of wilderness and by the human aspects traditionally excluded from or kept beyond the bounds of such locations, what could be interpreted as "sub-stance." Presented as such, McCarthy's wilderness landscapes and experiences coincide with and are thrown into relief by traces and marks of humanity. Second, within these integrative places, McCarthy's portrayals of nature and frontier spaces broaden definitions of wilderness, thereby expanding the set of values associated with concepts of wilderness. Abandoned mining equipment, ruins of a former cabin, and remains of a previous ranch augment wilderness rather than diminish it. Third, particularly through McCarthy's syntax and diminishment of humans-as-grammatical-actants, his novel shifts away from a hierarchal relation between humans and natural spaces and moves toward constructing horizontal or rhizomatic connections. Although this redefined landscape "flattens hierarchies" between environments and human presences, it also suggests that a return of nature, what Cloyd calls "a rewilding" that occurs as human artifacts decompose. As this movement toward decay is reflected in the physical diminishment of the novel's characters, McCarthy's novel presents a model for relating to rewilding wilderness spaces that shifts the focal point from humanity to considering how humans might be enfolded into the rhythms of an environment rather than remaining removed.

Comparative analysis of literary works is an unavoidable act. Indeed, readers and critics, in an attempt to make sense of their own attraction to a work, find the act of discovering archetypes and precursors to that work to be a primary consideration. No artist since Shakespeare, as noted critic Harold Bloom says, "comes without a literary forebear, and even artists as stylistically unique as McCarthy demand consideration of just how their genius has evolved." In the essay, "Cooper, McCarthy, and the Nineteenth-Century Roots of *All the Pretty Horses,*" Jericho Williams notes not only that *All the Pretty Horses* represents McCarthy's transition from an Appalachian regionalist writing to the more universal, as it were, American Western genre. He then goes on to trace, in chronologically backward fashion, how Faulkner's influence, recognizable from the outset of McCarthy's career, remained present, while more fruitful comparisons began to take shape. He notes in his work how Jonathan Swift and Washington Irving are his earliest precursors, while also recognizing how McCarthy makes room for his own work by swerving away from the Western genre as well. Williams contends that, as McCarthy "delved deeper into American history, and particularly in relation to the American West, he employed new modes and means of writing stories that also suggested connections with American literary history."

Williams traces the Western's evolution to Owen Wister's 1904 novel, *The Virginian*, and contends that *Blood Meridian* only *begins* to move away from the traditional Western. Although compelling and convincing as a neo-Western, *Blood Meridian* gives way, Williams suggests to the more "experimental" Western Romance that *ATPH* represents. In creating John Grady Cole as the centerpiece of *ATPH,* Williams argues that McCarthy subtly recreates the genre, and that Cole's "outlook recalls prior classic characters with strong moral viewpoints grappling with rapidly changing environments." The bulk of Williams's analysis then centers on a comparison with what he calls "American literature's first popular romantic literary hero," Natty Bumppo, of James Fenimore Cooper's *The Leatherstocking Tales* fame (1823–41). Each protagonist, Williams says, "intuits uncomfortable changes in his surroundings, maintains a strong moral compass, relocates as necessary, and never quite seems at home or grounded in one place, largely because the America he idealizes and desires to inhabit exists ephemerally, if at all." He also traces the development of a personal code that elevates each idealistic hero to mythic status in American literature.

Critical Readings of *All the Pretty Horses*

As this volume ventures into an explanation of individual critical analyses, it begins with a necessary ecocritical examination, Seth Forrest's "'one thing more of things she lay among': Ecological Form in McCarthy's *All the Pretty Horses.*" Drawing on the work of Angus Fletcher and Timothy Morton, Forrest develops an analysis of McCarthy's use of polysyndetic and paratactic grammar as it relates to the geologies and topographies of the Rio Grande watershed and the Madrean bioregion. McCarthy's language plumbs what Morton calls the "ambience" of this setting, casting human events among a Wordsworthian "earth's diurnal course," thus creating an ecological text. McCarthy exhibits that linear, additive storytelling is, in fact, a complex undertaking, as he analyzes McCarthy's famed use of polysyndeton and parataxis. "While the sentences themselves emerge from simple grammatical constructions of simple subjects and active verbs," Forrest argues, "they also combine and add upon each other to evoke rich and detailed descriptions." McCarthy's *Border Trilogy*, he says, utilizes "a structural principle of addition and accumulation and accretion" from the most minute constructions through the larger conceptions of plot and theme.

Allison Harl delves deeper into ecocriticism with her lucid essay, "Aldo Leopold's Land Ethic in Cormac McCarthy's *All the Pretty Horses.*" Analyzing *ATPH* through an ecocritical lens, Harl explores the characterization of John Grady Cole as a reflection of the degraded American landscape in a fragmented new world. "Fences like sutures" crisscross the bygone open frontier, foreshadowing the stitches across John Grady's wounded body after a knife fight in prison, and Harl eloquently provides that "McCarthy's use of subtle metaphors depicts an enduring life force, a natural wildness inherent in the wounded terrain marred by mechanization." McCarthy's charged prose, Harl goes on to say, "reveals the inherent natural energy at play in the interdependent systems of land and people." She then accesses Leopold, father of wildlife ecology, in his explaining the life force of all living beings works within a symbiotic cyclical balance, which ensures the health of the greater biota. John Grady then, in his disillusionment with the deteriorating landscape, demonstrates a lost code of integrity in a rapidly changing America. This ethical code, Harl says, echoes Leopold in his 1949 essay, "The Land Ethic," wherein the latter defines a "moral responsibility that derives from the conscious understanding of the interdependence of all creatures and the lands they inhabit." Yet, as his family, love, and future unravel, John Grady becomes increasingly disenfranchised, and it is only the judge who acknowledges and recognizes Cole's tenacious moral code. Ultimately, Harl celebrates John Grady's transcendent resilience, and argues that the novel presents the possibility of regeneration on the wounded landscape of American consciousness.

Rosa Parker continues the important act of analyzing the nuances of McCarthy's prose and his masterful use of polysyndeton, while tracing that practice back to McCarthy's forebear, William Faulkner. Her essay, "The Use of Polysyndeton and Cinematic Montage in William Faulkner's *As I Lay Dying* and Cormac McCarthy's *All the Pretty Horses*" highlights McCarthy's success not merely in mimicking, but in developing one of Faulkner's experimental prose stylistics. With reference to Eisenstein's pioneering films, *Strike!* (1925) and *Battleship Potemkin* (1925), her analysis sheds further light on the rich cinematic montage first established by Faulkner and developed across time and landscape within McCarthy's prose. She argues that McCarthy's style is uniquely cinematic, and suggests that his use of an Eisensteinian montage, as it relates to McCarthy's use of polysyndeton, has been overlooked to this day. In pointing to the often-revisited sentence "they rode on" in *Blood Meridian* (44), Harl evinces McCarthy's attention to sequences of events over plot, and suggests that in *ATPH,* he develops a "uniquely cinematic yet nonconformist mode of montage, exploring the effects of nontraditional uses of language." One of the central elements in Parker's analysis revolves around the concept of linguistic rhythm; she notes that, in John Grady's coming-of-age quest, he at one point "breathes in rhythm with the horse as if some part of the horse were within him breathing" (222). Parker asserts this merging of man and animal as comparable to Jewel in *As I Lay Dying*, who becomes "shaped to his horse" (9). Both Faulkner and McCarthy, she then says, draw from Eisenstein's use of intellectual montage; in *Strike!*, she recognizes, images of slaughtered cattle are juxtaposed with massacred workers, suggesting the powerlessness of both animals and humans. Throughout Parker's analysis, she maps McCarthy's cinematic montage, while drawing from Faulknerian rhythms and Eisenstein's montage style.

Elissa Greenwald then places McCarthy within a wider context in her cogent essay, "The Landscape of Grief: Dispossession and Self-Discovery in McCarthy's *All the Pretty Horses* and Virginia Woolf's *To the Lighthouse.*" In both novels, she notes, familial death opens fissures in the remaining family that threatens to tear apart each individual. She traces the similarities between McCarthy's John Grady Cole, and Woolf's adolescent protagonist, Cam Ramsay. In each novel, the teenager continues on a discrete quest to find something to reconcile their loss in a way that will inform them of the future. Greenwald's insight lies not as much in comparison, however, as it does in contrasts between the two iconic authors. McCarthy's hero, Greenwald notes, "eventually returns home to face even greater loss," while in *To the Lighthouse* there is some reconciliation for the Ramsay family. "Nature is both a nurturing and antagonistic force," Greenwald recognizes, and "both writers translate overwhelming human emotions into tumultuous and unpredictable weather and landscapes." Whereas in Woolf's novel there is at least a tentative peace within the Ramsay family, in McCarthy's, the ending remains tragic, as symbolized by the horses whose wild nature can only be intermittently tamed, thus asserting a natural world that will not yield to human desires.

Next, Stephen Daly notes the confluence between Melville's *Moby Dick* and McCarthy's *Border Trilogy*, and his analysis suggests a convergence between Melville's early novels of exploration (*Typee, Omoo), Moby Dick*, and *All the Pretty Horses.* From the opening paragraph, Daly asserts, which alludes to the "glass, darkly" of Corinthians, there is a pronounced ocularcentrism, or privilege of vision over other senses. "The visual is central to Melville not only because Melville's narrators are conduits of pictorialism," Daly says, "but because visuality forms part of the nexus of the exploratory apparatus of colonialism and its cultural offshoots—travel writing, the guidebook, and anthropology." What Daly calls "scopophilia" gives rise to a masculinist, libidinal vision of the world, and goes on to analyze various binary oppositions of presence and absence, light and dark, et al., that are inherited from Melville. Daly also recognizes how McCarthy's narrative is framed by absence and John Grady Cole is a victim of modernizing/revolutionizing processes. McCarthy's putative hero is then, for Daly, a scion of the evangelizing colonist, a figure satirized by Melville and McCarthy alike, via the doubled figure of Blevins. Grady's agency, and that of other characters, is called into question, evoking Melville's reflexive, "who ain't a slave?" McCarthy ultimately uses the genealogy and tradition of the sublime against itself—that the form's gesturing towards ineffability neatly suggests the possibility of an ethics of representation in the face of a literary tradition always and inevitably ideologically imbued.

Shubham Singh stays focused on dualities in his essay, "The Cowboy and the American Dream: Charting the Binaries of the

West in McCarthy's *All the Pretty Horses.*" Throughout the *Border Trilogy*, he asserts, each novel is "synthesized by the repetition of the act of crossing of a physical frontier: the Mexican American border." Singh asserts that the border, in each and every crossing by each and every person, represents a crossing of ideological boundaries, as well. McCarthy's cowboys pursue the American dream, Singh says, even as the textual binaries undermine the myth. The privileged North (America) dwarfs the Mexican South, with America's "civilization" in conflict with Mexico's undeveloped "wilderness." John Grady Cole, caught up in the midst of the clash between cultures and ideologies, struggles to move to the uncharted Western territory, "for the cherished ideals of civilization and industrialization in the American society challenge his own existence." The result of moving through and between these clashing ideals, Singh says, is violence, death, and suffering. The horses, meanwhile, play a unifying role in the novel for Singh: they represent a past era that is beautiful, natural, and glorious with a deeper connection to the natural landscape. They also represent constancy, and as a result, the horses become the link between dualities, and between characters.

Amanda Zastrow continues the examination of dualities, particularly those of male-female binaries, in her essay, "John Grady Cole as an Example of (Non)Traditional Western Masculinity in McCarthy's *All the Pretty Horses.*" She begins by recognizing that the term "cowboy" immediately evokes the image of a powerful, muscular, and weather-beaten man that often is synonymous with the traditional consideration of what is "masculine." He acts confidently, speaks little, and moves definitively. His clothing also implies a no-nonsense, pragmatic approach to existence; it hides the flesh out of necessity, but also as a symbolic troping of sensuality; in short, there is little sensuality in the cowboy. Zastrow asserts that a cowboy's masculinity is thus defined by what can be seen of him, while at the same time recognizing that the individual cowboy is not recognizably different from the hypothetical cowboys nearby. This concept is one that McCarthy effectively obliterates by bringing to light the "inner self" of John Grady Cole, thus un-troping the trope. In *ATPH,* Zastrow then asserts, John Grady is a person who "wants to fit the role of a traditional masculine cowboy . . . [but] emerges, rather, as a character who, on his path to coming of age, dismisses this traditional type of masculinity and adopts instead a feminized perspective of what it means to be a cowboy."

Elissa Greenwald returns to continue the necessary discussion of the masculine and feminine in her essay, "The Quest for Romantic Love: The Role of Women in *All the Pretty Horses.*" She begins by saying, "Romantic love is the catalyst that makes John Grady seem real to himself and others for the first time in his life," while acknowledging that "it is also the agent that undoes men." She then juxtaposes the story of Alejandra's grand-aunt, Dueña Alfonsa, with the life story the reader knows of John Grady; Dueña Alfonsa asserts that female independence only serves to endanger them. For John Grady, however, the loss of love "means being sentenced to an independence that seems less like freedom and more like imprisonment in the self against the empty spaces of the West."

Greenwald discerns John Grady's acquisition of his mother's empowerment and sexuality as an echo of an Edenic fall, as well as a Miltonic allusion: "They hand in hand with wand'ring steps and slow,/Through Eden took their solitary way" (Book XII, ll. 648–49). John Grady's expulsion from Eden immediately transforms him "into a different plane of being." Greenwald also recognizes how this theme—that of the banished young man seeking existential meaning—continued to be a theme throughout McCarthy's corpus and does well to provide a strong foundation for that theme here.

Amy Leshinsky also returns to share deeper insight into the role of the mother "Puppets Upon Puppets Upon Puppets: Forces at Play in the Mother's Construction in *All the Pretty Horses*," calling McCarthy a man's novelist. Early reviews of his works criticized his "limited engagement with his female characters," as he pursued the Western genre and devoted pages to understanding horses (and presumably not women). Leshinsky acknowledges that the consideration of women is something that divides critics, some claiming he lacks knowledge of them, while others suggesting his seeming avoidance of limning women in his novels actually reveals a deeper respect for women than others give him credit for—i.e., by avoiding misinterpretations and representations.

Unquestionably, Leshinsky states, while males are the primary consideration in *ATPH,* it is female characters who propel the story: "The female desire for independence controls the trajectory of John Grady's quest for self-discovery." John Grady's initial existential quest is of course necessitated by the actions of his estranged mother, to sell the ranch. In Mexico, then he seeks respite in the home of Don Héctor where his daughter, Alejandra, and Dueña Alfonsa control his fate. It is the latter who arranges his release from prison, and his decision to return to Don Héctor's home is spurred by Alejandra. Leshinsky focuses her attention on the two mother figures in the story, and the power of rejection on the young man's life to spur him to the pursuit of meaningfulness. Ironically, she suggests, Dueña Alfonsa's "resounding thoughts on the interconnectedness of humankind and the infinite tensions at play in one's actions and decisions" teaches him more about mothering and the mother-son connection than the relationship he has/does not have with his own maternal parent. "The depth and critique of women cannot be divorced from the myriad forces at play in their creation," Leshinsky says, noting that John Grady's mother "is not an invisible force in the text. Though her body remains unseen by the reader, she, like a puppet, is a visible icon on stage, residing at a hotel steeped in history, and born from a family of adventurers." In her analysis, Leshinsky sheds light on how the mother figure continues to make important statements about the myriad forces at play in American society, even as old motifs are replaced by new ones, and as previous symbols of motherhood evolve into the new century.

Sakti Sekhar Dash rounds the collection and then leaves the reader of this volume with a broad and compelling discussion of sociopolitical forces in her, "Confronting the Capitalocene: Capitalism, Culture, and Codes in *All the Pretty Horses.*" After providing perhaps the most lucid of summaries, Dash asserts that *ATPH* narrates the loss of tradition and the destruction of livelihoods. The cowboys are banished from a society that she says is steadily embracing the Capitalocene. The events of the novel coincide with the American oil boom that displaced farmers and ranchers from the pastoral life, as open spaces were replaced by oil rigs. As modernization and industrialization gained pace, Dash asserts, the pastoral gave way to a Capitalocene society. The loss of love, Dash recognizes, is not the only absence in the novel; as one of the last cowboys, John Grady belongs to the past—the tradition of farmlands, agriculture, horses, cattle, and ecology—that fades with each passing day. The inevitability of the present and anxiety of the future compel him to seek out a new way of life that ultimately involves a rejection of the pastoral. His mother has already done so, coerced by the lure of capitalism, and has sold the ranch in the opening section of the novel. Though John Grady subsequently searches for his next pastoral paradise, instead he finds a post-Edenic world of violence, selfishness, and nihilism. The ranch he joins, Dash asserts, "is nothing more than a commercial establishment driven by capitalist interests." Nature and ecology have lost their value, and are relevant only as financial institutions, and land becomes meaningless when it is no longer profitable.

McCarthy's Ongoing Legacy

The reader, fan, and critic of McCarthy all return to his work repeatedly to plumb increasingly more from his literary fiction. In *ATPH,* the more we, the editors, have read from those who proposed and submitted essays that shed new light on the novel, the more appreciation we came to have for its nuance. It continues to be a novel that eludes summary, and rewards reconsideration. Works that revise a genre, as *ATPH* is widely claimed to have done for the Western Romance, often achieve a place in history's canon, but cease to be valuable in and of themselves. *All the Pretty Horses* avoids that fate, at least for the first 30 years of its life, because it is so profound, so grim, so haunting, so esoteric, that it has not spawned many direct successors. In this way, McCarthy's work remains unique and uncanny, and thoroughly canonical. Only one-of-a-kind work such as his avoid being categorized with others like it. There are few others like it, and few other writers like him. The novel, and the author, essentially stand alone, and his recent death (in the summer of 2023) was acknowledged around the world with well-deserved tributes and accolades. We hope this volume helps to continue reaching readers with new and unique insights into this magnificent work.

All the Pretty Horses: McCarthy's Breakthrough into the American Canon

Laura Nicosia and James F. Nicosia

Dwight Garner's obituary in *The New York Times* labels Cormac McCarthy a "formidable and reclusive writer of Appalachia and the American Southwest, whose raggedly ornate early novels about misfits and grotesques gave way to the lush taciturnity of *All the Pretty Horses* and the apocalyptic minimalism of *The Road*" (1). It is certainly true that *All the Pretty Horses* stands as a pivotal work in American literature. A massive bestseller that won both the National Book Award and the National Book Critics Circle Award, the novel was the first installment of McCarthy's *Border Trilogy* series (including *The Crossing* and *Cities of the Plain*). As of this writing, Amazon ranks the novel as #27 of all-time in the Westerns category and #226 overall in the category of literary fiction.

In *All the Pretty Horses* (*ATPH*), McCarthy's narrative famously transcends the canonical definitions of westerns or cowboy literature and in the process forges a new type of western that may or may not have any descendants. It certainly does not have any rivals. In its exploration of the American landscape (a frequently visited topic in this history of American literature and cinema), McCarthy is unexpectedly successful at capturing the essence of the American spirit, defining both modernism and postmodernism, and plumbing the slippery, evolving definitions of masculinity. As in most of his works, many hardships befall the characters in this novel, but what stands out as unique to McCarthy as a writer of this particular novel is that his visions of tragedy, violence, and death transcend the well-worn genre's typically simplistic dualisms of black vs. white, hero vs. villain, civilization vs. nature, Mexican vs. American, male vs. female. A good person can do bad things, and a bad person can do good; there is more than an equal share of ethically and morally neutral actions, as well. Yet McCarthy does not merely obliterate dualities, either, as many of his contemporary writers might have been content to do; there is no throwing up of hands here to abandon the world to indeterminacy. Yet, where the needle actually falls in terms of ethics and morality is compellingly vague; in the words of critic Harold Bloom, literary novels that transcend summary and classification have some element of the "uncanny," and McCarthy's *ATPH* has the uncanny in spades.

In *ATPH*, life is full of gray zones that blur moral and ethical judgments. As Western writer James Wade explains, "[McCarthy] included all those elements from traditional Westerns, like cowboys and horses, but he also almost single-handedly brought the Western into the literary realm. . . . As Western writers we can now take chances on more metaphysical topics, and not just heroes and villains" (qtd. in Italie). What McCarthy recognizes, here and in most of the equally compelling, confounding fiction of his corpus that follows, is the randomness that surrounds contemporary existence has always been present; that marriage of modernist angst and subtly postmodern existentialism serves not so much, therefore, as a revision of twentieth-century modernist sensibilities as a correction of them. In short, his genius in reconsidering the American past suggests that this is what writers, in the vein of his forebear William Faulkner, should have been writing all along.

At its core, *ATPH* solidified McCarthy's position as one of the most esteemed writers of contemporary American letters, and perhaps even American literary history. The novel touches on numerous themes that are ingrained in the universal experience: love, loss, and the search for identity. But it also pursues these themes through a uniquely American lens using the western frontier as not just its backdrop, but also its theme. Some critics insightfully argue that the frontier, the border, and nature itself are characters in his novel. Certainly, the horses are. The novel is set in the America of 1949 and follows the story of John Grady Cole, the sixteen-year-old Texan on a horseback quest of self-discovery through the Texas and Mexican badlands. Left homeless by his family and by an America that is abandoning nature in favor of civilization, Cole is free to determine his path, even as ironically he comes to recognize that there is no literal path, westward or otherwise.

John Grady Cole's Search for Identity

Though the novel begins in a familiar place for an American Western, the reader learns along with the protagonist that life at the border between Mexico and Texas is not a Romance and that the mythology of the Western Frontier is not accurate to real life. Gordy Sauer says,"[McCarthy] stripped away the romance and the idea of romance. He forced us to look beyond the fabric of the genre and into the stitching, to understand how it was made" (qtd. in Italie). In short, it is a novel that does not merely destroy myths, or prop up convenient ones to replace them, but a novel that asks readers to revisit myths, and the novel itself; repeated readings of the novel and reconsiderations of its characters and themes reward multiple reconsiderations. Only the strongest works of literature achieve such summits.

All the Pretty Horses traces the protagonist, sixteen-year-old John Grady Cole, on his physical and existential quest to find himself and his evaporating legacy—concomitant with the modern erosion of the mythology of the frontier borderlands. Cole has lost his grandfather (on page one of the novel) and consequently, through a series of guilt-ridden divorce terms, he also loses control of his family ranch. His mother abandons the young boy to find her life's purpose and in so doing, sets the young man adrift in a world that does not care about his need for security and safety.

Despite his near psychic connection to the ranch's horses, Cole sets out with his best friend Lacey Rawlins to make his mark as a ranch hand and work his way back to eventually owning his own property (again) and reclaiming his family's legacy. Along his journey, Cole finds love, tempts fate, and flouts social conventions, stands for a personal code, and pays the price for his choices. At each moment, whether he is pondering his place in the universe, looking to earn his badge of manhood, or fighting the good fight, *ATPH* has been called a "meta-Western" by Rachel Kushner (qtd. in Italie). Such hyphenated phrases venerate the literature of our times that transcend simple classification, even works such as those that may anger critics who do not like what they read.

Juxtaposing the Silent Landscape and Gruesome Human Violence: A Liminal Space

McCarthy uses the overwhelming and poignant silence of the landscape as a liminal place for introspection, contemplation, and awareness of an "existential compulsion" (Italie). His mastery of sensory data and silence as narrative tools, hint at the unsaid and accentuate the characters' internal struggles along their quest:

> He lay on his back in his blankets and looked out where the quartermoon lay cocked over the heel of the mountains. In that false blue dawn the Pleiades seemed to be rising up into the darkness above the world and dragging all the stars away, the great diamond of Orion and Cepella [sic] and the signature of Cassiopeia all rising up through the phosphorous dark like a sea-net. He lay a long time listening to the others breathing in their sleep while he contemplated the wildness about him, the wildness within. (McCarthy 60)

There are no direct thoughts, no comments. All the reader experiences, with uncanny McCarthian immediacy—is what Cole experiences—immense skies, rolling hills, powerful thunderstorms, desert heat, predatory animals, and so on that evoke a sense of how small humans are in this universe. Yet, despite the harshness of that landscape, John Grady longs for and pursues a love of this American frontier and mourns its steady disappearance in the face of westward expansion, and the encroachment of technology and civilization.

The nostalgia McCarthy evokes through his vivid descriptions, lyrical syntax, and artistic use of silence, makes room in its absenting for the construction of a new American mythology. This mythology echoes an aching melancholy for the bygone era of Stetson-wearing cowboys astride magnificent steeds, the simplicity of good overcoming evil, and landscapes that were once lush and untainted by western civilization. Hillel Italie has said that McCarthy, throughout his corpus, "captured the duality of the gritty realism alongside the stark beauty and power of the landscape" and showed "how a place can belong to a person as much as a person can belong to a place." McCarthy's portrayal—the word seems more accurate for him than "description"—of landscapes and horses offer a literary portal through which both characters and readers are immersed within the natural while the distinctions between the things "out there" are blurred with the interiority of the individual. McCarthy frequently juxtaposes the expansiveness of the universe with the smallness John Grady feels, and the existential angst he feels is palpable. But it does not completely defeat him.

McCarthy's Literary Heritage: Melville, Faulkner, and Hemingway

It has been said that " Cormac McCarthy is the worthy disciple both of Melville and Faulkner. I venture that no other living American novelist, not even Pynchon, has given us a book as strong and memorable" (Bloom). McCarthy exhibits Melville's and Faulkner's tendencies toward being what Italie calls "excavators of the American spirit whose biblically influenced prose raised their narratives to tragic and poetic heights." Superlatives seem to find a way into critics' descriptions of McCarthy at every turn.

In *The New York Times* review of the novel, Madison Smartt Bell praises McCarthy's diction, language, and syntax:

> Powered by long, tumbling many-stranded sentences, his descriptive style is elaborate and elevated, but also used effectively to frame realistic dialogue, for which his ear is deadly accurate. This mixture builds on Faulkner's work, yet, more than Faulkner ever did, Mr. McCarthy seems to be pulling the language apart at its roots. He's noted for archaisms so unfamiliar they appear to be neologisms. His diction and phrasing come from all over the evolutionary history of English and combine into a prose that seems to invent itself as it unfolds, resembling Elizabethan language in its flux of remarkable possibilities. (9)

Considering McCarthy's lyrical language, existential quest, ethical codes, and deferral to the powers of all mighty nature, it is common to recognize an almost biblical sacredness to his storytelling. It is easy to recognize, of course, the stylistic qualities of stream-of-consciousness inherited from Faulkner; writers have, after all, mimicked the Faulknerian style that eliminates much punctuation, including and especially quotation marks. However, McCarthy succeeds, in ways few since Faulkner before him does, in bringing an immediacy into the work via its internality. In short, readers experience the world along with John Grady Cole, with little sense of narrative intervention. It is a quality that realistic writers of the turn of the twentieth century aimed to achieve, but only a handful of writers pursued—or succeeded at—afterward.

In this way, the novel also echoes the distinctly American narrative style expertly deployed by Hemingway. Garner is insightful in his assessment: "His prose was now rich but austere, shorn of most punctuation. It owed more to Hemingway than to Faulkner." The sparse dialogue, lack of quotation marks, richly descriptive passages, and poetic diction of *ATPH* are aimed at evoking an immediate, visceral response from the reader, one that coincides with McCarthy's protagonist. In this way, McCarthy proves the phenomenological insight that Georges Poulet famously (but perhaps unpopularly for twenty-first century cultural critics) states, "Whenever I read, I mentally pronounce an *I,* and yet the *I* which I pronounce is not myself" (60). Author and reader soon achieve a Pouletian "common consciousness" (62), thanks to McCarthy's withdrawal of an active narrator out from between the reader and the text. There is an authenticity here, then, that belies the stylistics; one is inclined to believe that literary prose obscures the realism of a narrative experience, yet here it is just that literary quality that ironically confirms the immediacy of the experience.

As with some of Hemingway's prose, there are moments of confusion about who-is-speaking-with-whom. Take for instance, this passage from the second page of the novel:

> I appreciate you lightin the candle, he said.
> Cómo?
> La candela. La vela.
> No fui yo, she said.
> La señora?

Claro.
Ya se levantó?
Anges que yo. (McCarthy 4)

There are no names offered, no identity for who "he" or "she" might be. There are no quotation marks, and no clear relationship between the two speakers. There is no Spanish translation and no key to help build language comprehension. This is the way listeners would, and do, experience the world. Much like Hemingway's iconic short stories "A Clean Well-Lighted Place" and "Hills Like White Elephants," readers are allowed, as it were, to build their own understanding through immersion and context over the span of the narrative—and over the span of the landscape as they traverse borders with John Grady Cole.

Additionally, like Hemingway's heroes, McCarthy's John Grady learns the steep price he must pay for believing in and living by a personal and heroic code that may not coincide with the ethics and morals of the place and era to which he belongs/does not belong. From the outset, one recognizes how, despite his age and seeming representation of new ideas, John Grady possesses ideals that are passé, and thus earns him sympathy, and perhaps even pity. Consequently, both he and the readers must confront the harsh realities of life along the border and oftentimes, must shatter any romanticized notions of what it means to be a hero or to live a life of sacrifice for a "greater good."

John Grady Cole's sidekicks—his lifelong friend, Lacey Rawlins, and tagalong troublemaker, Jimmy Blevins—are foils and provocateurs for him. One might even declare that Blevins is the trickster figure, too. Peter Matthiessen even goes as far as saying, "Jimmy Blevins will take a place as one of the great characters of American literature" (back cover McCarthy). For his part, Blevins is reminiscent of any number of characters readers may encounter in any number of the darker stories by Mark Twain. Blevins has even been referred to as an "urchin" in his mischievous nature ("*All the Pretty Horses*"). He is alternatingly funny and a troublemaker, an enigma and a stock character. Throughout the narrative, Blevins's mere presence causes the John Grady/Lacey Rawlins duo to experience both danger and adventures.

The Power of McCarthy's Prose

As a craftsman of words, McCarthy's command of the English language and his ability to limn vivid landscapes with his words is akin to poetry: "The novel's hero, as in the five [novels] that came before, is the English language—or perhaps I should say the American language" (Shelby Foote, qtd. on the back cover). It is true that the language of *ATPH* is elevated even as it possesses an almost ethereal, transparent quality; it captures a stark beauty of the southwestern frontier. Concomitantly while probing this nearly metaphysical rendering of the landscape, McCarthy delves into the oftentimes contradictory depths of the human condition—the powerful emotions of love and despair, anger and happiness, desire and contentment. John Grady Cole is a simple man—yet, as limbed, he is as complex and thoroughly rounded as any literary hero.

With his economy of words, the author constructs a worldview that exudes an enduring impact on reader response, hearts, and minds. There are moments of quiet awe in the text:

> He [John Grady] lifted the blanket and placed it on the animal's back and smoothed it and stood stroking the animal and talking to it and then he bent and picked up the saddle and lifted it with the cinches strapped up and the off stirrup hung over the horn and sat it on the horse's back and rocked it into place. The horse never moved. He bent and reached under and pulled up the strap and cinched it. The horse's ears went back and he talked to it and then pulled up the cinch again and he leaned against the horse and talked to it just as if it were neither crazy nor lethal. (McCarthy 106)

Along with depictions that are hauntingly beautiful, there are moments of and enervating brutality, like the bloody assassination attempt made on John Grady in a Mexican prison that runs through pages 198–201. Throughout the four pages of violent action, there is not one word uttered—only narrative. The first words to break the silence of the struggle are John Grady's utterance: "no me moleste"

(202). In this moment of his physical vulnerability and near-fatal injuries, John Grady sounds almost childlike—closest to the sixteen-year-old that he really is.

Loss, Love, and Loneliness

All the Pretty Horses stands as a pivotal work in the canon of American literature. Its evocative prose, profound themes, meditations on the human experience, and moral, ethical, and sociopolitical considerations, each serve to transport readers to a liminal and swiftly eroding frontier landscape. The novel is quiet, has long and seemingly meandering sentences, uses no dialog markings, and rests firmly in a genre that many consider passé and antiquated. However, this first volume of the *Border Trilogy* is a masterpiece.

Although the titular horses of the novel are seemingly the most sacred and pure living creatures on the frontier, John Grady Cole is a horse breaker who also (perhaps) ultimately breaks the reader's heart; he takes the very beasts he knows better than himself and subdues them to his command. On his journey through loss, love, and exile, the reader sees through his eyes, feels through his emotions, yearns for his success, and exhorts him through his trials. It has been said that "it's John Grady's conscientious striving for [integrity] that makes him Mr. McCarthy's most appealing character" (Bell). This much is true; John Grady Cole is a simple, yet complicated young man worthy of sympathy and analysis.

Tragedy and incarceration follow his illicit affair with love interest Alejandra. Her dark beauty and air of sadness follow the couple throughout their passionate encounters. After their doomed affair is cut short, John Grady Cole is never quite the same. While he found love, and perhaps a sense of his growing manhood, his romantic involvement with Alejandra is the catalyst for loss, violence, and pain. The novel traces John Grady throughout his quest to fill the voids left by this encounter—and to right the many wrongs done to him and by him.

Like his pensive and private protagonist, Cormac McCarthy, the author, quietly avoided the limelight and shunned the publicity most authors pursue: "By [McCarthy's] single-minded commitment to his work and his apparent indifference to the rewards and aggrandizements quite openly pursued by the rest of us, he puts most other American writers to shame. The work itself repays the tight focus of his attention with its finely wrought craftsmanship and its ferocious energy" (Bell). *All the Pretty Horses* was the sixth of the twelve novels McCarthy wrote (among several screenplays, short stories, and two plays) and many would say that it changed the course of his storied and lauded career. He died at the age of 89, on 13 June 2023 in Santa Fe, New Mexico.

Works Cited

"*All the Pretty Horses*: Vol. 1 of the *Border Trilogy*." *Kirkus Reviews.* 1 Apr. 1992, kirkusreviews.com/book-reviews/cormac-mccarthy/all-the-pretty-horses/.

Bell, Madison Smartt. "The Man Who Understood Horses." Review of *All the Pretty Horses, by Cormac McCarthy. The New York Times.* 17 May 1992, p. 9, nytimes.com/1992/05/17/books/all-the-pretty-horses.html.

Bloom, Harold. "Introduction." *Blood Meridian,* by Cormac McCarthy. Jan. 2002, penguinrandomhouse.com/books/110472/blood-meridian-by-cormac-mccarthy/.

Garner, Dwight. "Cormac McCarthy, 89, Literary Loner in a Dark World Is Dead." *The New York Times*, Section A:1, 14 June 2023.

Italie, Hillel. "For Novelists of Westerns, Cormac McCarthy Transcended—and Reinvented—the Genre." *Britannica,* britannica.com/news/353897/bac0f386d742d33ddd413ab3030ff6f2.

McCarthy, Cormac. *All the Pretty Horses*. Alfred A. Knopf, 1992.

Cormac McCarthy: A Biography

J. Gavin Paul

Early Life

Charles Joseph McCarthy was born in Providence, Rhode Island, on July 20, 1933, at a time and in a place that seem worlds remote from the violent, lush landscapes that have come to define his fiction. The first-born son and third child of six (three sisters and two brothers) born to Charles McCarthy and Gladys Christina McGrail McCarthy, he was named after his father but at some point before the publication of his first novel later legally changed his name to Cormac, a Gaelic nickname that some of his Irish aunts used for his father. The McCarthy family moved to Knoxville, Tennessee, in 1937 when his father, a Yale-educated lawyer, took a position with the Tennessee Valley Authority (TVA), a federally owned agency devoted to developing the infrastructure and industry of the state as part of President Roosevelt's New Deal.

McCarthy's intense curiosity and keen perception of the natural world flourished during his adolescence in Knoxville. He remarked in a 1992 *New York Times* profile, "I had every hobby there was. There was no hobby I didn't have, name anything, no matter how esoteric, I had found it and dabbled in it" (qtd. in Woodward 31). Despite, or perhaps because of, his aptitude and wide-ranging pursuits, McCarthy had little interest in school or academic achievement, a point that no doubt created some tension in his relationship with his parents: "I was not what they had in mind. . . . I felt early on I wasn't going to be a respectable citizen. I hated school from the day I set foot in it" (qtd. in Woodward 31). As he explored the woods and vales near his family's acreage, McCarthy's imagination gravitated toward those living on the ragged edges of society, clinging to sensibilities and ways of life that were coming under threat by the mid-point of century. Perhaps we catch a glimpse of his wanderings in the young protagonist of *The Orchard Keeper*, McCarthy's first novel (published in 1965): "These nights he could not bear to be in the house. He would go out after dinner and come back at bedtime—and then out again . . . walking the dark roads, passing by the shacks and houses, the people illuminated yellowly behind the window lights in gestures mute and enigmatic" (66). The downtrodden and rural poor would populate his early novels, the first four of which are all set in Appalachia, primarily in Tennessee.

Education

McCarthy graduated from Catholic High School in Knoxville in 1951 and entered the liberal arts program at the University of Tennessee. He would leave university after one year, enlisting in the Air Force in 1953. He served for four years, two of which were spent stationed in Alaska where he worked as a radio disc jockey. McCarthy described his time in the Air Force as "too grim an experience" (qtd. in Luce and Turpin 114) to inspire much creative work, but he used his downtime in the service to read extensively. The relative independence of his position in Alaska meant that he could "work at night and fish in the daytime" (Luce, *Vocation* 4). In his words, "I read a lot of books very quickly" (qtd. in Woodward 31). Although no writing survives from this period, McCarthy has described his voracious reading habits as essential to the development of his craft; in a 1969 interview, his "practical advice" for aspiring writers is "to read. You have to know what's been done. And you have to understand it. I like the gutsy writers—Dostoyevski [sic], Tolstoy, Joyce, Faulkner. I like Melville, particularly, and . . . Flannery O'Connor. She has a wonderful sense of the macabre" (qtd. in Luce and Turpin 116). McCarthy's aesthetic appreciation for O'Connor's unsettling depictions of the morbid and grotesque speaks to his own interest in uncompromising representations of abject horror and violence. That McCarthy's sonorous prose is so frequently in the service of describing humanity's darkest impulses is, it must be said, at the heart of his unique affective aura. In the words of Steven Frye, "one must reconcile the lyrical power of the author's language and narrative style, which blends words and imagery in a remarkable alchemy of the sublime and the picturesque, with a rendering of violence and depravity largely unparalleled in Western literature" (70).

After his discharge in 1957, McCarthy returned to the University of Tennessee, where he would spend the next three years (though he would leave without taking a degree). It was during this second stint at university that he began to write in earnest. Using the name "C.J. McCarthy, Jr.," he published two short stories in the university's literary magazine, *The Phoenix*: "Wake for Susan" (1959) and "A Drowning Incident" (1960); he received the Ingram-Merrill Award for creative writing in 1959, a $125 prize that was renewed the following year. The earliest surviving drafts of *The Orchard Keeper* are dated 1959. McCarthy left Tennessee in 1960, moving to Chicago, where he revised this first novel while working in an auto parts warehouse. He married Lee Holleman, a fellow U of T student, in early 1961; their son, Cullen, was born in 1962. McCarthy describes "living in cellars, on unemployment and welfare" (qtd. in Luce *Vocation* 13) in a 1962 letter, and by the end of that year the new family had returned to Tennessee, though their marriage would soon be over, with the couple divorcing in 1963. McCarthy's submission of *The Orchard Keeper* was accepted by Random House and published in 1965. His editor for the first two decades of his career would be Albert Erskine, the longtime editor of William Faulkner, whose stylistic and thematic influences—dense descriptive passages, long and complex sentences with ornate diction, a fascination with the grotesqueries of human nature, traumatized protagonists, and fading southern societies haunted by the past—are conspicuous in McCarthy's earliest work.

Writing Career: *The Orchard Keeper* and Other Publications

The reception of *The Orchard Keeper* would establish a general pattern for the first half of McCarthy's career as a novelist: critical acclaim accompanied by essentially no commercial success. The story tracks three individuals living in rural spaces around Knoxville in the late 1930s and early 1940s, none of whom ever completely understands the full significance or ramifications of their actions in the lives of the others: bootlegger Marion Sylder has killed young John Wesley Rattner's father, dumping the corpse on the property of aged Arthur Ownby. Rattner finds distorted paternal models in both Sylder and Ownby against a larger thematic backdrop that "criticizes the destructive forces of industrial civilization, implicitly embodied in the various improvement projects of the Tennessee Valley Authority" (Frye 21). Reviewers of the novel tended to laud McCarthy's lyrical engagements with Faulkner specifically and southern literature generally (the book would win the 1966 William Faulkner Foundation Award for notable first novel). While McCarthy's arresting linguistic and stylistic talents were evident from the outset, the dense narrative threads of this first novel proved less than popular with readers. Nevertheless, McCarthy's promise won him an American Academy of Arts and Letters travel fellowship worth $5000. In August 1965, he would set sail for Ireland; while on board the *Sylvania*, he would meet Anne DeLisle, an Englishwoman who worked on the ship as a singer and dancer. The two would marry in England in 1966.

McCarthy worked on revisions of his second novel, *Outer Dark*, and also began to compose what would become his third and fourth novels—*Child of God* and *Suttree*—while he and his wife ventured through Europe. They saw Italy and Switzerland, lived in London and Paris, and spent a year in Ibiza, off the coast of Spain. The two returned to the United States in late 1967 and eventually settled in Rockford, Tennessee, in 1968, the year *Outer Dark* was published. McCarthy and Anne bought an abandoned dairy barn that McCarthy slowly and steadily renovated into something that suited their needs. The appeal of this unconventional living space was both the relative solitude that it afforded McCarthy, as well as the opportunity to shape the space to his creative vision. They gathered bricks, stones, and roofing slates from nearby properties that had been abandoned; planks for the ceiling were from a local mill; a one-ton rock was hauled in to serve as the hearth (Luce and Turpin 122). The house was built "of refuse and rubble," said McCarthy in a 1971 interview (qtd. in Luce and Turpin 122), adding that "My ideal would be to be completely independent. . . . But I don't want to be cut off from society and have to make some compromise" (qtd. in Luce and Turpin 121). As McCarthy continued to write and work on the new home, reviewers weighed in on *Outer Dark*. This second novel has an archaic, recognizably southern setting, though no precise details are given in terms of time period or specific locations. At its core is a primal sin: a brother (Culla) and sister (Rinthy) produce a child born of incest, which the brother deserts in the forest, telling his sister it has died. The surviving newborn is, in fact, taken by an itinerant tinker, and Culla and Rinthy wander separately through a folkloric, often nightmarish world that is terrorized by a murderous "triune" of outlaws who loom in the shadows of the narrative and bring forth infernal judgement. Although some critics were dismissive of McCarthy's experiments in the southern gothic and the southern grotesque, the prevailing sentiment was that the novel was proof of McCarthy's burgeoning talents and his ability to grapple with enduring human themes. This promise took a more material form when McCarthy was awarded a Guggenheim Fellowship for creative writing in 1969, a welcome financial boost.

McCarthy might have been willing to "compromise" by maintaining some contact with society while living in rustic seclusion, but his artistic vision held no room for concessions or half measures. Evidence of this can be seen in McCarthy's next novel, *Child of God*, published in 1974, an unflinching look at humanity's most horrific impulses. Thought to be loosely based on an actual murder in Sevier County, Tennessee, *Child of God* centers on Lester Ballard, a twenty-seven-year-old outcast who finds himself dispossessed of his family's property and driven to commit increasingly violent and perverse crimes against the community that has rejected him. A voyeur, a murderer, a necrophile: Ballard's alienation is absolute and no boundary—physical, social, or moral—is safe from his transgressions. McCarthy's devilish twist is that, like nearly all of his protagonists throughout his career, Ballard's thoughts and interiority are hidden from readers, greatly complicating matters of either outright condemnation or sympathy. That Ballard might be "A child of God much like yourself perhaps" (6) is the novel's central, haunting challenge that readers are invited to consider.

McCarthy had received a $6000 advance for *Child of God*, and an additional $6000 when he submitted the manuscript (Luce, *Vocation* 240). He would use some of these funds to travel west, working out of Tucson, Arizona, in 1974 as he began meticulously researching what he cryptically referred to in correspondence as his "Western," the novel that would eventually become what is generally thought to be his masterpiece, *Blood Meridian*. McCarthy's work had gained the attention of director and producer Richard Pearce, who in 1975 hired the novelist to produce a screenplay, *The Gardener's Son*, for public television. Set in a South Carolina town in the late-nineteenth century, the film is based on historical events: the murder of a mill owner by an impoverished young man. Describing his tragic hero in 1975, McCarthy noted, "Robert McEvoy grows up being a black sheep, the bad boy of the town. That was familiar to me. . . . The kid was a natural rebel, probably just a troublemaker in real life. But in our film he has a certain nobility" (qtd. in Luce and Turpin 127). The screenplay experience was evidently a positive one for McCarthy, as he remained interested in producing them throughout his career; Pearce and McCarthy planned to team up again to produce a film version of Faulkner's *As I Lay Dying*, but the requisite financing was never secured. Two novels from later in McCarthy's career—*Cities of the Plain* (1998) and *No Country for Old Men* (2005)—both began as screenplays, and McCarthy's original screenplay, *The Counselor*, was directed by Ridley Scott and released in 2013.

McCarthy and DeLisle separated in 1976 and formally divorced a few years later. After another stop in Tucson, McCarthy moved to El Paso, Texas, in 1978. The following year *Suttree* was published, a story that McCarthy had been drafting since the early 1960s. This novel shifts the focus from rural Tennessee to urban Knoxville in the 1950s, tracing the misadventures and existential musings of Cornelius Suttree, a hard-drinking member of a wealthy family who prefers the company of the wastrels and drunks of McAnally Flats and other Knoxville slums. It is tempting to mine this novel for autobiographical details, especially since it is populated with characters who share names with McCarthy's associates from his time in Knoxville. A widespread readership for his work remained elusive, but McCarthy was steadily gaining recognition as a major voice in American letters. In 1981, he was awarded a MacArthur Fellowship—what is now often referred to as a "genius" grant. The financial support was substantial: $236,000 over a five-year period. McCarthy met Nobel-prize winning physicist Murray Gell-Mann at a dinner for MacArthur fellows and the two became friends. Gell-Mann later became a founder of the Santa Fe Institute, a meeting place for intellectuals in the arts and sciences that would come to play an increasingly significant role in McCarthy's life—he would become a member of the Institute in 2001 and remains a trustee to this day.

The MacArthur prize enabled McCarthy to move to El Paso permanently in 1982, where he bought a house and continued researching and writing *Blood Meridian*. This novel would mark the beginning of his "western" phase of books, all of which refashion and undermine familiar archetypes of the American West. *Blood Meridian; or, The Evening Redness in the West* was published in 1985. McCarthy once again turned to history to find his subject matter, this time setting his sights on the Glanton gang, a group of marauders and scalp hunters who terrorized both sides of the Texas-Mexico border in the 1840s and 1850s. The ostensible protagonist is known only as "the kid"; although he regularly slides from view in the episodic narrative, the kid bears witness to, and participates in, an unfathomable series of atrocities against Native Americans and Mexicans. Acts of horrific violence are the central engine driving the narrative, punctuating seemingly every page. The book's unforgettable character is Judge Holden, a massive albino (and perhaps otherworldly) figure who waxes poetic and philosophic on all manner of topics as the gang wanders from bloodbath to bloodbath across a pitiless landscape. Amidst the relentless violence is McCarthy's majestic language; readers have found echoes in the novel of Faulkner, Shakespeare, Dostoyevsky, Milton, Melville, and the King James Bible.

It would take some time before *Blood Meridian* came to be recognized as one of the greatest novels of the twentieth century. McCarthy's popular and commercial breakthrough, however, was not far away: it would happen with his next publication, *All the Pretty Horses* (1992), the first installment in his *Border Trilogy*.

After his longtime editor at Random House, Albert Erskine, retired, McCarthy began a new partnership with Gary Fisketjon at Knopf. A publicity campaign for McCarthy's most accessible work to date led to 100,000 copies being sold in under a year, with 300,000 paperback copies being sold by 1994 (Arnold and Luce 9, 10); this success also sparked interest in McCarthy's back catalogue, which began to be reprinted with more diligence. *All the Pretty Horses* won the National Book Award for Fiction (1992) and the National Book Critics Circle Award (1993), and a film adaptation would be produced in 2000. After thirty years of writing and six novels, McCarthy was now a household name. John Grady Cole is sixteen years old when *All the Pretty Horses* begins; dispossessed of his family's ranchlands he heads south into Mexico hunting the cowboy's way of life that is fast disappearing in 1948. His quest yields a temporary glimpse of the paradise he is seeking, but he must eventually return to the United States, his innocence shattered by heartbreak and death. The next volume in the trilogy, *The Crossing* (1994) was greatly anticipated, with a first printing of 200,000 copies (Arnold and Luce 10). This book moves backwards in time, beginning just prior to World War II, and introduces a new central figure, Billy Parham; after trapping a wolf on his family's property, Billy makes the first of a series of increasingly ruinous crossings into Mexico in an attempt to return the wolf to the wild. The final volume of the trilogy, *Cities of the Plains*, was published in 1998; it brings John Grady and Billy together as ranch hands in Alamogordo, New Mexico, in 1952, where John Grady's desire for a Mexican prostitute leads to a final shattering of whatever frail, romantic idealism either man still possesses.

The year 1998 marked another change in McCarthy's life: he married Jennifer Winkley and his son, John Francis, was born. The new family would move to Santa Fe in 2001; there, McCarthy continued to write and settled into an ongoing residency at the Santa Fe Institute (he drafted an institutional mission statement in 2014). McCarthy and Winkley divorced in 2006. Creatively, the first decade of the new century would prove to be a prolific one: two more novels were published—*No Country for Old Men* in 2005, and *The Road* in 2006—each of which exemplified a sparser, less ornate style of writing, and each of which would contribute to McCarthy's soaring fame. *No Country for Old Men* transported McCarthy's fascination with Texas-Mexico border crossings to the 1980s; raging drug wars provide the backdrop to the story: Llewellyn Moss happens upon the aftermath of a drug deal gone bad and leaves the scene with a satchel of two million dollars. He is hunted by assassin Anton Chigurh—another unforgettable entry in McCarthy's pantheon of philosophizing, psychopathic villains—and by an aged sheriff, Ed Tom Bell, who is overwhelmed by the inexplicable violence of the modern world. Acclaimed directors Joel and Ethan Coen filmed a very faithful adaptation of the novel that won four Academy Awards in 2008, including Best Picture and Best Director. McCarthy attended the awards with John Francis, and it is to his son that *The Road* is dedicated. John Francis would have been around eight years old at the time of its publication, likely the same age as the nameless boy in the novel who is moving through a lifeless, ashen world with his nameless father. The fable-like quality of a father and son's enduring love in a post-apocalyptic setting struck a chord with readers and *The Road*'s success was guaranteed when Oprah Winfrey made it a selection for her influential Book Club. McCarthy sat down for his first televised interview with Winfrey where he answered questions about his writing process, the origins of *The Road* and its message—"we should be grateful"—and his belief in God—"it would depend on what day you ask me. I don't think you have to have a clear idea of who or what God is in order to pray" ("Cormac"). *The Road* won the Pulitzer Prize for literature in 2007, and a film adaptation was released in 2009.

After the success of *The Road*, each passing year brought with it an increased possibility of it being McCarthy's final published work. Clearly content to be out of the public eye and amongst scientists at the Santa Fe Institute, he produced an essay, "The Kekulé Problem," on the relationship between language and the unconscious mind in 2017. There had long been rumors of another novel, *The Passenger*, set in New Orleans, perhaps with a female protagonist, which would be a first for McCarthy. Remarkably, this book, references to which exist in McCarthy's correspondence as far back as 1980 (Luce, *Vocation* 13) was published as two, linked novels in 2022: *The Passenger* and *Stella Maris*. Together, the two books tell the story of Bobby Western, an itinerant salvage diver, and his younger sister, Alicia, a brilliant mathematician—both Westerns are haunted by their desire for each other and their father's participation in the creation of the atomic bomb. Given their extensive gestation period and the fact that their story crisscrosses (amongst many other places) Knoxville, Chicago, New Orleans, Paris, London, Ibiza, Texas, Mexico, and even Providence, Rhode Island, where McCarthy was born, they might very well be thought of as his life's work. Cormac McCarthy died June 12, 2023, at home in Santa Fe, New Mexico. He was 89.

Works Cited

Arnold, Edwin T., and Dianne C. Luce. "Introduction." *Perspectives on Cormac McCarthy*. Edited by Edwin T. Arnold and Dianne C. Luce, 1999, pp. 1–16.

"Cormac McCarthy on Writing." *Oprah.com*, www.oprah.com/oprahsbookclub/cormac mccarthy-on-writing.

Frye, Steven. *Understanding Cormac McCarthy*. U South Carolina P, 2009.

Luce, Dianne C. *Embracing Vocation: Cormac McCarthy's Writing Life, 1959–1974*. U South Carolina P, 2023.

__________, and Zachary Turpin. "Cormac McCarthy Interviews in Tennessee and Kentucky, 1968–1980." *The Cormac McCarthy Journal*, vol. 20, no. 2, 2022, pp. 108–35.

McCarthy, Cormac. *All the Pretty Horses*. Alfred A. Knopf, 1992.

__________. *Blood Meridian*, or *The Evening Redness in the West*, Random House, 1985.

__________. *Child of God*. 1973, Picador, 2011.

__________. *Cities of the Plains*. Alfred A. Knopf, 1998.

__________. "Cormac McCarthy's Venomous Fiction." Interview by Richard B. Woodward. *New York Times Magazine*, 19 Apr. 1992, pp. 28–31+.

__________. *The Crossing*. Alfred A. Knopf, 1994.

__________. *The Gardener's Son*. Adapted from a Screenplay (*Blood Meridian*) by Cormac McCarthy. Directed by Richard Pearce. PBS Series "Visions," 1975.

__________. *No Country for Old Men*, Alfred A. Knopf, 1995.

__________. *The Orchard Keeper*. 1965, Vintage, 1993.

__________, *Outer Dark*. Random House, 1968.

__________. *The Passenger*. Alfred A. Knop, 2022.

__________. The Road. Alfred A. Knopf, 2006.

__________. Stella Maris, Alfred A. Knopf, 2022.

__________. *Suttree*. Random House, 1979.

CRITICAL CONTEXTS

All the Pretty Horses: McCarthy's Vision of Frontier Myths and Revolutionary Struggles

Melinda Knight

Cormac McCarthy's novel, *All the Pretty Horses,* was published in 1992 and quickly became a bestseller as well as the winner of two prestigious literary prizes (the U.S. National Book Award and the National Book Critics Circle Award). The novel takes its title from a traditional lullaby, also known as "Hush Hush-a-bye," that has generated many recordings and adaptations, most of which focus on the promise of what will occur if children go to sleep without resisting authority by crying. In the most well-known version, the opening lyric asks babies to "hush" and not "cry," and promises that when they wake, they will have "all the pretty horses." The writer Dorothy Scarborough believes the tune had African American origins, and she documents several versions she collected in her compilation of folksongs (145–48). Though McCarthy does not mention the lullaby directly in the novel, the protagonist John Grady Cole captures the wish fulfillment of the lullaby in a scene toward the end. On his return journey to Texas, he encounters a group of children near the border who want to know more about him, and he "told them how he had come from another country, two young horsemen riding their horse, and they had met with a third who had no money or food to eat nor scarcely clothes to cover himself and that he had come to ride with them and share with them all they had" (243). John Grady tells the children everything that happened, and they debate what he could do now—"find a wise man" or "perhaps a curandera[1] [female folk healer]" or "pray to God" (244). Although horses do figure prominently in the novel, they serve primarily as plot devices, to move the plot along, rather than as the primary subject. What the lullaby signifies, then, is the promise of a reward, which in the case of John Grady is never fulfilled. Understanding the historical context of the novel requires an analysis of two competing narratives: the frontier myth in American culture and the events of the Mexican Revolution.

The Frontier Myth in American Culture

The image of the frontier, the promise of open land, has had a long history in American culture. Colonial settlers imagined the New World as a site for reinvention, with unlimited possibilities for exploiting the land, which coincided with eradicating Indigenous inhabitants who were the first Americans. The frontier hero mediates between the settled and unsettled world, as Richard Slotkin has suggested. In his view, the frontier presents a "wide-open land of unlimited opportunity for the strong, ambitious, self-reliant individual to thrust his way to the top" (5). Open land is an important image, as it presents an alternative to Thomas Jefferson's concern that cities are "pestilential to the morals, the health and the liberties of man." The idea of open , unsettled land promised endless opportunity, individual freedom, and wealth from boundless natural resources of mythic proportions; this myth of the frontier, as Slotkin explains, embodies "a set of narratives that acquire through specifiable historical action a significant ideological charge" (19).

Related to the frontier myth is the "safety-valve" theory, in which it was understood that potential violence and social upheaval in overcrowded Eastern areas could be "relieved" by migration to the open spaces offered by "free" land in the West. The Homestead Act of 1862 provided 160 acres to almost anyone (excluding those who fought for the South in the Civil War) willing to farm the land, build a home, and make improvements over a period of five years, a process known as "proving up." About 10 percent of the total land of the United States was eventually given away, a giveaway that primarily benefitted White people and later large corporations. Although the frontier was officially declared closed in 1893, as Frederick Jackson Turner argued in his famous address to the American Historical Association at the World's Columbian Exhibition, the frontier myth has persisted. Turner was highly concerned about what the loss of open land would mean for American democracy, and what became known as the Turner Thesis reinforced the mythic status of the frontier at the same time it provided a justification for continued expansion even beyond the continental borders of the United States, a philosophy termed Manifest Destiny—which led to the annexation of Hawaii and the Philippines.

The iconography of the unbridled West has long dominated American cultural production. Early examples of frontier heroes include Daniel Boone (who inspired William Fenimore Cooper's protagonist Natty Bumppo in his five Leatherstocking novels), Davy Crockett, and Kit Carson, and later in the nineteenth century Buffalo Bill Cody, whose Wild West Shows did much to reinforce archetypes and stereotypes of the American West. Cowboys were not a uniquely American phenomenon, for the job of herding cattle and transporting them to market originated in Europe and most prominently in Spain. Cowboys in America learned their trade from *vaqueros* in Mexico, who were often Indigenous peoples trained by the Spanish conquerors in horse riding. With the end of the Civil War, cattle were in great demand; this coincided with the development of vast cattle ranches in Texas, which required cowboys to manage the herds. It is estimated that a third of nineteenth-century cowboys were Mexican, and another quarter were African American. The mythic cowboy of fiction and film, however, was distinctly White, though Nat Love's 1907 account of his adventures countered that trend. In the 1860s to 1890s, so-called dime novels were enormously popular, often portraying fictionalized exploits of historical characters such as Kit Carson and Buffalo Bill. Owen Wister's 1902 novel *The Virginian* did much to produce the mythical cowboy, the heir to the frontiersman, and its influence on publishing, film, and television was enormous.

The frontier myth has not gone unchallenged by American Studies scholars. In the late 1980s, a group who became known as the New Western Historians—including William Cronon, Patricia Nelson Limerick, Richard White, and Donald Worster—reinterpreted the West through the analytical categories of race, gender, class, ethnicity, and the environment to demonstrate that what had been seen as a land of adventure and opportunity was, in fact, a site of conflict and violence. Western expansion should be seen not as triumphant progress but instead as eradication of Indigenous peoples and destruction of Native habitats. Nevertheless, frontier images continue unabated, and the term "pioneering spirit" retains its power to portray American exceptionalism, a belief that the United States is uniquely superior for political, ideological, and moral reasons.

The two protagonists of *All the Pretty Horses*, John Grady and Lacey Rawlins, would seem to believe in the "the image of the frontier man, the old waddies," as Megan Riley McGilchrist has suggested (126). McCarthy's narrator does not explain the term *waddie*, but it originally connoted a thief or rustler, then evolved into a hired hand on horseback, and today probably refers more generally to cowboys. We first meet John Grady in his dark suit in 1949 as he encounters the corpse of his grandfather, with whom he had lived since his parents divorced. The house was built in 1872, and John Grady passes through a hallway with portraits of "forebears only dimly known to him." He walks out onto the prairie, and his thoughts are interrupted by the sound of a train, a modern technological intrusion. This opening scene reveals that John Grady is from a family of considerable status, owning a cattle ranch that was 2,300 acres in 1886 expanding to 18,000 acres some five years later. He learns that his mother, who has inherited the property, is going to sell it to an oil company. She tells him that at sixteen he cannot run a ranch and besides, it has not been profitable for longer than he has been alive. John Grady decides to leave with Lacey, who is clearly of a different social class as evidenced by the way he talks, and the two ride off "at once jaunty and circumspect, like thieves" (30), or, as they might like to see themselves, as waddies riding off into the sunset.

The contradiction in this story, of course, is that there is no more real need for cowboys in West Texas, and, as they will find out, they cannot find their calling in Mexico either. Cattle drives ended before the twentieth century (the last documented one was in Deadwood, South Dakota in 1893), and cowboys themselves were more wage laborers than gun slinging adventurers. One can be reminded of the epic story of *Don Quixote*, about a nobleman who has read so many romances that he deludes himself into thinking that he himself can become a knight-errant in search of chivalric adventures on board his horse Rocinante. For reasons left unexplained in the novel, John Grady and Lacey set out for Mexico, apparently to escape the modern world of West Texas, and eventually reach the Hacienda de Nuestra Señora de la Purísima Concepción. The two young men are quickly taken in by workers on the ranch. John Grady excels in breaking horses, a skill that has not been previously noted, whereas Lacey fits in well with the vaqueros—another marker of the class differences between the two friends. It would seem that they have realized their cowboy dream here, but John Grady forms a secret relationship with Alejandra, daughter of the hacendado's owner, and both he and Lacey are eventually arrested and imprisoned for an earlier episode involving a boy they met on their journey. The boy, Jimmy Blevins, lost his horse and pistol, and eventually, with the help of John Grady and Lacey, attempts to recover both, but in the process, he has killed a man. The real reason, of course, is that Alejandra's family wants to be rid of John Grady.

John Grady appears to be imitating classic cowboys in movie westerns—of which there were plenty examples by the time of the events in this novel. He speaks in short sentences, rarely reveals any feelings, and particularly "repudiates the authority of women," a characteristic of Western movie heroes Jane Tompkins has noted (39). His seduction of Alejandra reveals the irony of the hacienda's name and becomes a conquest, just as domination of horses suggests the taming of the wilderness, the goal of frontiersmen. What he does not understand is that Mexico is not a virgin land but is an already settled society with its own codes and customs. He cannot comprehend that Alejandra would choose her father over her lover and that her grand-aunt would both rescue him from jail and refuse to allow him to marry her goddaughter. The novel thus becomes not a celebration of a frontier hero or cowboy who overcomes all adversity and wins in the end but a mockery of the entire tradition.

John Grady is forced to leave Mexico and return to Texas. Instead of demonstrating that he has grown into an adult, which would be the logical conclusion of a coming-of-age story, he instead is left not knowing his purpose, as he replies in the end to Lacey's question about where his country is: "I dont know where it is. I don't know what happens to country" (299). His adventure has been a failure. Although he can tame horses, he cannot interact successfully with humans. He is unable to prevent the murder of Jimmy Blevins, the boy whose bay horse served to put John Grady and Lacey in jail; he cannot leave prison without Alfonsa's help; and he cannot convince Alejandra to go against her word to her grand-aunt that she would give him up. Protecting loved ones is a major component of cowboy masculinity, and so in this respect John Grady has become emasculated.

McCarthy presents another inversion of an iconic image in the last scene of the novel. John Grady has left San Angelo and is continuing on his search for country in the western plains. As the narrator comments, "[a]t that time there were still Indians camped on the western plains and late in the day he passed in his riding a scattered group of their wickipiups. . . ." The Native Americans, undoubtedly from the Comanche Nation, watched him but had "no curiosity about him at all. As if they knew all that they needed to know" (301). The Comanches have long been known for their identification with horses. They continue to watch him and see him "vanish upon that landscape because he was passing. Solely because he would vanish" (301). This striking image suggests the famous 1904 photograph by Edward Curtis entitled "The Vanishing Race," which shows a group of Navajos riding on into the sunset. As Curtis explains in a caption to the photograph, "The thought which this picture is meant to convey is that the Indians as a race, already shorn in their tribal strength and stripped of their primitive dress, are passing into the darkness of an unknown future." The American cowboy, as envisioned by John Grady, was also vanishing. Although he and Lacey try to recreate the past, they are unable to do so, as John Grady is left without either an identity or a country.

Events of the Mexican Revolution

Just as John Grady does not realize that his adopted persona imitates a role that never existed, he fails to appreciate the significance of

Dueña Alfonsa's story in Part IV of *All the Pretty Horses,* which, to my mind, provides the most important historical background to the novel. Alfonsa is Alejandra's grand-aunt, and she is referred to as Dueña, which means owner, not as Doña (the latter being the usual honorific for Mexican women of her class). John Grady has previously met with Alfonsa when she invites him in for a chat and a game of chess, though her real motive is to tell him to stay away from Alejandra, for in Mexico, "a woman's reputation is all she has" (136). She goes on to explain that "[t]here is no forgiveness. For women. A man may lose his honor and regain it again. But a woman cannot. She cannot" (137). John Grady ignores Alfonsa's warnings about "consequences," for he begins a sexual relationship with Alejandra anyway, which results in his eventual imprisonment and subsequent rescue by Alfonsa. Also during this visit, Alfonsa tells him about the shooting accident that caused her to lose several fingers, but she does not reveal anything else about her past, other than to imply that she had been rebellious at one time.

John Grady's second visit with Alfonsa comes on his return to la Purísima after his imprisonment and release, and he wishes to see Alejandra. That will not happen according to Alfonsa. But in telling him this she begins to tell him what happened to her many years prior, a story embedded in the Mexican Revolution. She explains that her family are considered "guachupines," or original immigrants from Spain—colonial settlers, in other words. In a different life she believes she could have been a *soladera* (232), a woman who actively participated in the Mexican Revolution, a struggle that began in 1910 and lasted until 1920. The hundred years preceding this uprising represented an extremely chaotic period, as Mexico attempted to transition from a colony into a nation state. This history is quite complicated, but a few highlights will help provide some background to understand Alfonsa's long story.

The Mexican war for independence from Spain began on September 16, 1810. This day commemorates the Grito de Dolores, a call for independence from Spain issued in the village of Dolores by Miguel Hidalgo y Costilla, a Catholic priest known as Father Hidalgo. In Mexico, it is celebrated every year but is often confused in the United States with Cinco de Mayo.[2] John Grady's last meeting with Alejandra takes place in Zacatesas just before Independence Day, a date that seems to have no significance for him. Although Mexico achieved independence from Spain in 1820, the primary beneficiaries were the upper classes or criollos, as opposed to the mestizos and Indigenous peoples who represented the majority of the population. During a period known as *la Reforma* from 1854 to 1876 the government (ostensibly to undermine the power of the clergy and military) began dividing the communal lands known as *ejidos* into smaller farms or incorporated them into haciendas and making them available even to foreign investors. Hacendados (owners of haciendas), such as Alejandra's grandfather and great grandfather, undoubtedly would have benefitted from these kinds of transactions.

A coup led by General José de la Cruz Porfirio Díaz in 1876 then led to what has been called the *Porfiriato*, a period during which he was elected president on seven separate occasions until he was forced into exile in 1911. Díaz put the country on a path to modernization but that did not lead to industrialization, as raw materials from Mexico were shipped out to foreign companies in exchange for manufactured goods (Fehrenbach 470). Díaz continued the so-called land reforms that destroyed the *ejidos*, leading to the formation of even larger haciendas and increased land holdings by foreign investors. By 1910, the standard of living in Mexico was lower than it had been at the time of independence. As Gilbert Joseph and Jürgen Buchenau note, "the average life expectancy was thirty years in 1910, a shocking comment on the high level of infant mortality at the end of the Porfiriato (30 percent of live births)." In addition, "real wages in the agricultural sector were a quarter of what they had been a century before, at the end of the colonial period. Thus, while prices had increased significantly, wages were up only slightly, if at all" (25). In McCarthy's novel, Alfonsa confirms the level of poverty all around her:

> When I was a girl in poverty in this country was very terrible. . . . In the towns there were tiendas which rented clothes to the peasants

> when they would come to market. Because they had no clothes of their own and they would rent them for the day and return home at night in their blankets and rags. They had nothing. (231)

The conditions of urban workers were equally dire, as foreign workers displaced skilled Mexicans. The origins of the Mexican Revolution can be found in significant anger about economic inequality but also in the inability of the elites to continue increasing their fortunes in the face of foreign investment. Thus, the Madero family, one of the wealthiest in Mexico, "bitterly chafed at the preferential treatment Díaz gave to the Guggenheim mining and smelting interests and to other rivals in the fluctuating investment climate of the North" (Joseph and Buchenau 30).

We hear more about the Madero family through Alfonsa's eyes: "Teníamos compadrazgo con su familia. You understand? There is no translation" (232)[3]. Here, McCarthy is interjecting an actual historical family, one that played a key role in the beginning of the Mexican Revolution, into the narrative, and what is said about them appears to be largely accurate. In other words, while Alfonsa is a fictional character and her interactions with the Madero family did not actually happen, what she reports about the role of the Maderos in the Mexican Revolution is based on fact. Francisco's grandfather Evaristo Madero, served for a brief time as Governor of Coahuila during one of the periods that Díaz could not continue as president. In the novel, Evaristo took Alfonsa along with other girls from local haciendas to California the same year the Maderos sponsored her quinceañera. Francisco and his brother Gustavo studied in California and Maryland and then for five years in France. When they returned, Alfonsa "first heard the full expression of those things closest" to her "heart" (233). She begins to "see how the world must become" if she "were to live in it" (233). Presumably, she is speaking of the brothers' well-known philanthropy: "Francisco began to set up schools for the poor children of the district. He dispensed medicines. Later he would feed hundreds of people in his own kitchen. It is not easy to convey the excitement of those times to people today" (233). And in every endeavor he was "seconded by Gustavo" (233).

Alfonsa has developed a special relationship with Gustavo, for they share something in common. Both have been disfigured as a result of accidents, Alfonsa having lost some fingers and Gustavo his eye—a loss that resulted in his nickname "Ojo Parado" [staring or glass eye]. Alfonsa's father sends her to Europe and will not bring her home unless she dissociates herself from both Madero brothers. Although she and Gustavo were never engaged, it is clear he was the only love of her life. While she says at one point in her story "the rest" is "not so difficult to imagine since the facts are known" (236), she goes on to describe how both Francisco and Gustavo were killed, as they were crucial figures in the start of the Mexican Revolution.

Francisco Madero published a book entitled *The Presidential Succession in 1910,* in which he laid out a political and economic critique of the Díaz regime. He had previously attempted to counteract the official Díaz slate in his home state of Coahuila several years before only to see the election rigged in the end. With the support of the new Anti-Reelection Party, Francisco Madero challenged Díaz in the 1910 election, which was receiving enormous support from many sectors. In June of that year, Díaz arrested Madero for sedition and then won an eighth term in an election widely seen as rigged. Many began to see the jailed Madero a successor to Father Hidalgo, as Mexico was celebrating the hundredth anniversary of the Grito de Dolores. Madero escaped from jail and fled to the United States, where he wrote the *Plan of San Luis Potosí*, which called for a wide-scale revolt. The plan called for people to rise up on November 20, a date now celebrated as Revolution Day in Mexico, and the Porfirian regime collapsed within six months. New elections made Madero president in November 1911, but he was then forced to resign in 1913 and then assassinated as a result of an armed coup by one of his generals in the period known as *La Decena Trágica* [Ten Tragic Days] in what became the second phase of the Mexican Revolution. The leader of the coup, Victor Huerta, had the support of both those loyal to Díaz and the United States. Francisco's brother Gustavo suffered the fate reported by Alfonsa in the novel:

> Gustavo was turned over to the mob in the courtyard of the ciudadela [citadel]. They crowded about him with torches and lanterns. They abused and tormented him, calling him Ojo Parado. . . . They burned him. When he begged them again to cease one of them came forward with a pick and pried out his good eye and he staggered away moaning in his darkness and spoke no more. Someone came forward with a revolver and put it to his head and fired but the crowd jostled his arm and the shot tore away his jaw. . . . Finally, a volley of rifle shots was fired into him. . . . One of them pried out his artificial eye and it was passed among the crowd as a curiosity. (237)

Alfonsa says a bit more about the Madero family, but not about later events in the Mexican Revolution. Huerta served as president for only a brief time, and eventually had to flee the country. The Governor of Coahuila, Venustiano Carranza, then entered the conflict, and his Constitutional Army, together with the help of Álvaro Obregón eventually overcame the forces of the revolutionaries Pancho Villa and Emiliano Zapata. The constitution of 1917 was "one of the world's most progressive" at the time (Gilbert and Buchenau 11), but the country did not reach political stability until the formation of the *Partido Revolucionario Institucional* [Institutional Revolutionary Party] in 1929, which remained in power for seventy-one years.

Throughout Alfonsa's long story, John Grady remains almost entirely silent. At the end of one section he wants to know what has happened to Francisco, and Alfonsa tells him about the murders of the two brothers. At the end of her story, she begins to explain why "she wont accept a conventional marriage" for Alejandra, which is also related to "a certain extravagance in the female blood" of her family. John Grady replies, "you wont let me make my case" (240). But Alfonsa says she knows his case: "Your case is that certain things happened over which you had no control "(240). Further, she has "no sympathy with people to whom things happen." She insists that Alejandra will not see him, but she also expresses some sorrow that she will not see him again, for she has "been at some pains" (240) to tell him about herself, since we "should know who our enemies are" (241). She appears to want for Alejandra what she could not have herself.

Alfonsa's long story would seem to be a parable about Mexico itself. Had the Madero brothers known who their enemies were, could they have survived? Does she want to demonstrate her sympathy for the goals of the revolution while at the same time maintaining her privilege as a dueña? At the beginning of this second meeting, Alfonsa reminds John Grady that he had lied about what had happened prior to his arrival at the hacienda. She clearly considers him to be a criminal, or at least one who allows events he cannot control to make him one. She insists that her rejection of him is not because he is "young or without education or from another country," though she seems not to recognize his similarities in social class; she instead wants Alejandra to "value what is true above what is useful" (240). To Alfonsa's long story about the Mexican Revolution, John Grady seems to have no reaction at all. What appears to motivate him in Mexico is to have what he could not have in Texas, a living hacienda to replace the failing ranch he did not inherit, and a beautiful but selfish woman to replace his mother, an argument that McGilchrist has persuasively made (154). John Grady seems not to identify in any way with what Alfonsa is telling him, nor does he appear to have any interest in Mexico as a nation state; similarly, he does not appear to be moved by the economic inequality that precipitated the revolutionary conflicts.

Ultimately it would seem that John Grady's inability to react to what happened to Alfonsa and Mexico reinforces his feeling of statelessness, a longing for a country for which he is still searching at the end. Some scholars, such as Jeffery Herlihy-Mera, argue that John Grady should be considered Mexican and not Anglo, but that does not explain his lack of interest in the history of the Mexican Revolution. San Angelo, where John Grady was born, is somewhat north of the region of South Texas that has been called a Mexican American "homeland," and before 1950 Texas was the state with the largest number of people of Mexican descent (Arreola 44). Although John Grady does appear to have native fluency in Spanish, as a result of being raised by a family who has long been employed at the cattle ranch, he nevertheless uses the two languages strategically. He is careful to say that Abuela (who also cared for his mother) and

Luisa and her husband Arturo "worked for his family." He does not call them servants, but their social position is clear. He can eat with them in the kitchen but also join his mother in the formal dining room. This situation is analogous to plantation owners, who often used enslaved people for child rearing and as childhood companions and then separated everyone along class and racial lines once the children were grown.

John Grady was born in the United States, lives briefly in Mexico, and in the end is a man without a country. In some respects, he would seem to be able to live only on the margins, or in the border, as Nicholas Monk has suggested. Gloria Anzaldúa's definition of the border is worth considering: "It is in a constant state of transition. The prohibited and forbidden are its inhabitants." John Grady has failed to live his dream of being a cowboy, and now he continues perpetually to wander. Both the long-studied frontier myth and the events of the Mexican Revolution, which he does not appreciate, illuminate the existential dilemma at the heart of *All the Pretty Horses.*

Notes

1. Throughout, McCarthy's narrator intersperses Spanish words without translation, including a good deal of spoken dialogue. This essay will provide definitions as needed.
2. France invaded Mexico in 1861 ostensibly to collect some national debts. The Mexican army then defeated the French invaders in the Battle of Puebla on May 5, 1862—a date commemorated as Cinco de Mayo, although the victory was brief, as French reinforcements then arrived and helped to establish a monarchy presided over by Maximilian I.
3. Compadrazgo usually translates as godparenthood or co parenthood, so she is emphasizing the close relationship between the two families.

Works Cited

Anzaldúa, Gloria. *Borderlands/La Frontera: The New Mestiza.* Aunt Lute Books, 1987.

Arreola, Daniel D. *Tejano South Texas: A Mexican American Cultural Province*. U of Texas P, 2002.

Cronon, William, and George A. Miles. *Under an Open Sky: Rethinking America's Western Past*. Edited by William Cronon, et al., W. W. Norton, 1992.

Curtis, Edward S. *The North American Indian, Being a Series of Volumes Picturing and Describing the Indians of the United States and Alaska*. Edited by Frederick Webb Hodge, Cambridge UP, 1907–30.

Fehrenbach, T. R. *Fire and Blood: A History of Mexico*. Macmillan, 1973.

Herlihy-Mera, Jeffrey. "'Mojado-Reverso' or, a Reverse Wetback: On John Grady Cole's Mexican Ancestry in Cormac McCarthy's *All the Pretty Horses*." *MFS Modern Fiction Studies*, vol. 61 no. 3, 2015, p. 469–92.

Jefferson, Thomas. "From Thomas Jefferson to Benjamin Rush, 23 September 1800." *National Archives*, Founders Online, founders.archives.gov/documents/Jefferson/01-32-02-0102.

Joseph, Gilbert, and Jürgen Buchenau. *Mexico's Once and Future Revolution*. Duke UP, 2013.

Limerick, Patricia Nelson. *The Legacy of Conquest: The Unbroken Past of the American West.* Norton, 1987.

Love, Nat. *The Life and Adventures of Nat Love, Better Known in the Cattle Country as "Deadwood Dick."* U of Nebraska P, 1995.

McCarthy, Cormac. *All the Pretty Horses.* Knopf, 1992.

McGilchrist, Megan Riley. *The Western Landscape in Cormac McCarthy and Wallace Stegner: Myths of the Frontier*. Routledge, 2010.

Monk, Nicholas. "*All the Pretty Horses*, the Border, and Ethnic Encounter." *The Cambridge Companion to Cormac McCarthy*. Edited by Steven Frye, Cambridge UP, 2013, pp. 121–32.

Scarborough, Dorothy, and Ola Lee Gulledge. *On the Trail of Negro Folk-Songs.* Harvard UP, 1925.

Slotkin, Richard. *Regeneration Through Violence: The Mythology of the American Frontier, 1600–1860.* Wesleyan UP, 1973.

Tompkins, Jane P. *West of Everything: The Inner Life of Westerns.* Oxford UP, 1992.

Turner, Frederick Jackson. "The Significance of the Frontier in American History." *The Frontier in American History.* 1893/1920. *Project Gutenberg,* www.gutenberg.org/files/22994/22994-h/22994-h.htm.

White, Richard. *"It's Your Misfortune and None of My Own": A History of the American West.* U of Oklahoma P, 1991.

Worster, Donald. *Under Western Skies: Nature and History in the American West.* Oxford UP, 1994.

All the Pretty Horses Alters the Reception and Prestige of McCarthy

Amy Leshinsky

Although little attention had been paid to Cormac McCarthy's earlier works, *All the Pretty Horses* thrust McCarthy into the public spotlight. The novel won the 1992 National Book Award and the 1993 National Book Critics Circle Award for Fiction. His work was reviewed in scores of newspapers in 1992 and was propelled into the spotlight again in 1993. Random House Audiobooks released a two-cassette audiobook in 1993 narrated by internationally acclaimed actor and film producer, Brad Pitt. Columbia Pictures sought film rights immediately after the book's publication and released their film after a series of challenges in 2000. Though reviews of the film underperformed those of the book, the film had a strong budget and an impressive cast with Matt Damon as John Grady Cole and Penelope Cruz as Alejandra Villarreal.

It is well documented that McCarthy did not seek out the spotlight; Richard B. Woodward did interview McCarthy, however, prior to the release of *All the Pretty Horses*. The resulting article published in April of 1992 in the *New York Times Magazine* provided a candid profile of McCarthy and touched upon components of his writing that would be explored and discussed in early reviews. Woodward's fascinating and valuable interview with McCarthy charts his journey as a writer and provides valuable insight into McCarthy's demeanor just prior to the release of *All the Pretty Horses*, the novel that cemented McCarthy's value in contemporary American literature.

First, this essay explores McCarthy's writing style, which was examined in early reviews of his work. Second, this essay highlights the impact of *All the Pretty Horses* on the academic and public perception of McCarthy as one of the greatest living American writers. Finally, nearly thirty years after the publication of *All the Pretty Horses*, McCarthy's work remains a continuously explored piece in U.S. classrooms and academic spaces, which requires an examination of the contemporary lens receiving and processing this great American work of fiction.

All the Pretty Horses

Prior to the May 11 release of *All the Pretty Horses*, McCarthy was profiled by writer Richard B. Woodward in *The New York Times Magazine*. While *All the Pretty Horses* was not the focus of this interview, the esteem of *The New York Times Magazine* and the prestige of Woodward captured the attention of other media outlets. Woodward's interview, published as "Cormac McCarthy's Venomous Fiction," hailed McCarthy as "the best unknown novelist in America" (28). The Woodward interview touched upon components of McCarthy's narrative style that would be examined in the subsequent weeks. Though previous reception of McCarthy's works highlights his contributions to Southern Gothic style and human cruelty, Woodward works to juxtapose the "world-class talker," who is quick to laugh, with his "terse and crude" characters. Many reviews of *All the Pretty Horses* would comment on the "stylized sparseness" of Cormac's works; Woodward's interview highlights the ability of McCarthy's prose to "magnify the force and precision of his words." This precursory interview to *All the Pretty Horses* was the first of many mainstream media outlets to positively review McCarthy's writing within the novel.

The limited punctuation and long, winding sentences packed with description were examined in early reviews of the work. As Woodward notes in his work on McCarthy, readers take less than a page of reading McCarthy's works to know his writing is "minimally punctuated." The absence of punctuation is noted by *Boston Globe* writer Gail Caldwell writes that McCarthy's "laconic dialogue is stripped of speakers and quotation marks" (B41). This style of writing, Caldwell notes, creates a "voice that is unmistakably and torrentially [McCarthy's]." Caldwell explains that while his descriptions often become too extravagant, "a moment of understated gravity comes along, when all the silence in the world can't do justice to the feeling beneath it." Madison Smartt Bell writes in the *New York Times* that McCarthy's prose is "powered by long, tumbling many-stranded sentences" with an elaborate and elevated descriptive style (9). The language McCarthy employs "come[s] from all over the evolutionary history of English and combine[s] into a prose that seems to invent itself as it unfolds."

However, not all reviewers immediately took to McCarthy's writing style. *New York Times* writer Herbert Mitgang was "put off at first by the author's all too writerly writing" (18). Despite the "unpunctuated, breathless sentences," Mitgang found the work "attain[ed] heroic dimensions" once John Grady Cole and Lacey Rawlins depart from Texas. While Mitgang's review ended with positive accolades, not all reviews of his style ended favorably. In John Southerland's article in the *Times Literary Supplement*, Southerland remarks that the style was "laconic and artfully lazy, like the speech of the region" (qtd. in Frye 99). In his thorough examination of McCarthy's critical reception, writer Stephen Tatum explains that the narrative style of McCarthy aligns with his thematic interests, drawing attention to the point that "everything, whether on the landscape of the page or in the world beyond, finally counts" (76). This interest in McCarthy's narrative style refers not only to his syntax and grammar, but also to the impact the prose style has on the development of setting.

The setting of McCarthy's text is much enhanced by his prose. Richard Eder shared that McCarthy's "elevated prose does wonders for deserts, mountains, freezing winds, night landscapes and the tangibility of food, a bath and clean clothes" (3). Similarly, Madison Smartt Bell references the descriptions of the landscapes, calling them "breathtakingly beautiful." Along with these accolades, Geoff Dyer's review is particularly telling because he aligns the setting with a beauty found within American literature. Unlike British literature, which Dyer claims is "restricted by the climate," American literature portrays adventures in the wilderness. He writes: "Step out of your front door in an English novel, and you're on your way to the newsagent; in an American you're headed off, headed out." Dyer cites that merely 30 pages into *All the Pretty Horses*, the journey begins with the phrase: "They rode out" (30).

This section of McCarthy's work is deeply attuned to the beauty of place. The boys who confide in one another that they are "ready" for this moment, hear the leather saddles creaking in the cold, watch lights falling "away behind them," and exist within solitude where "the stars swarmed around them out of the blackness" (30). Reviews describe McCarthy's landscape as breathtaking and elevated; Dyer notes that: "In McCarthy, landscape is a verb" and the landscape, friendships, and horsemanship contain a force and beauty that leaves readers seeking to continue the journey.

Within early reviews, writers tackle the sparse use of dialogue through different lenses; however, the use of dialogue in the text is considered largely successful. Bell writes that the sentence structure and descriptive style of McCarthy are "used effectively to frame realistic dialogue" and Newsweek staff writes in their review, "Literary Lion in the Desert," that the "laconic exchanges" between Cole and his father are "particularly fine" (9; 68). In addition to an exploration of dialogue, early critics also considered the relationship between dialogue and writer. This idea emerged in Woodward's pre-publication interview, which humanized McCarthy and examined the way McCarthy's authentic voice departs from his characters. Bell writes that McCarthy's elaborate prose, for example, stands in stark contrast to the dialogue of the characters. Similarly, Eder notes "a disconcerting contrast between [John Grady's] down-home speech and the baroquely elaborate thoughts which the author puts in his head" (3).

Unique to note, and perhaps unintentional, early reviews are infused with religious imagery. For example, Christopher Zenowich writes that *All the Pretty Horses* is a "prayer in prose fiction, a homage to the world" and later writes that the work is "a genuine miracle in prose." The end of Caldwell's *Boston Globe* article uses similar phraseology when calling *All the Pretty Horses*, McCarthy's "eloquent lament." Bell refers to the "unusual vision" that persists within the text, and likewise, Dyer's work in the U.K.'s *The Guardian* concludes with similar phraseology, stating McCarthy's prose contains "visionary richness." In addition to visionary references, Bell writes of parallels between La Purísima in *All the Pretty Horses* and paradise within the Old Testament, as La Purísima is a paradise "complete with its Eve, Don Héctor's daughter, Alejandra." Toward the end of the review, Bell writes: "The deity that presides over Mr. McCarthy's world has not modeled itself on humanity; its voice most resembles the one that addressed Job out of the whirlwind." Finally, Jones Jr. concludes his *Newsweek* article by aligning the book with a "hymn to youth and times past." Ultimately, the religious connotations found within multiple news articles indicate the beauty of McCarthy's prose and his ability to capture the spirit of his readers.

All the Pretty Horses Alters the Reception and Prestige of McCarthy

Prior to the release of *All the Pretty Horses*, McCarthy's five novels, *The Orchard Keeper*, *Outer Dark*, *Child of God*, *Suttree*, and *Blood Meridian*, sold fewer than 15,000 copies. Edwin Arnold and Dianne Luce share in their work *Perspectives on Cormac McCarthy* that *All the Pretty Horses* resulted in more than 180,000 copies in hardcover and 300,000 copies in paperback over a two-year period. A survey of reviews of McCarthy's work praised the writer, and though he had published numerous works prior, *All the Pretty Horses* was hailed as "the most accessible of Mr. McCarthy's six novels" (Smartt Bell). On May 31, 1992, the *New York Times* listed *All the Pretty Horses* under the "And Bear in Mind: Editors' Choices of other recent books of particular interest" (Best Sellers: 31 May). One week later, *All the Pretty Horses* took the fifteenth spot on the *New York Times* Best Seller list with works by Danielle Steel, Dr. Seuss, Toni Morrison, and John Grisham (Best Sellers: 7 June). With sustained public interest, Tatum explains in *Cormac McCarthy's All the Pretty Horses* that Vintage International republished McCarthy's works *Suttree* and *Blood Meridian*. *All the Pretty Horses* was instrumental in establishing McCarthy's place in the American literary canon and the anticipation for the remaining works of the *Border Trilogy* sustained public interest.

Although reviews in U.S. newspapers helped increase the sales, *All the Pretty Horses* also received praise from nationally acclaimed

Texas radio host Don Imus, who recommended McCarthy's work on his radio program, *Imus in the Morning*. Imus's promotion of McCarthy's work highlights the book's popularity in the public sphere. Despite a reputation for an uncouth demeanor, Imus appreciated literature and "push[ed] to establish himself as the male Oprah Winfrey, in recommending books" ("Imus Sets Book Award Finalists"). In 1998, Imus established the Imus American Book Awards in conjunction with Barnes and Noble after "a book he liked didn't win a National Book Award" (Tracy 278). Placed on this list was McCarthy's 1998 book *Cities of the Plain*, the third book of the *Border Trilogy*. The promotion of literature was typical of Imus, and as his radio program highlighted his personal ruminations, he would "frequently talk about the books he had read, both good and bad" (Tracy 274). *All the Pretty Horses* received attention on his show, as it tapped into his appreciation for his home state of Texas and love of cowboys. On the Official Web Site of the Cormac McCarthy Society, Rick Wallach shared that Imus plugged the book on his show, and said, "I am so sure you will love this book that if you don't, I will personally buy it back from you" (qtd. on The Official Web Site of the Cormac McCarthy Society).

The first major publication dedicated to McCarthy was by Vereen Bell, who published *The Achievement of Cormac McCarthy* prior to the release of *All the Pretty Horses*. Bell justifies the need for this work because: "McCarthy needs to be written about, both because his work is major work and yet still unknown and because he himself is so unwilling—in his work and outside it—to meet his readers halfway" (xiii). Thus, Bell's work was a study of McCarthy with no direct thesis, but with a goal to "close up some of the space between the uncompromising novelist and his uncourted audience" (xiii). Vereen Bell provides a close study of each of McCarthy's first five novels. In Edwin Arnold's 1989 review of Bell's text, Arnold knowingly predicts: "*The Achievement of Cormac McCarthy* will be seen either as a footnote to a forgotten author or as a groundbreaking, prescient appreciation of one of our greatest novelists" (262). Given the prestige that has followed McCarthy since *All the Pretty Horses*, Arnold's latter prediction proves correct.

Dianne C. Luce writes in the piece, "Remarks on the State of Cormac McCarthy Scholarship," that in addition to Bell's work, there was only one dissertation, two thesis, and about thirty short pieces on McCarthy prior to the release of *All the Pretty Horses*. Despite the various novels McCarthy had produced, Luce writes that before *All the Pretty Horses*, scholarship focused the most attention on *Suttree*. After the 1992 publication, the number of articles on McCarthy doubled "with a special Cormac McCarthy issue of *Southern Quarterly*" (Luce 7). The *Southern Quarterly* designed a special issue to examine McCarthy, which "had been in production almost simultaneously with *All the Pretty Horses*" (7). Later, this edition of the *Southern Quarterly* was expanded and published in book form in Edwin Arnold and Dianne Luce's *Perspectives on Cormac McCarthy*. While the publication had limited chapters on *All the Pretty Horses*, the book was "surrounded by the rumors of its imminent publication" (Arnold and Luce, 14). The purpose of Arnold and Luce's work was to "cover all of McCarthy's available work and to represent a variety of critical readings of that work" by writers who "shared convictions that McCarthy was an underread and underappreciated writer of stunning talents" (14).

After the release of *All the Pretty Horses*, McCarthy scholarship blossomed. The success of the first volume of the *Border Trilogy* would be discussed further after the successive trilogy publications, resulting in McCarthyism as a field of study. Academic research increased with discussion on his treatment of violence, women, and landscape. According to The Official Web Site of the Cormac McCarthy Society, the society informally began at the first conference focusing on McCarthy's work, which was held in October of 1993 at Bellarmine College, Louisville, Kentucky, and organized by Wade Hall and Rick Wallach. The Cormac McCarthy Society was founded with a mission that focuses on furthering scholarship and appreciation for scholars and enthusiastic readers. In 1995, Hall and Wallach published: *Sacred Violence: A Reader's Companion to Cormac McCarthy*, which printed essays from the first McCarthy Conference at Bellarmine College.

In 1997, Robert L. Jarrett published *Cormac McCarthy* as part of the Twayne's United States Author Series. Within the work, the first two books of the *Border Trilogy*, *All the Pretty Horses*, and *The Crossing*, are unpacked in chapter five. While *Cities of the Plain* had not yet been published, the book comments on the relationship and popularity of *All the Pretty Horses* and *The Crossing*. Jarrett shares: "The *Border Trilogy*'s first strategy is to openly imitate the popular western, while the second is to critique from within the western its belief in the autonomous individual" (96). The *Cormac McCarthy Journal* provides recommendations for further reading to pique the interest of their audience. In the spring of 2001, Jarrett's work was sold and available from the Cormac McCarthy Society Online Bookstore and promoted in the spring 2001 edition of the *Cormac McCarthy Journal.*

While McCarthy's *All the Pretty Horses* garnered strong interest in the United States, international appreciation for McCarthy prevailed as well. In *Irish Catholic Writers and the Invention of the American South*, writer Bryan Giemza shares that acclaimed Irish writers John Bainville and Roddy Doyle had listed McCarthy in a *London Times* poll as "one of the greatest living novelists writing in English" (qtd. in Giemza 217). This news had been delivered to McCarthy in a letter dated March 24, 1994, from Howard J. Woolmer, which is now part of the Wittliff Collections at Texas State University. In 2015, after *The Guardian* published a list of "The 100 Best Novels Written in English: The Full List," leaving out all works by McCarthy, Martin Doyle, writing for *The Irish Times*, responded to this list, questioning why there was nothing by McCarthy among other writers like Ian McEwan.

As the twentieth century came to a close, *All the Pretty Horses* had altered McCarthy's popularity in the United States and abroad. In 1998, the peer-reviewed *Cormac McCarthy Journal* was founded and published online, and at the turn of the century, the Cormac McCarthy Society published the first hard copy of the journal. In the fall of 1999, *Southwestern American Literature* published a special issue on McCarthy and in the spring of 2000, the *Southern Quarterly* published a special issue on the *Border Trilogy*. As the United States turned to the twenty-first century, McCarthy's *All the Pretty Horses* would continue to be examined in scholarship.

Twenty-first Century Reception and Continued Impact

Twenty-first century scholars continue to analyze McCarthy's *All the Pretty Horses*; however, there is more work to be done on understanding this valuable American novel and the relationship between *All the Pretty Horses* and his more recent works. In 2009, McCarthy received the prestigious PEN/Saul Bellow award for his contributions to American literature. With the integration of *All the Pretty Horses* into secondary schools and colleges, current research considers ways of applying pedagogical approaches to his works, and academic research continues to flourish. With the recent publication of two new books, *The Passenger* and *Stella Maris* in 2022, it is likely renewed interest in *All the Pretty Horses* will surface, as readers work to extract all the detailed nuances of his writing and compare his new books to the style of his award-winning publications.

In 2001, Luce shares there were "over 180 English-language books and articles" on McCarthy, however, Luce notes a discrepancy exists in the examination of his earlier, Southern works and his Western novels, the latter of which received far more press (7). Around the same time, the *Cormac McCarthy Journal* published its first hard copy printing of the journal. The irony that the first hard copy of the journal "coincide[d] with the release of the Billy Bob Thornton's big screen adaptation" was noted by John Wegner on the Editor's Page (4). Thus, *All the Pretty Horses* was thrust into the spotlight again nearly a decade after the initial publication.

The production of *All the Pretty Horses* film proved challenging. Several days before the Christmas Day premiere in 2000, Rick Lyman published an article in the *New York Times*, "After Choppy Seas, a Film Nears Port." The article detailed the potential impact abridging the story had on the adaptation, which was condensed from an initial run time of 3 hours and 48 minutes to just shy of two hours. This decision to reduce the film was discussed in Peter

Biskind's 2004 book, *Down and Dirty Pictures* where he shares the tense exchanges occurring behind the silver screen.

Reviews of the film did not meet the praise attained by McCarthy's book. *New York Times* writer A. O. Scott wrote, "Film Review: Lost Souls Adrift Across a Barren Mesa," which highlights the weaknesses of the film. Within the review, Scott writes that "in spite of thoughtful performances and a handsome sense of scale, the picture is, for the most part, as slick and superficial as a Marlboro advertisement on the back of a glossy magazine." Marty Priola reviewed "All the Pretty Horses, the film" in *The Cormac McCarthy Journal*, and the review touched upon the challenges of putting together the film and the successes and failures of the work. Like Lyman and Scott discuss in their *New York Times* articles, Priola writes of the "wrangling about the editing, about the film's length, about violence and sex in the film, about distribution and marketing, about, it seems, just about everything" (69). Noticeable structural alterations impacted the film's pacing, which Priola believed to be the movie's greatest flaw. However, the film captured the textured dialogue of the book, and the details "from the costumes to the sets to the props—it's all 'right'" (70). Priola ends by sharing that while the film contains "hints of genius and glimmers of greatness," the pace moves too quickly and makes the viewer feel "as though he is watching a very elaborate trailer for the 'real film'" (71).

Shortly after his first released publication since the *Border Trilogy*, *No Country for Old Men*, McCarthy sat down again with Richard B. Woodward, the writer who had initially interviewed him prior to the release of *All the Pretty Horses*. This interview, published in *Vanity Fair* and titled, "Cormac Country," was "his first interview in 13 years —since *All the Pretty Horses* turned him from cult figure into literary star." The interview highlighted McCarthy's presence at the Santa Fe Institute, where he attends workshops, engages in discussion, and reads pre-publication work. Ironically, Woodward writes that "McCarthy would rather hang out with physicists than other writers. He doesn't do blurbs, book tours, or even Oprah;" however, in 2007, McCarthy accepted an interview with talk show host Oprah Winfrey. McCarthy's interview with Winfrey came after

Winfrey selected McCarthy's *The Road* for her book club. The interview provided background on the creation of *The Road* and sought to understand McCarthy's process of writing.

Perhaps the most unexpected interview with McCarthy regarding *All the Pretty Horses* came out of Arizona when two Advanced Placement English students at Catalina Foothills High School were tasked with completing a rhetorical analysis of a novel, and *All the Pretty Horses* was an option on the list. One of the students had a boyfriend who lived next door to an individual who was friendly with McCarthy. The individual took a list of questions from the students to McCarthy and then sent an email back to the students with McCarthy's responses. In some cases, the responses mirrored ideas McCarthy had shared in his interview with Winfrey. For example, when asked if he could describe the process for developing ideas into stories, McCarthy responded, "Writing is very subconscious and the last thing I want to do is think about it" (*Literary Hub*). Another question the students asked McCarthy was whether music had an influence on his style since his "syntax has sometimes been described as musical" (*Literary Hub*). While McCarthy shared that "everything in life influences style," his friend candidly remarked in a side comment that McCarthy is too modest to admit this, but he has a "beautiful singing voice and plays the guitar very well" (*Literary Hub*). The friend went on to share that McCarthy particularly likes old bluegrass music and country ballads.

Nearly a quarter into the twenty-first century, McCarthy, who published his first book *The Orchard Keeper* in 1965, is still writing. His recent works *The Passenger* and *Stella Maris* were both published in 2022. Executive Editor Jenny Jackson at Knopf shared with NPR writer John Burnett that the process of working with McCarthy was "cloak-and-dagger" and that they would walk down the hall and "hand off manuscripts in person" in order to keep the books a secret (qtd. in Burnett). The archives of McCarthy were sold in 2008, the Associated Press reported, and had been bought by the Southwestern Writers Collection of Texas State University–San Marcos. The literary curator at the Witliff, shared that the university has "about a hundred boxes of Cormac material . . . his collection begins with his first book, *Outer Dark*" and also includes edits made to *The Passenger* (qtd. in Burnett). It is likely that as scholarship continues to examine McCarthy's works that the archives will play an increasingly valuable role.

In 2001, Luce wrote in "Remarks on the State of Cormac McCarthy Scholarship" that regarding McCarthy scholarship "we have done much good work, but there is a great deal more to do—and good heads and hands to do it" (11). Luce's words remain true today, as McCarthy scholarship is a continuously altering field with, as of 2022, two more works to explore. As Luce predicted, good heads and hands continue the demanding work. In February 2023, the Southwest Popular/American Culture Association was scheduled to host a conference in Albuquerque, New Mexico, and in May of 2023 the American Literature Association Annual Conference is scheduled to include three panels sponsored by the Cormac McCarthy Society at their conference in Boston, Massachusetts. The continuous effort placed on McCarthy studies will have a significant impact on the shape and direction of the field for future generations. The continuous effort put forth by scholars today will provide great insight for future generations unpacking the critical reception of McCarthy, as they work to complete the picture of his arrival and presence in the American literary canon.

Works Cited

"About the Cormac McCarthy Society." The Official Web Site of the Cormac McCarthy Society, www.cormacmccarthy.com/about-the-society/.

Arnold, Edwin T. "Review: The Achievement of Cormac McCarthy, by Vereen M. Bell." *Appalachian Journal,* vol. 16, no. 3, 1989, pp. 262–64. *JSTOR*, www.jstor.org/stable/40933153.

__________, and Dianne C. Luce. *Perspectives on Cormac McCarthy*. UP of Mississippi, 1999.

Associated Press. "Texas State Acquires McCarthy Archives." *Daily Freeman*, 24 Jan. 2008, www.dailyfreeman.com/2008/01/24/texas-state-acquires-mccarthy-archives/.

Bell, Madison Smartt. "The Man Who Understood Horses." Review of *All the Pretty Horses,* by Cormac McCarthy." *The New York Times*, 17 May 1992, p. 9, www.nytimes.com/1992/05/17/books/the-man-who-understood-horses.html.

Bell, Vereen M. *The Achievement of Cormac McCarthy*. Louisiana State UP, 1988.

"Best Sellers: May 31, 1992." *The New York Times*, 31 May 1992, p. 40, www.nytimes.com/1992/05/31/books/best-sellers-may-31-1992.html.

"Best Sellers: June 7, 1992." *The New York Times*, 7 June 1992, p. 32, www.nytimes.com/1992/06/07/books/best-sellers-june-7-1992.html.

Biskind, Peter. *Down and Dirty Pictures: Miramax, Sundance, and the Rise of Independent Film*. Simon and Schuster, 2005.

Burnett, John. "After 16 Years, Author Cormac McCarthy Gifts Two New Novels to Readers." Review of *The Passenger* and *Stella Maris*, by Cormac McCarthy. *NPR*, 22 Oct. 2022, www.wfae.org/2022-10-22/after-16-years-author-cormac-mccarthy-gifts-two-new-novels-to-readers.

Caldwell, Gail. "Cormac McCarthy's High Frontier: The Novelist's Unmistakable Voice Brings Majesty to the Badlands: [City Edition]." *The Boston Globe*, 3 May 1992, p. B41.

Dempsey, John. "Imus sets book award finalists." *Variety*, 4 June 1999, variety.com/1999/biz/news/imus-sets-book-award-finalists-1117489896/.

Doyle, Martin. "The 100 Best Novels in English? Irish Writers and Critics Have Their Say." *The Irish Times*, 20 Aug. 2015, n.p., www.irishtimes.com/culture/books/the-100-best-novels-in-english-irish-writers-and-critics-have-their-say-1.2322884.

Dyer, Geoff. "Books: *All the Pretty Horses* by Cormac McCarthy." Review of All the Pretty Horses, n.p. *The Guardian,* 6 Apr., 1993.

Eder, Richard. "John's Passion: *All the Pretty Horses*." Review of *All the Pretty Horses, by Cormac McCarthy. Los Angeles Times*, 17 May 1992, p. 3, www.latimes.com/archives/la-xpm-1992-05-17-bk-562-story.html.

Frye, Steven. *Understanding Cormac McCarthy*. The U of South Carolina P, 2009, p. 99.

Giemza, Bryan. "Cormac McCarthy, An Irish Southerner Among the Heresiarchs." *Irish Catholic Writers and the Invention of the American South*, Louisiana State UP, 2013.

Hall, Wade, and Rick Wallach. *Sacred Violence: A Reader's Companion to Cormac McCarthy: Selected Essays from the First McCarthy Conference, Bellarmine College, Louisville, Kentucky, October 15–17, 1993*, U of Texas at El Paso, 1995.

Jarrett, Robert L *Cormac McCarthy. Twayne's United States Author Series.* Twayne, 1997.

"Literary Lion in the Desert." Review of *All the Pretty Horses*, by Cormac McCarthy. *Newsweek*, vol. 119, no. 20, 17 May 1992, p. 68, www.newsweek.com/literary-lion-desert-199164.

Luce, Dianne C. "Remarks on the State of Cormac McCarthy Scholarship." *The Cormac McCarthy Journal*, vol. 1, no. 1, 2001, pp. 7–11.

McCarthy, Cormac. *All the Pretty Horses.* Vintage International Edition, 1992.

__________. *Blood Meridian*. Random House, 1985.

__________. *Child of God*. Random House, 1974.

__________. *Cities on the Plain*. Knopf Doubleday Publishing Group, 1998.

__________. "Cormac Country." Interview by Richard B. Woodward. *Vanity Fair.* 1 Aug. 2005, www.vanityfair.com/culture/2005/08/cormac-mccarthy-interview.

__________. "Cormac McCarthy's Venomous Fiction." Interview by Richard B. Woodward. *The New York Times Magazine*, 19 Apr. 1992. p. 28, www.nytimes.com/1992/04/19/magazine/cormac-mccarthy-s-venomous-fiction.html.

__________, "Interview with Cormac McCarthy." Interview by Oprah Winfrey. The Oprah Winfrey Show, 5 June 2007.

__________. *No Country for Old Men*, Knopf Doubleday Publishing Group, 2005.

__________. *The Orchard Keeper*. Random House, 1965.

__________. *Outer Dark*. Random House, 1974.

__________. *The Passenger*. Knopf Doubleday Publishing Group, 2022.

_________. "Rare Thoughts on Writing from Cormac McCarthy in This Unlikely Interview." Interview by Murray Carpenter. *Literary Hub*, 15 Mar. 2022, lithub.com/rare-thoughts-on-writing-from-cormac-mccarthy-in-this-unlikely-interview/.

_________. *The Road*. Knopf Doubleday Publishing Group, 2006.

_________. *Stella Maris*, Knopf Doubleday Publishing Group, 2022.

_________. *Suttree*. Random House, 1979.

McCrum, Robert. "The 100 Best Novels Written in English: The Full List." *The Guardian*, 17 Aug. 2015, www.theguardian.com/books/2015/aug/17/the-100-best-novels-written-in-english-the-full-list.

Mitgang, Herbert. "Books of the Times; Boys on Horseback, Loose in Mexico." Review of *All the Pretty Horses*, by Cormac McCarthy. *The New York Times*, 27 May 1992, p. C18, www.nytimes.com/1992/05/27/books/books-of-the-times-boys-on-horseback-loose-in-mexico.html.

Morrison, Gail Moore. "*All the Pretty Horses*: John Grady Cole's Expulsion from Paradise." *Perspectives on Cormac McCarthy*, UP of Mississippi, 1999.

Priola, Marty. "Review of All the Pretty Horses, the film." Directed by Billy Bob Thornton. *The Cormac McCarthy Journal*, vol. 1, no. 1, 2001, pp. 69–71.

Tatum, Stephen. *Cormac McCarthy's 'All the Pretty Horses.'* Continuum Contemporaries, 2002.

Tracy, Kathleen. Imus: *America's Cowboy*. Carroll and Graf Publishers, 1999.

Wallach, Rick. "Don Imus, RIP." The Official Web Site of the Cormac McCarthy Society, 27 Dec. 2019, www.cormacmccarthy.com/topic/don-imus-rip/.

Wegner, John. "Editor's Page." *The Cormac McCarthy Journal*, vol. 1, no. 1, 2001, pp. 4–6.

_________. "'Whatever I was going to be I wanted to be really good': Cormac McCarthy's Life in Writing." *The Guardian*, 22 Oct. 2022, www.theguardian.com/books/2022/oct/22/cormac-mccarthy-life-in-writing-books-the-passenger.

Woolmer, Howard J. "Woolmer to McCarthy." 24 Mar. 1994, Texas State University, Woolmer Collection of Cormac McCarthy 1969–2006, www.thewittliffcollections.txst.edu/research/a-z/woolmer.html.

Zenowich, Christopher. "Coming of Age: A Lyrical Tale of the Southwest from Cormac McCarthy." Review of *All the Pretty Horses*, by Cormac McCarthy. *Chicago Tribune*, 10 May 1992, pp. 5, 10, www.chicagotribune.com/news/ct-xpm-1992-05-10-9202110419-story.html.

Wilderness 2.0: Redefining and Rewilding Wilderness in McCarthy's *All the Pretty Horses*

Aaron A. Cloyd

Wilderness is complicated territory in Cormac McCarthy's novel *All the Pretty Horses.* Even though the novel takes place in deserted regions of southern Texas and northern Mexico, the characters ride mostly to the west of legally designated wilderness areas in Texas. Their closest proximity to an official wilderness occurs as they cross into Coahuila, Mexico, and ride east of Maderas del Carmen. However, even if John Grady Cole, Lacy Rawlins, and Jimmy Blevins were to encounter a designated wilderness area within their travels, "wilderness" would be anachronistic, in a legal sense of the word, as none of these areas were legally recognized as wilderness in 1949, the timeline of the novel. Confounding this discussion more, the word "wilderness" does not appear in the novel.

Rather, wilderness is present implicitly throughout the novel, occurring by way of qualities traditionally associated with wilderness such as "barren" (59), "open" (256), and "wild" (87). These terms further imply wilderness to be a site beyond human influence, an idea that has long existed, but that was legally set down in the 1964 Wilderness Act. Yet, the presence of human artifacts in these areas such as abandoned ranches (23), an apple orchard (226), and a collapsing cabin (226) contest these ideas of wilderness. Further complicating matters, these human objects are crumbling or rusting, fading into the land around them. Their movement toward decay and the implied reciprocal reinstatement of natural elements indicate that wilderness in this novel is not a static site but a process where both elements of nature and humanity are fluid, visible, and even valued. Given this complex imaging of wilderness, this chapter argues that *All the Pretty Horses* is a novel that redefines wilderness in multiple ways but, most importantly, as a site that can be identified as a rewilding wilderness.

Images of Nature and Wilderness in *All the Pretty Horses*

Throughout *All the Pretty Horses*, nature gains prominence in two ways. One, the narrator continuously draws the reader's attention to particular vegetation and precise geological features. Two, the characters raise awareness of nature by repeatedly interacting with it.

Attending to Nature

To cite one example of the narrator's attention toward nature from early in the novel, John Grady and his father go riding, and the warm weather has brought the "yellow mexicanhat" into bloom (22). They begin riding "along Grape Creek," that is "clear and green with trailing moss braided over the gravel bars," before riding into "open country among scrub mesquite and nopal," a land "dotted with cedar" and covered with "traprock" (22–23). A similar focus on specific flora occurs later in the novel as the narrator describes terrain with "evergreen ash growing in the rocky draws" (59). "Persimmon, mountain gum" grows there as well, and the path before the boys is described as a series of "shaly rock switchbacks" that ends on a "gravel shelf" (59). Preparing camp that night, they hear "three long howls" of a wolf (59–60).

In both passages, the narrator's attention to specific vegetation, particular environments, and concise features of those locations, raises nature beyond a generalized backdrop or some aspect overshadowed by other features of the narrative. The exactness of the language in these sections, and others similar to them, helps foreground the importance of nature throughout the novel, and, as implied in both sections, the characters throughout the novel pay nature a similar level of attention, heightening its prominence.

Similar to the narrator, characters repeatedly deal with nature. Through sight, speech, thought, and bodily movement, they grant significance to natural elements in the narrative. Throughout the novel, the landscape is continually "looked out over" (59, 62, 70), and "looked out to" (45); it is "admired" (93), "studied" (57, 279), "took in" (49), discussed in multiple contexts (25, 34, 55, 93, 226), "watched" (88, 283), "gestured at" (88), thought and dreamed about (118, 161), and "passed into" (302). With the inclusion of admiration, study, internal reflection, discussions, and thoughts and dreams, the novel presents nature as an element with which the characters substantially interact. Nature is not a prop on the periphery or a decorative edge for the plot but is integral to these characters and the narrative itself. With each look or gesture, nature becomes ever-present in the novel rather than a soon forgotten background set up in the initial stages of the narrative but thereafter ignored.

Wilderness by Association

This attention of the narrator and characters establishes the significance of nature in the novel. However, with the absence of the term "wilderness" from the novel, wilderness exists by association through words that are typically linked with wilderness: bareness, openness, and wild. Taken as a cluster, these frames of reference point toward a key assumption of wilderness: it consists of lands outside or beyond humanity. To cite language from section 2c of the 1964 Wilderness Act, wilderness is taken to be a place "untrammeled by man" and a site "retaining its primeval character and influence." To be fair, the Act does acknowledge "recreational, scenic, scientific, educational, conservation, and historical use" under section 4b, but when these activities do occur, the Act assumes them to be temporary and secondary to the preservation of "wilderness character." As will be seen below, the novel draws on these frames of reference to stage scenes of wilderness, while also gesturing toward human presences in those locations, in order to redefine ideas of wilderness.

Bareness is first introduced into the novel through a frame of nothingness. Frequently, as the characters are looking toward or watching the land around them, the text notes that there is nothing for them to see. In one example, as the boys ride through northern Mexico, the narrator relates that "there was nothing along the road save the country it traversed and there was nothing in the country at all" (57). Although this continual presence of nothing—an absence—might be related to several characteristics of land, it most directly conveys the idea of bareness, a description of land frequently repeated. Early in their trip, after leaving Reforma, the boys cross mountainous terrain through a "barren windgap" (59). In a similar scene toward the end of the narrative, as John Grady rides north to return home, he rides along a "barren gravel ridge" (269), and the novel ends with him riding through a desert where there are "few cattle in that country because it was barren country" (302). This rugged and harsh territory—barren land—is unable to support and sustain much life, suggesting a location beyond the reach or dwelling of humanity.

As Grady rides across this "barren gravel ridge," the land is also described as "open country," implying an unbounded place, vast in size and removed from human-based environments (269). This connotation is clarified when Grady travels beyond a small town named Torreón to sleep in a "field far from any town," in the "open country," where he watches the "stars trace the arc of the hemisphere" (256). While the confined and human site of Torreón provides a contrast to emphasize the openness of Grady's evening camp, the stars and the vastness of the sky above act to reinforce the openness of the country that unfolds beyond a human presence.

Barrenness and openness imply a presence of wilderness by way of association, but the use of "wild" throughout the novel is linked to wilderness etymologically, and it directly forms a connection to that which is beyond the reach or influence of humanity. As Roderick Frazier Nash details in his cultural history of wilderness, "will," as an English root of "wilderness," derives from "early Teutonic and Norse languages" and conveys ideas of being "self-willed, willful, or uncontrollable" (1). According to Nash, the word "wild" derived as an adjective from this root word, which was initially applied to animals, specifically those "creatures not under the control" of humanity (1). Completing the form that we use today, "'wilder' gave rise to 'wildern' and finally 'wilderness'" (2).

McCarthy's novel mirrors these historical uses of the wild and their association with wilderness to mark environments throughout the novel, but it is specifically applied to animals or vegetation outside the control of humanity. As the boys ride through "old lava country" in search of water, they discover the "senseless tracks of birds or wild pigs" (87). In this context, "senseless" signifies the same as "wild" as both are beyond the meaning or structures of humans, and by extension, so is the land in which they ride. The term *wild* is similarly applied to horses the boys locate during their ranching work in Coahuila as they must ride into mountainous territory, away from the presence of the ranch, to track the animals. In addition to describing animals, the wild also applies to vegetation. For example, toward the end of the novel, John Grady rides through an old apple grove, but the apples have "gone wild and brambly" (226). The implication in this use is similar to the wild animals, but the order is reversed. The wild animals have always been or are initially outside human control, but the apples that were at one time tended by humans, are now neglected. This scene of the apple orchard is an important lens for broadening a reading of wilderness throughout the novel and for examining how the narrative reimages wilderness.

A Wilderness of Interrelation

As implied by the abandoned apple orchard, while *All the Pretty Horses* stages scenes of wilderness through attributes of bareness, openness, and wildness, it simultaneously complicates those same places by gesturing toward human traces that remain. In this presentation of wilderness, McCarthy's novel is not only situated within wilderness spaces, but it also reimages wilderness by tracing interconnections between spaces traditionally defined as beyond human influence and vestiges of human work and habitation in the form of ranch animal bones and in the ruins of former ranches.

This reimaging of wilderness is initiated in the early pages of the novel when John Grady rides south with "the sun coppering his face and the red wind blowing of out the west" (5). Dismounting atop a small hill, he picks up an old horse skull that has become "frail and brittle. Bleached paper white," and as he turns the skull in his hands, he looks at the "comicbook teeth loose in their sockets" and hears the "muted run of sand in the brainbox" (6). The sun, sand, and wind emphasize nature while the horse skull represents human culture, for the horse is likely linked with the ranches in the area.

Nature and human culture intertwine here, as the sand resides within the skull and the skull rests in the sand.

A more direct relation between nature and humanity is visible in the ruins of old ranches. Early in the novel, Grady and his father ride across a "stony mesa" and pass through the "ruins of an old ranch" where "crippled fenceposts" that carry "remnants of wire not seen in that country for years" are propped among the rocks in the midst of an "ancient pickethouse" and the "wreckage of an old wooden windmill" (23). They ride past these objects and rouse "ducks up out of potholes," and by evening they descend "through low rolling hills and across the red clay floodplain" (23). The ranch ruins, the ducks, and the geographical landforms mark and define this land as a location of nature and human culture, existing simultaneously at the same time, in the same location.

Redefining Wilderness

The presentation of wilderness throughout *All the Pretty Horses* thereby consists of a double move: gesturing toward traditional images and markers of wilderness while also reimaging those spaces through the inclusion of human influence and artifacts. Within this image of wilderness, the novel works toward redefining wilderness in three ways: by adding additional sites of value, by shifting definitions from a hierarchical to a horizontal structure, and by considering wilderness as a fluid space, a place of rewilding.

Additional Sites of Value

By intertwining aspects of barrenness, openness, and wildness with images of apple orchards and remnants of human work and habitation, the novel is combining what is typically considered intrinsic to wilderness with aspects taken as extrinsic. To return to the language of the Wilderness Act, wilderness is seen as a contrast or even an opposition to "those areas where man and his works dominate the landscape." Throughout section 2c, wilderness is defined as a place "without permanent improvement or human habitation," a site that has been "affected primarily by the forces of nature." By considering elements that are both intrinsic and extrinsic to wilderness, the novel broadens the scope of what is considered significant to wilderness, and, as a result, the traces of humanity shift from an undesired and invasive extra to a site of value that aids understanding and clarifies perception of wilderness areas.

To revisit the scene when John Grady and his father ride through the ruined ranch with "crippled fenceposts" and a wrecked windmill, they have recently passed through "broken hills" and "cobbled" ground (23). Although "cobbled" can designate the action of bringing together and repairing, as in "cobbling together" or in reference to a repairer of shoes, it also speaks of a fracturing. A cobbled road is one paved with parts of brick or stone. The context of the sentence leans toward this second connotation of "fracturing" by placing "cobbled" in relation with "broken," with both adjectives similarly signifying a ruined or derelict aspect of the land. As such, the "crippled fenceposts" and wrecked windmill aid in understanding a broken and fractured land, each reinforcing meaning found in the other.

The most poignant reference to an extension of wilderness values occurs when Grady rides through the aforementioned abandoned apple orchard; beyond which, he walks his horse inside the "ruins of an old cabin" (225–26). Roof beams lie partially dismantled in the room, former fires have claimed window frames and sashes, and tacks hold an old calf hide to a wall. There is a "strange air to the place," and Grady's horse "liked nothing about it" (226). The scene ends as Grady turns in the room, leaves, and rides out past a marshland where "doves called in the winey light" (226).

The transition into and away from the abandoned orchard and cabin might suggest that Grady experiences two distinct locations in this passage: a site of wild nature and a site of human culture. Yet, it is just as accurate to argue that the orchard and cabin do not separate Grady from a sense of the wild, for these aspects emphasize a sense of a wild nature that he has experienced throughout his ride. The apple trees that have gone "wild and brambly" doubly signify; they represent human culture in the former cultivation of them while also referencing a wild condition beyond the care of humans as they have become gnarled and entangled (226). Similarly, the cabin indicates the presence of human culture in the walls that remain as well as a sense of the wild by what is now missing. The holes where roof joists, windows, and doors once were now intertwine with sun, rain, and other natural elements. Moreover, the horse and Grady are psychologically attuned to the elements of the wild in the "strange air" throughout the place. In these ways, the strange cabin and brambly apple trees sharpen and accentuate John Grady's experience of a wild place.

From Hierarchical to Horizontal

A second way that McCarthy's novel works to redefine wilderness is by challenging preferences of natural elements to aspects related to humanity. As indicated at the start of this chapter, definitions of wilderness, such as the 1964 Wilderness Act, tend to prioritize what is natural in wilderness over what is related to humanity, often to the point that any history or trace of humanity is erased so that wilderness spaces can appear more natural. McCarthy's novel, however, offers a different image and definition of wilderness, a space where the natural and human co-exist without a ranking. Said differently, and to borrow the language of Gilles Deleuze and Félix Guattari, *All the Pretty Horses* represents a move from arborescent (tree-like) systems to rhizomatic (horizontal) interactions. According to Deleuze and Guattari, "Arborescent systems are hierarchical systems," in which different parts are seen as an "*opposed segment*" [emphasis in the original] (16, 21). A rhizomatic relationship is "acentered, nonhierarchical"; it "connects any point to any other point," which can be indicated through repeated conjunctions such as "and . . . and . . . and" (21, 25). Like a ginger root, the novel's redefinition of wilderness situates sites of value as parallel and horizontal nodes or hubs that share equal significance and meaning. It creates this relationship in two ways: by collecting the human and nonhuman into a single category of "thingness" and by grammatical form.

Throughout the novel, humans are equated with water, ground, and horses with each expression of life being equalized with others as it is placed within a single grouping of "thing." During a thunderstorm, for example, Blevins strips off his clothes and huddles on the ground in fear, and the text identifies him as a "thing . . . in that landscape" (70). This equating of all things occurs even more overtly later in the novel when John Grady shoots a doe. Sitting next to the dying deer, Grady thinks about his lover Alejandra, and he also recalls the "birds and the cattle standing in the grass and the horses on the mesa" (282). As the sky darkens, "a cold blue cast had turned the doe's eyes to but one thing more of things she lay among in that darkening landscape. Grass and blood. Blood and stone" (282). The fading light casts an equalizing light over the doe, grass, and stone alike, shading each object similarly and assembling them into a nonhierarchical category. Likewise, as Grady remembers Alejandra and the live animals on the mesa, they are connected through themes of physical absence and loss. Like the birds and cattle in the grass, and similar to the horses on the mesa, Alejandra is now lost to Grady. Just as the fading light flattens hierarchies between the doe's eyes, grass, and rocks, so the memories of John Grady situate Alejandra within a coordinating relationship—rather than a hierarchical one—with the land, animals, and vegetation.

What the content and category of "thingness" indicate, the novel's grammatical form also implies in a writing style of McCarthy's that is often labeled as "optical democracy." The phrase derives from the author's 1985 novel, *Blood Meridian*, as riders encounter a land in which "all phenomena were bequeathed a strange equality" (247). Such equality proceeds from a vision where no one thing is more "luminous" or "enshadowed" than another, resulting in an "optical democracy" where "a man and a rock become endowed with unguessed kinships" (247). This observation and argument about McCarthy's writing style has long been discussed by literary critics, but to cite one example, as a way of defining optical democracy, David Holloway writes that "optical democracy first of all means looking at landscape, and then writing about landscape, in such a way that any anthropocentric assumption of human primacy over the natural world is rejected" (192). In McCarthy's optical democracy, the hierarchy of human over nature is collapsed into a horizontal relationship of equity.

Applying optical democracy to McCarthy's grammatical forms, Phillip and Delys Snyder argue that his writing "tends to privilege coordination rather than subordination" through his ubiquitous use of coordinating conjunctions in the creation of lists that equate all items in the list in a "linguistic democracy" (33). As the Snyders highlight, the use of "and" produces a "democratic compound subject" between humans and rocks (33). These observations return the analysis of McCarthy's wilderness spaces back to the previous point about rhizomatic organization and its use of conjunctions to create alliances rather than oppositions.

The novel's subject-verb structure complements this use of conjunctions in supporting nature-human coordination by downplaying the typical focus of English sentences: a human who acts. As Nancy Kreml observes, McCarthy's sentences often lack direct objects, "actions happen . . . without an actor, who acts upon something else" (39–40). When actors do appear, they do not act as "agents" (40). I would go farther and add that McCarthy often strips his sentences of action altogether, granting more attention to objects, raising them to a similar value to humans. To revisit the example used earlier in this chapter, before the boys reach the hacienda, "they rode down through the cooling blue shadowland of the north slope. Evergreen ash growing in the rocky draws. Persimmon, mountain gum" (59). This passage progressively becomes void of action and actants, or what Kreml identifies as agents. The actants of the first sentence are missing by the final phrase, placing the focus on objects: the plants, which balances the overall emphasis on the humans in the early part of the passage.

Rewilding Wilderness

In its action to redefine wilderness by assigning value to nature and human culture alike and by flattening hierarchies between those aspects, *All the Pretty Horses* presents a wilderness of interrelation and interchange. Human aspects are folded into rhythms of nature just as those same natural aspects reflect the presence and influence of humanity. To reference recent work from the field of environmental history, McCarthy's novel redefines wilderness as a space that is rewilding.

"Rewilding" was first used in a 1990 *Newsweek* article by Jennifer Foote to describe actions of environmental advocacy groups, and since then, the word has come to be linked with a wide array of environmental actions, policies, definitions. One such use of the word relates to a reintroduction of animals into an environment. The focus in this sense of the word is a reestablishment of keystone species, as seen in the vision of The Rewilding Institute, with the overall goal to reestablish a presence of large carnivores in areas where they have been eliminated, reintroducing a sense of wild into such locations. A second, related, but distinct use of "rewilding," pertains to land itself, as described in the anthology *Wilderness Comes Home* . The focus might be replanting native grasses in prairies or helping to reforest part of a mountainous terrain, but the intent is similar: a reintroduction of some natural element that has gone missing and is deemed foundational to defining a space as wild.

While these understandings of rewilding are significant and continue to guide much of the discussion around this topic, a third use of the term is more pertinent to McCarthy's novel, a use that has been developed by the environmental historian James Feldman. According to Feldman, rewilding is a return of wild nature in places of previous human habitation and work, but such landscapes "should be interpreted as evidence neither of past human abuse nor of triumphant wild nature, but as examples of the ongoing impact of human choices on natural processes and of natural conditions on human history" (9). To make his point more direct, Feldman goes on to say that rewilding wildernesses "represent both history and nature, working simultaneously and together" (9). Taking Feldman's point within the context of this chapter and McCarthy's novel, a rewilding wilderness is a site where the traces of humanity are fading, giving way to nature, but also a site that upholds both the natural and the human to examine the dynamic interchange between them.

In the various scenes described earlier in this chapter, a declining human presence within wilderness is implied. As Grady picks up the "frail and brittle" horse skull, as the characters discover ranch ruins with “crippled fenceposts” and the “wreckage” of an ancient windmill, and as Grady rides through the abandoned apple orchard and decaying cabin, these scenes and objects indicate sites where the human is waning. The sun bleaching the horse skull slowly turns it white, and the UV rays weaken the skull, a process abetted by the sand and its etchings inside the “brainbox.” Such interactions remove the skull from its associations with ranching practices, moving it toward dust and the natural elements of which it is composed. The “crippled” fence posts and wrecked windmill indicate movement toward a rewilded state as they break down, folding back toward nature.

Yet even as the novel presents and redefines wilderness as such, it also portrays these places as sites of interchange between human and natural elements, which can be seen in two ways: John Grady’s interaction with horses and his efforts to be folded into or to become part of landscapes.

Soon after Grady and Rawlins begin their work at the hacienda in Coahuila, local vaqueros bring in sixteen “wild” colts (98). When the boys begin to work with them, they rope one and “the other horses flared and bunched and look back wildly” (103). They smelled like “wild animals” (103). If Robert Jarrett’s claim that in *All the Pretty Horses* the “horse is a particularly complex symbolic representation of the relation between the human and the natural” is admissible, then Grady’s and Rawlins’s horse-breaking represents a significant encounter between humanity and wild nature (107). This encounter, similar to Feldman’s idea of nature and humanity working together, demonstrates the dynamic interchange present in wilderness rewilding sites in this novel. Grady’s work with the horses shows his desire to intermingle with and become part of horses, and, by extension, nature. Initiating his work with the horses, Grady presses a horse’s head against his chest where its “hot sweet breath” rises up, over his “face and neck,” where he can feel the horse’s blood and speak to it (103). By noon on the first day, the “voice of the breaker [is] still running in their brains like the voice of some god come to inhabit them” (105). Like the skull in the sand

and the decaying fenceposts in the rocks noted above, Grady and the horses—human and nature—are intermingling here.

An even more direct version of this dynamic interchange between nature and human occurs later in the novel, during a trip into the mountains above the hacienda, when John Grady lies on the ground, watching the stars overhead. He places his "hands on the ground at either side of him and pressed them against the earth," and in this position he "slowly turned dead center to the world, all of it taut and trembling and moving enormous and alive under his hands" (119). Comparable to his interaction with the horses, Grady pulls himself close to the earth, pressing into it. As he allows the horse's breath to rise up over him in the previous scene, and as he locks into the rhythm of the blood in the horse, so, too, in this scene Grady's movements come to resemble those of the earth as he "centers" himself within its rhythms. This interchange between Grady and the land about him holds throughout the final pages of the novel, until a last interaction occurs when he "passed and paled into the darkening land" (302).

Wilderness Reimagined

The Wilderness Act of 1964 collected and ratified images and ideas of wilderness, presenting wilderness as a site set apart, a place preserved from the ravages of humanity. Although this Act is crucial for protecting invaluable lands, it simultaneously sets up unrealistic expectations of and experiences in lands supposedly free of human influence. In contrast to these assumptions, to access wilderness is to encounter a place bearing the stories of human history, the traces of human experiences, and the evidence of significant interactions between natural and human elements. To recognize both aspects: the land set aside and the human echoes in those spaces, and to borrow a phrase from William Cronon's now-famous essay "The Trouble with Wilderness, or, Getting Back to the Wrong Nature," "The time has come to rethink wilderness" (69).

Narratives and stories are crucial to such a rethinking of wilderness, and Cormac McCarthy's novel *All the Pretty Horses* is one example where this takes place. By carefully attending to nature and wilderness, the novel reminds us that such places are not peripheral to the often more-emphasized plots of humanity. Conversely, the novel also displays human elements present within wilderness areas. For McCarthy, narratives of wilderness are stories of interaction and dramatic interchange between nature and humanity. As John Grady encounters and becomes part of the land around him, *All the Pretty Horses* narrates a posture in a rewilding wilderness that does not place the human in a position of opposition to nature, as an element removed from the land, or as the focal point. Rather, the novel moves that human figure toward finding the rhythms of an environment, enfolding the self into them, and thereby coexisting within natural elements.

Works Cited

Cronon, William. "The Trouble with Wilderness, or, Getting Back to the Wrong Nature." *Uncommon Ground: Toward Reinventing Nature*. Edited by William Cronon. Norton, 1995, pp. 69–90.

Deleuze, Gilles, and Félix Guattari. *A Thousand Plateaus: Capitalism and Schizophrenia*. Translated by Brian Massumi. U of Minnesota P, 1987.

Feldman, James. *A Storied Wilderness*. U of Washington P, 2011.

Foote, Jennifer. "Trying to Take Back the Planet." *Newsweek*, 5 Feb. 1990, pp. 24–25.

Holloway, David. "Modernism, Nature, and Utopia: Another Look at 'Optical Democracy.' in Cormac McCarthy's Western Quartet." *Southern Quarterly*, vol. 38, no. 3, Spring 2000, pp. 186–205.

Jarrett, Robert Lee. *Cormac McCarthy*. Twayne, 1997.

Klyza, Christopher McGrory, editor. *Wilderness Comes Home: Rewilding the Northeast.* UP of New England, 2001.

Kreml, Nancy. "Stylistic Variation and Cognitive Constraint in *All the Pretty Horses*." *Sacred Violence: Cormac McCarthy's Western Novels*. Edited by Wade Hall and Rich Wallach, vol. 2, Texas Western P, 2002, pp. 37–49.

McCarthy, Cormac. *All the Pretty Horses.* Vintage, 1993.

__________. *Blood Meridian*. Vintage, 1992.

Nash, Roderick Frazier. *Wilderness and the American Mind.* 4th edition, Yale UP, 2001.

"The Rewilding Institute's Vision and Work." *Rewilding Institute*, rewilding.org/about-tri/vision/.

Snyder, Phillip A., and Delys W. Snyder. "Modernism, Postmodernism, and Language: McCarthy's Style." *The Cambridge Companion to Cormac McCarthy*. Edited by Steven Frye. Cambridge UP, 2013, pp. 7–40.

"The Wilderness Act." *Wilderness Connect*, wilderness.net/learn-about-wilderness/key-laws/wilderness-act/default.php.

Cooper, McCarthy, and the Nineteenth-Century Roots of *All the Pretty Horses*

Jericho Williams

Blood Meridian (1985) marked a major transition for Cormac McCarthy from writing about the Appalachian region of the United States to the American West. Prior to the publication of this book, critics cited the novels and short stories of southern author and Modernist William Faulkner (1897–1962) as obvious precursors to McCarthy's work. *Blood Meridian*, though, suggested other influences from long before Faulkner's lifetime. For example, the novel's detailed subheadings for each of its chapters mirror a fictional style popular in the eighteenth century and common in narratives such as Jonathan Swift's *Gulliver's Travels* (1726), as well as Washington Irving's western works [*A Tour on the Prairies* (1835), *Astoria* (1836), and *The Adventures of Captain Bonneville* (1837)] from the nineteenth century. As McCarthy delved deeper into American history, and particularly in relation to the American West, he employed new modes and means of writing stories that also suggested connections with American literary history.

Although technically also a western, or perhaps better described as a neo-western or experimental western, McCarthy's next novel, *All the Pretty Horses* (1992), the first of what became known as the *Border Trilogy* along with *The Crossing* (1994) and *Cities of the Plain* (1998), differs significantly from *Blood Meridian* in story, approach, and character. It is arguably the most romantic book in McCarthy's oeuvre and features John Grady Cole, one of the author's most memorable characters. As in the case of *Blood Meridian*, though, *All the Pretty Horses* also bears some resemblance to works that predate Owen Wister's *The Virginian* (1904), which is sometimes described as the first prominent novel within what became known as the western genre in American literature. Gone are the detailed chapter subheadings of *Blood Meridian*, but central to the story is Cole, whose distinctly American outlook recalls prior classic characters with strong moral viewpoints grappling with rapidly changing environments.

Cole's spirit and situation harken back to nineteenth-century American fiction and invite a comparison with American literature's first popular romantic literary hero, Natty Bumppo from James Fenimore Cooper's *The Leatherstocking Tales* (1823–41), a five-novel series. Like Bumppo, Cole appears in multiple books in The *Border Trilogy*, including *Cities of the Plain*, and shares a strong likeness with Bumppo, who intuits uncomfortable changes in his surroundings, maintains a strong moral compass, relocates as necessary, and never quite seems at home or grounded in one place, largely because the America he idealizes and desires to inhabit exists ephemerally, if at all. The book that best reveals this likeness is Cooper's *The Deerslayer* (1841), which features Bumppo at his youngest stage of life, or "just arriving at manhood" (493) as Cooper describes in the preface of an 1850 edition. Though technically the final book that Cooper wrote about Bumppo, *The Deerslayer* not only depicts his hero as roughly the same age as Cole but has also been considered the most romantic and environmentally evocative novel of the series. Although Cooper and McCarthy's diction choices and narrative styles remain starkly different, the stories they tell of American protagonists coming to terms with shifting societal values and realities are remarkably similar. The following discusses the origin and development of a personal code that elevates the idealistic Natty Bumppo (aka Deerslayer) and John Grady Cole to mythic status in American literature and accounts for the ways that both Cooper' and McCarthy's novels explore the possibility and perils of romance and violent tests to ensure survival.

The Formation of a Personal Code

A key difference between *The Deerslayer* and *All the Pretty Horses* is that by the time readers during James Fenimore Cooper's time read the fifth and final book of *The Leatherstocking Series*, *The Deerslayer* functioned more or less as a prequel to a set of adventure stories many had previously read. Between *The Deerslayer*'s initial release date and the present, critics, scholars, and readers have debated the merits and drawbacks of reading the series in publication order, which is 4-2-5-3-1, versus following the life span of Cooper's hero, which entails reading the novels out of publication sequence (i.e., 1841, 1826, 1840, 1823, and 1827). Depending upon one's point of view, arguable cases can be made for both approaches. From one perspective, two of the first three novels Cooper wrote detail Natty Bumppo's final years, and so it seems that they might be best read following the stories of his youth and middle age. From another angle, though, and particularly if one is interested in Cooper's life trajectory and writing career, the two 1840 novels feel distinctly different from the prior three from the 1820s, undoubtedly because the author lived abroad for the bulk of the 1830s. As Daniel H. Peck notes, Cooper spent much time during his decade writing books with a strong emphasis on social and political commentary (ix). In *The Pathfinder* and then *The Deerslayer*, published one year apart in 1840 and 1841, Cooper returned to his popular series with stronger and more conflicted opinions about the United States than during the 1820s, but perhaps, too, as a means of retreat. Like McCarthy, who moved to the American Southwest a little less than a decade prior to writing *Blood Meridian*, a major relocation impacted Cooper's outlook and artistic development.

As a result, and in contrast to *All the Pretty Horses*, Cooper focuses on the early formation of his protagonist's values in *The Deerslayer* with Natty Bumppo's entire lifetime already in published form. Throughout *The Leatherstocking series*, although characters refer to Bumppo using a variety of sobriquets or names, including Deerslayer, Hawkeye, Pathfinder, Leatherstocking, and the trapper, Bumppo's personal code remains consistent. Readers coming to *The Deerslayer* in 1841 would have expected something akin to an origin story that would serve as a basis for a familiar hero. Describing the genesis of Bumppo and offering a glimpse of what he aimed to do throughout the series, Cooper later reflected, "The idea of delineating a character that possessed little of civilization but its highest principles as they are exhibited in the uneducated, and all of savage life that is not incompatible with these great rules of conduct, is perhaps natural to the situation in which Natty was placed" ("Preface" 489). Therefore, if *The Deerslayer* would account for Bumppo's coming of age, this called for detailing the formation of a perspective grounded in rugged values shaped by environmental impressions and Native American culture, as well as Christianity to some extent, mirroring Cooper's own "disdain for organized religion" but reverence for private and spontaneous spiritual moments between humans and God (Mann 7). In the process, he created a character template that would later serve as a basis for countless American protagonists found in various western novels and stories. Bumppo exhibits an unapologetic lack of formal education and formality, and in some ways offers a rebuttal of European civilization by embodying what Cooper imagined as the best of American culture.

The Deerslayer's many narrative twists and turns highlight Bumppo's developing ethic. Described succinctly, the story involves tension and violence between White settlers and members of Delaware and Mingo Native American tribes. It includes two White men with mysterious pasts or questionable ethics, Hurry Harry and Tom Hutter; two White sisters, Judith and Hetty Hutter; Bumppo and his closest companion Chingachgook, a Delaware chief; Hist, a Native American woman whom Chingachgook loves; and Rivenoak, chief of the Mingos; at the end of the novel, Uncas, Chingachgook and Hist's son. From the opening pages, however, the central character is Bumppo, initially referred to as Deerslayer in the novel. The first description of Bumppo conveys that his expression is "that of guileless truth, sustained by an earnestness of purpose, and a sincerity of feeling" (498). Cooper continues, "few came in serious contact with the man, without losing this distrust in respect for his opinions and motives" (499). In a similar manner as McCarthy adopts in his presentation of John Grady Cole in *All the Pretty Horses*, Bumppo appears upright and unblemished.

There is also no evidence of his inheriting positive attributes directly from either his parents or family members, yet it becomes clear that during the 1740s setting, Cooper views his protagonist as embodying the best of America. Questioning the novel's literary value more than a century later, George Dekker wrote, "how can a work of art that is so often gauche, improbable, crowded, bigoted, puerile—how can such a work form, as I believe *The Deerslayer* does, an aesthetic whole which is intensely moving and convincing?" (170). The answer to that question rests on Bumppo's shoulders within a narrative that celebrates his genuineness, morality, active nature, and outdoor skills within a picturesque setting on Otsego Lake, which Cooper refers to as Lake Glimmerglass in the novel and exists in reality outside of Cooperstown, New York, a village Cooper's father founded during the 1780s.

A young and idealistic central character also accounts for the success and popularity of *All the Pretty Horses*. Unlike Cooper, McCarthy wrote *All the Pretty Horses* near the end of a century that witnessed the rise of the American western, a literary subgenre that became one of a few distinct art forms associated with the United States and includes the blues and jazz music. Western films and television shows, arguably more culturally influential than novels and short stories that inspired some of them, peaked in popularity in the 1940s, 1950s, and early 1960s. By the mid-to-late 1960s and stretching into the 1970s and 1980s, the genre declined in cultural influence, though it still attracted artists interested in innovating it for new generations.

Antiheroes such as the Man with No Name, portrayed by Clint Eastwood in Sergio Leone's trilogy of Italian spaghetti westerns [*A Fistful of Dollars* (1964), *For a Few Dollars More* (1965), and *The Good, the Bad and the Ugly* (1966)], and movies such as Robert Altman's *McCabe and Mrs. Miller* (1971) presented uncommon main characters. And novels such as Charles Portis's *True Grit* (1968) and Ron Hansen's *The Assassination of Jesse James by the Coward Robert Ford* (1983) supported claims that some Westerns could be considered literary. Penning *Blood Meridian* (1985), McCarthy conveyed that he inherited and sought to innovate a literary and revisionist Western tradition. The antiheroic main character in that novel, known as "the kid" and later as "the man," navigates a bleak and hyper-violent world that stretches from during the late 1840s through the late 1870s. *All the Pretty Horses*, McCarthy's next book, places an entirely different and more sympathetic Cole at its center, and largely for that reason, immediately became more popular than its predecessor.

The setting of *All the Pretty Horses* is Texas and Mexico in 1949, and like *The Deerslayer*, the novel begins with a likable protagonist experiencing a conflict that sparks movement and adventure. Here, it is worth noting that McCarthy's writing style differs significantly from James Fenimore Cooper's. The earlier writer's style tends to be verbose and requires patience on the part of modern readers. Mark Twain famously quipped that "there are nineteen rules governing literary art in the domain of romantic fiction," (693) and that Cooper violated eighteen of them in *The Deerslayer*, including #18: "Employ a simple and straightforward style" (695). A simple and straightforward style is certainly more characteristic of McCarthy's approach in *All the Pretty Horses*, although like Modernist writers who appeared after Mark Twain, and Ernest Hemingway in particular, McCarthy's prose suggests carefully chosen scenes and details to convey character. The first two pages of the book feature a glimpse of Cole at his grandfather's funeral. McCarthy writes, "Lastly he looked at the face so caved and drawn among the folds of the funeral cloth, the yellowed mustache, the eyelids paper thin. That was not sleeping. That was not sleeping" (3). Stripping away common forms of punctuation such as apostrophes and commas, McCarthy places readers in the midst of a scene of a sixteen-year-old young man losing someone important to him. This is not fully clear, however, until the following pages present the conflict: the coming loss of a ranch central to Cole's youth and identity. Unlike Natty Bumppo, what prompts Cole's grand adventure is family related. Neither his father, a former World War II prisoner, or his mother, a struggling actress living more than two hundred miles away in San Antonio, have any strong interest in keeping the ranch. As the story continues, readers learn that just prior to Cole's grandfather's death, his mother appears to orchestrate a scheme to inherit and then sell the ranch.

Consequently, Cole faces the toughest predicament of his life, one that will inspire him to flee the area to avoid having to move and drastically change his lifestyle. McCarthy, via selectively revealing sparse details about Cole's family, conveys the great extent of his protagonist's identity crisis. Like Bumppo, Cole comes to appear not as the son of his parents so much as a child of surrogate parents and a mentor from another culture, in this case Latin American rather than Native American. In one of the most valuable critical responses to the novel, Jeffrey Herlihy-Mera notes that for fifteen of his sixteen years of life, a Latin American family residing and working on the ranch serve as Cole's family and guardians (473). Consisting of a married couple, Luisa and Arturo, and Luisa's mother, Abuela, who has lived there for fifty years or more, this trio of adults raises Cole while his parents are away at war and pursuing an acting career. After Cole's grandfather passes, Cole has no biological family members who share his passion for a ranch lifestyle, and like Bumppo, he retains a strong conviction that an outdoor-oriented lifestyle best allows him to pursue the life he desires to live.

The impetus for Cole's abrupt abandonment of both the ranch and Texas with Lacey Rawlins (his friend) is a love of horse culture (betrayed by parents, who abandon ranch life). Soon after his grandfather's funeral, Cole discusses the possibility of leasing the ranch from his mother, promising her to send her all of the earnings. She replies, "All the money. You don't know what you're talking about. There's not any money. This place has barely paid expenses for twenty years. There don't been a white person worked here since before the war. Anyway you're sixteen years old, you cant run a ranch" (15). Absent most of his life pursuing a career in California and then San Antonio, Cole's mother represents a stark rebuke to his grandfather's way of life. She understands the ranch only in monetary terms and plans to sell it.

Like Bumppo, Cole temporarily becomes homeless, electing to pursue an adventurous outdoor lifestyle that increasingly harkens back to the prior century rather than move to town and adapt to a modern way of life. While Cooper and McCarthy's writing styles differ significantly, the sense of independence that Cole feels while working outdoors functions as an extension of Bumppo's priorities nearly two centuries later. In both cases, their personal philosophies urge them to risk conflict and violence in unsettled or perilous places rather than accept inevitable unfulfillment they feel certain to find in settlements, villages, or towns. In this way, both characters become mythic figures capable of critiquing the American concept of progress that involves industrialization, rapidly expanding population growth, and the reimagining of the beauty of the wild landscapes as land for sale, to be managed, cultivated, and sold according to profit margins and speculation.

The Possibility of Romance and the Necessity of Violence

Although the stakes for Cooper and McCarthy differed significantly when composing *The Deerslayer* and *All the Pretty Horses*, both authors imply that the possibility of romance and necessary violence are formative experiences for each of their young protagonists. Near the conclusion of *The Deerslayer*, two situations occur that suggest that Bumppo might marry one of two women. During Cooper's time, readers of the prior *Leatherstocking* novels would have known that the chances of this ever happening would be slim. Nonetheless, in the prior novel, *The Pathfinder* (1840), Bumppo did fall in love with a character named Mabel Dunham, and so romance became more central in Cooper's development of the fuller Leatherstocking story. In contrast, during the first three novels published in the 1820s, a serious romance was never a concern for Bumppo, but it became a key narrative element of the final two novels that Cooper composed.

The strongest appeal for marriage in *The Deerslayer* comes from Judith Hutter. At the beginning of the novel, Henry "Hurry Harry" March, Bumppo's traveling companion, expresses romantic interest in Hutter, and he hopes that she will eventually come to consider him a potential marriage partner throughout the story. However, Hutter later denies his marriage request as March is an unacceptable companion and because of her strong attraction to Bumppo. Though only a few years apart in age and skilled in frontier activities such as navigating wilderness areas and hunting, Hurry Harry and Bumppo are otherwise opposites, and often considered as foil characters. The former is known for his physical stature and attractiveness, while the latter is not. Hurry Harry rushes into dangerous situations and resorts to aggression and unquestioned violence, while Bumppo is more conscientious and avoidant of violent actions, if at all possible.

From Hutter's perspective, these and Bumppo's other positive qualities such as sincerity, honesty, and courage make him a far more marriageable choice. At one point, she asks him bluntly, "do you think, Deerslayer, that you could be happy with such a wife as a woman like myself would make?" (901). At first, Bumppo does not take this request seriously given their differences in background. Later, though, when Hutter makes another more direct appeal, he declines, replying that he feels closer to the spirits of his dead parents than any potential marriage partner: "if father and mother was livin', which, howsoever, neither is—but if both was livin', I do not feel towards any woman as if I wish'd to quit 'em in order to cleave *unto* her" (1025). This rebuke angers Hutter, who replies, "This is enough!" (1025). Adhering to character, as someone not always skilled in conveying truth in a kind way, Bumppo pushes Hutter away. His priorities are focused on the greater romance of his life, which is the time he spends pursuing adventures in the frontier woods, relishing a state of mind that already seems antiquated to some of the book's White characters and will "soon be nullified by time and the proclivity of other men to populate and live as social animals in those once-free expanses to which he has led them" (Berger 438). These values are also likely to ensure perpetual bachelorhood.

Though Cooper devotes more narrative space to Judith Hutter's pursuit of Bumppo, there is another marriage suggestion for Bumppo that occurs as a consequence of a major event in the story, the first time he kills someone. Subtitled "The First War-Path," *The Deerslayer* is more preoccupied with Bumppo's thoughts about violence than some of the later novels, where such actions appear more necessary to ensure survival and uphold frontier justice. The opening chapter of *The Deerslayer* reveals what amounts to peer pressure related to violence, when Hurry Harry tells Bumppo, "I shall not frequent your society long, friend Natty, unless you look higher than four footed beasts to practyse [sic] your rifle on" (501). Like John Grady Cole, Bumppo first appears averse to violence. He has previously cultivated a reputation based on his hunting prowess, but sharply distinguishes between hunting for food and subsistence versus harming other humans. Later, when a Mingo man named Le Loup Cervier throws a tomahawk at him, though, Bumppo reacts quickly and shoots him. Cooper writes, "The sensations were novel; and regret, with the freshness of our better feelings, mingled with his triumph" (599). Afterwards, Bumppo demonstrates respect and shows compassion for Le Loup Cervier by placing him close to the nearby Glimmerglass Lake as he dies. However, the social consequences of this tragic event also resurface later in the story. After Bumppo becomes a prisoner of the Mingo tribe, Chief Rivenoak urges him to marry Sumach, Le Loup Cervier's widow, and to help support her and her children with his hunting abilities. As in the case of Judith Hutter, Bumppo declines, citing insurmountable racial differences and lifestyle preferences on his part. Though not a surprise, this is certainly a moment of discomfort—and one that validates Hillary Soames's criticism that underneath Bumppo's "idealism, his innocence, his natural love for the natural world, lies the bedrock of racism" (n.p.). Bumppo's denial of Rivenoak's request to support Sumach also inspires strong objections and begets more violence. Her brother attacks him, and as a result, Bumppo kills another man in self-defense. This scene features a much more complicated murder, one which reveals Bumppo as flawed and self-centered. Cooper's intermingling of violence and romance within a frontier novel heightens the emotional stakes, and it also offers a template that later Western writers, including McCarthy, would explore.

In John Grady Cole's case, a passionate romance eventually prompts his deepest engagement with violence. It begins at a ranch in Mexico, where he and Rawlins find work. Having crossed the border and experienced unexpected dramatic events involving Jimmy Blevins, a runaway who attracts trouble and is later partially responsible for the time they spend in jail, Cole and Rawlins are relieved to find the stability of an operating ranch. Like Bumppo, whenever he inhabits a new and lightly populated frontier area, whether that be in the forests of New York or open spaces now known as the Midwestern prairies in *The Prairie*, Cole's new surroundings are ideal at first glance. The ranch seems like a safe haven in the midst of an "older culture in which it appears that modernity" has not yet begun to render the American ranching life obsolete for members of Cole's generation (Monk 123). If Bumppo's preferred outdoor sport is hunting, Cole's is riding, training, and breaking horses.

Similar to Bumppo, he excels at this activity and receives a promotion that brings him close to the ranch owner Don Héctor Rocha y Villareal's house, where he meets the man's daughter Alejandra and her grand-aunt and godmother Alfonsa. After some time passes, Cole and Alejandra begin a short-lived but passionate affair. Her presence completely alters Cole's behavior, inspiring him to purchase new clothes, attend a dance, and risk his job to see her. At one point, Rawlins cautions him, "I know the old man likes you . . . But that don't mean he'll set still for you courtin his daughter. . . . What I see is you fixin to get us fired and run off the place" (McCarthy 138). Drawing from a lifetime of personal experience and justifying her effort to keep Alejandra at a distance from Cole, Alfonsa provides a stronger and sterner warning: "There is no forgiveness. For women. A man may lose his honor and regain it again. But a woman cannot. She cannot" (137). Cole's reply—"I guess I'd have to say that don't seem right"—is not the right one, from Alfonsa's point of view, and his continued pursuit of a relationship with Alejandra leads to his and Rawlins's arrest (137). As in the case of Bumppo in *The Deerslayer, All the Pretty Horses* encourages readers to side more with Cole's perspective rather than Alfonsa's. Clearly, there is a power struggle between the two, and one in which Alejandra has little-to-no voice. James Lilley argues that the young girl remains underdeveloped as a character because she represents Cole's "own Symbolic power growing" (277). Put another way, she seems less of an individual than a part of Cole's greater struggle to find belonging and a suitable lifestyle at a distance from Texas.

Cole faces a tougher and more violent test when he and Rawlins go to prison. First, they reunite with Blevins, whom they simultaneously consider a major safety liability but also someone they feel responsible for protecting, to some extent, and as one might a younger brother. Corrupt police officers beat them and then Cole and Rawlins experience Blevins's execution en route to a larger prison, where their lives, too, become threatened. During their first day, the pair fight with other prisoners continually. McCarthy writes, "Underpinning all of it like the fiscal standard in commercial societies lay a bedrock of depravity and violence where in an egalitarian absolute every man was judged by a single standard and that was his readiness to kill" (182).

Eventually, in a similar situation as the first time Bumppo kills someone, a prisoner attacks Cole with the intent to kill him, and Cole responds by stabbing the man in his heart. This scene functions as one of Cole's major tests in the story, a reminder of the consequences that have come from his decisions to flee from a society he better understood and pursue an illicit romance with an unapologetically American mindset. Beaten and in pain, Cole has experienced what is viewed as a central tenet of McCarthy's work: "an almost unbearable level of violence" (176).

Fortunately, Alfonsa intercedes on their behalf and Cole and Rawlins are released from prison. Cole attempts to locate and resume a relationship with Alejandra, which fails and sends him back in the direction of Rawlins and the United States. Along the way, he recovers Blevins's horse and suffers from being shot during another violent encounter. Cole finally crosses the border, attempts to locate the owner of Blevins's horse, and has one final conversation with Rawlins, where his friend asks him, "Where is your country?" (299). Cole replies, "I don't know . . . I dont know where it is. I don't know what happens to country" (299). Reflecting on Cole's journey, Linda Woodson maintains that "there is some evidence that he has understood some of the lessons he has been offered," particularly related to summoning courage and responsibility related to his "perceived role" in the death of Jimmy Blevins (19). Perhaps this is the case, as it certainly seems that Cole has matured and accepts changes that include the loss of his father and the passing of Abuela, a pivotal figure in his youth and coming of age on the ranch. He also receives some respite from trying to locate the owner of Blevins's horse. Yet, a new set of scars that Alfonsa once cautioned him about—"Scars have the strange power to remind us that our past is real"—adorn his body and Cole is psychologically impacted by his experience in Mexico (135).

The Deerslayer and *All the Pretty Horses* conclude in similar ways. After fifteen years, Natty Bumppo, now known as Hawkeye rather than Deerslayer, returns to Lake Glimmerglass and reflects on his past adventure and first warpath there. John Grady Cole, in the closing two paragraphs of *All the Pretty Horses*, appears to have been riding his horse for four days in the desert. McCarthy concludes the novel this way: "horse and rider and horse passed on and their long shadows passed in tandem like the shadow of a single being. Passed and paled into the darkening land, the world to come" (302). The future that Bumppo and Cole both face is the future of America, but not one where either will find complete comfort. As romantic heroes in a proto-Western and revisionist Western, different in origin, background, and circumstances and separated by two centuries, but both in love with open spaces and the landscapes of America, they convey similar personas and personal codes challenged by romance and violence.

As Donald Pease noted in 1987, modern American readers of *The Deerslayer* "must consider how and why and even whether they wish to remain" inheritors of national characters such as Natty Bumppo (xxv). Published five years later, the winner of the National Book Award, and a bestselling book that catapulted Cormac McCarthy's literary career to new heights, *All the Pretty Horses* provides a clear answer to Pease's question, at least for now; the romantic literary western novel that Cooper pioneered remains as relevant and revealing of the evolution of American character as ever.

Works Cited

Berger, Thomas. "Afterword." *The Pathfinder,* by James Fenimore Cooper. 1840. Signet, 1961, pp. 429–38.

Cooper, James Fenimore. *The Deerslayer*. 1841. Library of America, 1985.

_________. "Preface to *The Leather-Stocking Tales*." 1850. *The Deerslayer*, by James Fenimore Cooper. Library of America, 1985, pp. 489–92.

Dekker, George. *James Fenimore Cooper: The American Scott*. Routledge and Kegan Paul, 1967.

Herlihy-Mera, Jeffrey. "'Mojado-Reverso' or, A Reverse Wetback: On John Grady Cole's Mexican Ancestry in Cormac McCarthy's *All the Pretty Horses*." *Modern Fiction Studies*, vol. 61, no. 1, Spring 2015, pp. 469–92.

Lilley, James D. "'The Hands of Yet Other Puppets': Figuring Freedom and Reading Repetition in *All the Pretty Horses.*" In *Myth, Legend, Dust: Critical Responses to Cormac McCarthy.* Edited by Rick Wallach. Manchester UP, 2000, pp. 272-287.

Mann, Barbara. "James Fenimore Cooper and God." *Miscellaneous Papers of the James Fenimore Cooper Society*, vol. 30, May 2013, pp. 7–9.

McCarthy, Cormac. *All the Pretty Horses*. 1992. Vintage International, 1993.

Monk, Nicholas. "*All the Pretty Horses*, the Border, and Ethnic Encounter." *The Cambridge Companion to Cormac McCarthy*. Edited by Steven Frye. Cambridge UP, 2013, pp. 121–32.

Pease, Donald. "Introduction." *The Deerslayer*, by James Fenimore Cooper. 1841. Penguin, 1987, pp. vii–xxv.

Peck, Daniel. "Introduction." *The Deerslayer*, by James Fenimore Cooper. 1841. Oxford World's Classics, 1999, pp. vii–xxvii.

Reimer, Jennifer. "All the Pretty Mexican Girls: Whiteness and Racial Desire in Cormac McCarthy's *All the Pretty Horses* and *Cities of the Plain*." *Western American Literature*, vol. 48, no. 4, winter 2014, pp. 422–42.

Soames, Hillary. "Introduction." *The Deerslayer*, by James Fenimore Cooper. 1841. Wordsworth American Library, 1995.

Twain, Mark. "Fenimore Cooper's Literary Offences." 1895. *Collection Nonfiction: Volume I.* Edited by Adam Hochschild. Everyman's Library, 2016, pp. 693–704.

Woodson, Linda. "McCarthy's Heroes and the Will to Truth." *The Cambridge Companion to Cormac McCarthy*. Edited by Steven Frye. Cambridge UP, pp. 15–26.

CRITICAL READINGS

" . . . one thing more of things she lay among": Ecological Form in McCarthy's *All the Pretty Horses*

Seth Forrest

Near the end of *All the Pretty Horses*, John Grady Cole has returned to the Rancho de la Nuestra Señora de la Purísima Concepción, ostensibly to retrieve his belongings but primarily to pursue some degree of closure with Dueña Alfonsa. After speaking with Señora Alfonsa, John Grady leaves the hacienda with his meager belongings, an envelope of cash, and the grullo horse he had broken early in his days at La Purísima. Stopping outside a tiny village, he encounters a group of curious children, who share his sandwiches and ask to hear his story.

> Es una historia larga, he said.
> Hay tiempo, they said.
> He smiled and looked at them and as there was indeed time he told all that had happened. He told them how they had come from another country, two young horsemen riding their horses and that they had met with a third who had no money nor food to eat nor scarcely clothes to cover himself and that he had come to ride with them and share with them in all they had. This horseman was very young and he rode a wonderful horse but among his fears was the fear that God would kill him with lighting and because of this fear he lost his horse in the desert. He then told them what had happened concerning the horse and how they had taken the horse from the village of Encantada and there had killed a man and that the police had come to the hacienda and arrested him and his friend and that the grandmother had paid their fine and then forbidden the novia to see him anymore. (243–44)

Not only does this telling encapsulate the novel's basic plot up to this point, but it reproduces McCarthy's own prose style, as well.

The plot falls into a linear pattern, and for the most part, so does the grammar of sentence structures:

> He smiled and looked at them and as there was indeed time he told all that had happened. He told them how they . . . and that they had met with . . .and that he had come to ride with them. . . . He then told them what had happened . . . and how they had taken the horse . . . and there had killed a man and that the police had come . . . and that the grandmother had paid . . . and then forbidden the novia. . . (243–44)

The overall pattern and style of John Grady's storytelling—this happened, and then this, and because of that another thing happened, and then finally this last thing happened—fits the occasion. It is the kind of patterning that his young audience themselves might use to tell a story, a basic kind of patterning, suitable for oral storytelling. This style is referred to as "simple." Using ellipses here can serve to isolate the main clauses that drive the sentences, grammatically simple in their construction: "He smiled and looked. . . . he told . . . He told them how . . . they had met with . . . he had come to ride with them . . . he then told them . . . the police had come. . ."

Yet, McCarthy shows us that such a linear, additive storytelling can become incredibly complex. Although the sentences themselves emerge from simple grammatical constructions of simple subjects and active verbs, they also combine and add upon each other to evoke rich and detailed descriptions. His most powerful novels, including all three books in the *Border Trilogy*, utilize this overarching structural principle of addition and accumulation and accretion, from the sentence level on up through the novels' plotting. It serves well for plots that involve adventures and journeys and wanderings and repeated attempts to survive under difficult conditions. And as shown in this essay, this style serves well even at the level of the sentence to establish an earthbound and ecological understanding of the world and our place within it.

McCarthy's Style: Polysyndeton and Parataxis

"The magnetic attraction of Mr. McCarthy's fiction," writes the novelist Madison Smartt Bell, "comes first from the extraordinary quality of his prose; difficult as it may sometimes be, it is also overwhelmingly seductive." Bell goes on to describe how the essence of McCarthy's style is "powered by long, tumbling many-stranded sentences."

I want to examine a few of these sentences carefully in order to build up a clear sense of this writing style. From the novel's first page, take the following set of sentences:

> It was dark outside and cold and no wind. In the distance a calf bawled. He stood with his hat in his hand . . . Inside the house there was no sound save the ticking of the mantel clock in the front room. He went out and shut the door.
>
> Dark and cold and no wind and a thin gray reef beginning along the eastern rim of the world. He walked out on the prairie and stood holding his hat like some supplicant to the darkness over them all and he stood there for a long time. (1)

The mirrored first sentences of the two paragraphs present an incredibly basic structure. Indeed, the sentence that begins the second paragraph is a fragment, not an actual clause. The sentence beginning "It was dark" uses the typical *dummy pronoun* (also called a *pleonastic* pronoun) (OED) to describe the weather on the night of John Grady Cole's grandfather's wake. Following the simple subject and verb—*It was*—the predicate presents the weather conditions using a style known as *polysyndeton*, in which the items in a series—"dark," "cold," and "no wind"—are connected using basic conjunctions. We see this style often in McCarthy's writing and will review several more examples in what follows. The sentence beginning the second paragraph omits the *pleonasm* and gets straight to the polysyndetic (OED) set of descriptors, now adding a shelf of distant clouds: "Dark and cold and no wind and a thin gray reef."

Near the end of the novel, McCarthy uses *polysyndeton* to create a long compound predicate, as John Grady prepares himself to take back the horses and exact a measure of revenge on the captain from La Encantada:

> He dismounted and unrolled his plunder and opened the box of shells and put half of them in his pocket and checked the pistol that it was loaded all six cylinders and closed the cylinder gate and put the pistol into his belt and rolled his gear back up and retied the roll behind the saddle and mounted the horse again and rode into the town. (257)

McCarthy packs eleven different active verbs into the predicate of this sentence, connecting them only with the repeated coordinating conjunction "and." The effect is to heighten the detail of description, in a manner not unlike the way a cinematographer might zoom into and track a series of small actions in order to emphasize the level of care and planning being undertaken. The writing grounds us in the moment and slows the action to a series of deliberate movements.

As we see in the first example above, from the night of the wake, McCarthy often employs *polysyndeton* in descriptions of setting. Take this example from just before John Grady and Rawlings first arrive at La Purísima:

> "It rained in the night and the rain hissed in the fire and the horses came in out of the darkness and stood with their red eyes shifting and blinking and in the morning it was cold and gray and the sun a long time coming." (93)

Here we see more than just adjectives strung together in a sequence based on the polysyndeton. The *and* controls the movement of the sentence; indeed, seven of the forty-six words in this sentence are *and*, good for more than fifteen percent of the sentence. Here the *and* joins four simple independent clauses, one after another, in a style known as *parataxis*. (OED)

Polysyndeton and parataxis are the primary stylistic features that create what Bell calls the "long, tumbling many-stranded sentences." Bell goes on in his review to say that "McCarthy seems to be pulling the language apart at its roots. He's noted for archaisms so unfamiliar they appear to be neologisms. His diction and phrasing come from all over the evolutionary history of English and combine into a prose that seems to invent itself as it unfolds." Indeed, this archaic quality of McCarthy's writing also lies in the distinctive style built on *polysyndeton* and *parataxis*.

To further exemplify the style, here is a passage from the beginning of the novel's primary plot. In this scene, John Grady and Rawlings have just left home under cover of night to start their grand adventure into the wild borderlands of Mexico:

> They rode out along the fenceline and across the open pastureland. The leather creaked in the morning cold. They pushed the horses into a lope. The lights fell away behind them. They rode out on the high prairie where they slowed the horses to a walk and the stars swarmed around them out of the blackness. They heard somewhere in that tenantless night a bell that tolled and ceased where no bell was and they rode out on the round dais of the earth which alone was dark and no light to it and which carried their figures and bore them up into the swarming stars so that they rode not under but among them and they rode at once jaunty and circumspect, like thieves newly loosed in that dark electric, like young thieves in a glowing orchard, loosely jacketed against the cold and ten thousand worlds for the choosing. (30)

The first four sentences are constructed simply, almost like bullet points, out of simple subjects and active verbs. The fifth sentence follows this pattern but introduces coordinating conjunctions to create a compound sentence. (McCarthy, of course, omits commas before conjunctions.)

- They rode out . . .
- The leather creaked . . .
- They pushed the horses . . .
- The lights fell away . . .
- They rode out . . .
    - where they slowed the horses . . .
- and the stars swarmed around them . . .

This part of the passage is textbook *parataxis*, particularly the first four sentences, which are connected only by proximity. This is, specifically, *asyndetic parataxis*, meaning that there are no conjunctions at all. The fifth sentence, then, is *syndetic parataxis*, definable by the presence of the *where* and the *and*. Indeed, we could probably argue that the *where* is verging on *hypotaxis* because "where they slowed the horses to a walk" is not an independent clause, meaning that its grammatical completion relies upon a main clause, "they rode out on the high prairie." (*Hypotaxis* refers to sentence construction in which subordination occurs, as in this example: *Although the clause is not complicated*, the preposition "although prevents grammatical completion without a main, or independent, clause.") Similarly, the long last sentence of the passage contains a few spots in which a relative pronoun brings the sentence close to *hypotaxis*, but on the whole, the sentence is overwhelmingly *paratactic* with its backbone of *they heard . . . and they rode . . . they rode . . . and they rode*.

At least as far back as Aristotle's *Rhetoric*, linguists and literary critics have debated the nature and function and effect of *parataxis* and its antonym, *hypotaxis*, and far too much ink has been spilled on the subject to rehearse these debates at any length here.[1] The heart of the scholarly discussion over *parataxis*, though, has been that the style presents simpler structure that is more suitable for oral storytelling. Thoreau, throughout his Journals, mentions *parataxis* as an antidote for the opulence and decadence of the long and periodic, *hypotactic* sentences and paragraphs of nineteenth-century prose style. Richard Dillman, in his "Thoreau's Philosophy of Style," has plumbed the details of Thoreau's journals for his comments connecting grammar and style to the nature of the thought therein described: "[Thoreau] asks us 'Who is not tired of the weak and flowing periods of the politician and scholar, and resorts not even to the Farmer's Almanac to read the simple account of the month's labor, to restore his tone again?'" (qtd. in Dillman 91) Dillman suggests that Thoreau's preference is for sentences plain and forceful, undiluted by *hypotactic* twists and turns away from main clauses, with the "strength and compactness of masonry," "closeness to the physical fact," "a diamond found in the sand, or a pearl fished out of the sea" (qtd. in Dillman 91). Awash in the kind of American Transcendentalism that we see in Emerson and Whitman, Thoreau makes the case for "[s]entences which suggest far more than they say, which have an atmosphere about them . . . as durable as a Roman aqueduct . . . which lie like boulders on the page, up and down or across; which contain the seed of other sentences" (qtd. in Dillman 92).

Thoreau's comments, delivered with his usual acidic criticism for what he saw as the Old World dilettantism of academia in nineteenth-century America, are certainly not the final word on the nature and function of paratactic style, but they raise possibilities for stylistic analysis that have interested recent criticism, especially criticism that is interested in connections between literary style and environmental thought.

Nature Writing, *Chorographia*, and Ambient Poetics

As we might expect, there are a number of scholarly works focused on what McCarthy's fiction has to say about land, wilderness, histories of landscape, and cultural notions of nature. Andrew Estes's *Cormac McCarthy and the Writing of American Spaces* offers perhaps the best overall sense of McCarthy's writing on landscape, analyzing it within the broader context of American environmental culture. Other articles, like Adam Morton's "The Warp of the World," explore the *Border Trilogy* through the lens of a political geographer. And environment comes up sporadically in the essays included in Steven Frye's edited collection, *The Cambridge Companion to Cormac McCarthy*. Yet, most of the scholarship and criticism of nature in McCarthy's novels focus almost exclusively on content, on ideas about land and on interpretations of the meaning of landscapes and settings.

There is an *environmentality*, to use the term of contemporary ecologically oriented literary theory, to McCarthy's text. Certainly, across his best-known novels, McCarthy writes *about* place and space, *about* humanity's fraught relationships with environment, *about* the ways in which people can be determined and affected by places. This is especially true, Alfred Weidie states, of the extreme environments of the Sonoran basins and Madrean woodlands of the border country of New Mexico, Texas, Sonora, Chihuahua, and Coahuila. In addition to writing *about* these environments, their landforms, and their ecology, both human and otherwise, McCarthy employs his unique paratactic style *to write environments*.

Poetry scholar Angus Fletcher has resuscitated and re-envisioned the rhetorical term *chorographia* to describe the kind of writing that strives not merely to describe an environment but to become an environment. Fletcher, in *A New Theory for American Poetry: Democracy, the Environment, and the Future of Imagination*, describes the *chorographic* as "a genre where the poet neither writes *about* the surrounding world, thematizing it, nor analytically represents that world, but actually shapes the poem to *be* an Emersonian or esemplastic circle. . . . [T]hese environment-poems aspire to surround the reader, such that to read them is to have an experience much like suddenly realizing that one actually has an environment, instead of not perceiving the surround at all" (9). By "esemplastic" here, Fletcher refers to a concept of imaginative unity and holistic understanding that was theorized first by the Romantic poet Samuel Taylor Coleridge and developed further by Ralph Waldo Emerson. In practice, it means something like our contemporary understanding of ecology, an *e pluribus* in which the *unum* is understood to be an imaginary construction.

The Romanticist and ecocritical theorist Timothy Morton argues that this kind of writing cultivates what he calls "a poetics of *ambience*." In *Ecology without Nature*, he writes, "Ambience denotes a sense of a circumambient, or surrounding, *world*. It suggests something material and physical, though somewhat intangible, as if space itself had a material aspect" (Morton 33). Cormac McCarthy's writing achieves precisely this kind of writing the world, a *chorographia* that goes beyond description and interpretation of place. Take the following passage from *The Crossing*, in which Billy Parham has been wandering across Sonora following the death of the wolf that he sought to return to the wilds of the Madrean woodlands:

> At the eastern escarpment he dismounted and led the horse along a shelf of gray rock. The scrub juniper that grew along the rim leaned in a wind that had long since passed. Along the face of the stone bluffs were old pictographs of men and animals and suns and moons as well as other representations that seemed to have no referent in the world although they once may have. He sat in the sun and looked out over the country to the east, the broad barranca of the Bavispe and the ensuing Carretas Plain that was once a seafloor and the small pieced fields and the new corn greening in the old lands of the Chichimeca where the priests had passed and soldiers passed and the missions fallen into mud and ranges of mountains beyond the plain range on range in pales of blue where the terrain lay clawed open north and south, canyon and range, sierra and barranca, all of it waiting like a dream for the world to come to be, world to pass. (135)

The writing here establishes a narrative position that is all around Billy Parham *and* all around the reader and creates an ecological web of rock, geological formations, flora both wild and cultivated, human and animal presence. There are also presences of the spectrum we think of as time, both on a human scale and a geological scale. The ancient pictographs are paratactically aligned adjacent to the locomotive, as the plowed fields sit atop the floor of a Cretaceous-Period ocean. All of these things are equally present in this environment as they are present equally in a single paragraph. Landscape and history, both ancient and modern, are equally present here in an ecological togetherness, the human world buzzing at the surface of geological depths. The *chorographia* is rendered in McCarthy's polysyndeton and parataxis, creating the kind of ambient environmentality that Morton describes, and McCarthy does this not simply by writing *about* ecological relationships and geological strata, but by encoding ecology and geology in the *written-ness* of his language.

McCarthy's Ambience: *Parataxis* and Basin and Range

McCarthy achieves this level of *chorographia* and *ambient poetics* again and again in *All the Pretty Horses* and throughout the *Border Trilogy*. In this last section of the chapter, I want to study two passages from near the end of *All the Pretty Horses*. In both passages,

John Grady wanders back through the Parras Basin, a small region of desert terrain pocked by isolated freshwater wetlands known as ciénagas, and up into the mountain ranges of the Sierra Madre Oriental. Geologists know this area as the southern extension of the Basin and Range Province, a geological region that stretches north into modern-day Nevada and south into the heart of central Mexico. The Basin and Range is limited on its northern end by the Sierra Nevada Mountains of California to the west and the Laramide Mountains of the Rockies to the east, and on its southern end by the Sierra Madre Occidental and Sierra Madre Oriental. *All the Pretty Horses* and the entire *Border Trilogy* are set within the landscapes of the southern Basin and Range.

In the first passage, John Grady has already met with Dueña Alfonsa for the last time and has retrieved the horses from the Captain in La Encantada and has just been dispossessed of the Captain, who he held hostage, by the "hombres del país." Left alone, with no particular direction, no real home to return to in San Angelo and no beloved to pursue in Mexico, John Grady simply wanders the country: "By evening all the north country was black and the wind was cold and he picked his way across the rim country through the sparse swales of grass and broken volcanic rock and he sat above a highland bajada in the cold blue dusk with the rifle across his knee" (281). Deer wander into the shadows of the slope below, and John Grady shoots a small doe:

> When he reached her she lay in her blood in the grass and he knelt with the rifle and put his hand on her neck and she looked at him and her eyes were warm and wet and there was no fear in them and then she died. He sat watching her for a long time. He thought about the captain and he wondered if he were alive and he thought about Blevins. He thought about Alejandra and he remembered her the first time he ever saw her . . . and he remembered the birds and the cattle standing in the grass and the horses on the mesa. The sky was dark and a cold wind ran through the bajada and in the dying light a cold blue cast had turned the doe's eyes to but one thing more of things she lay among in that darkening landscape. Grass and blood. Blood

> and stone. Stone and the dark medallions that the first flat drops of rain caused upon them. (282)

The poignancy of the kill and the silence of the scene dredge up existential thoughts for the young protagonist, but the writing renders the fullness of the ambience in which memories and darkness and dead eyes and eroded mesa terrains and blood and love and stones and rain exist alongside one another in total coexistence. The paratactic writing renders all of this without the intrusions of subordination. The man and the deer and the "swales of grass" and "broken volcanic rock" are enmeshed, equals in the additive logic of the polysyndeton, "one thing more of things she lay among."

To emphasize that McCarthy's signature style is itself a written environment, let us compare McCarthy's writing to John McPhee's descriptions of the Basin and Range, the dominant geological formation extending from northern Nevada through the regions of southern New Mexico, West Texas, and into Coahuila, where most of *All the Pretty Horses* takes place: "Basin. Fault. Range. Basin. Fault. Range. A mile of relief between basin and range . . . Ondographic rhythms of the Basin and Range. . . . This country from afar is synopsized and dismissed as 'desert'—the home of the coyote and the pocket mouse, the side-blotched lizard and the vagrant shrew, the MX rocket and the pallid bat" (McPhee 42). This is more parataxis and polysyndeton. Clauses are lined up like sedimentary layers, joined by the simple, understated power of the *and*. McPhee, one of our great science writers, uses parataxis and polysyndeton briefly in *Basin and Range*, a splash of style for effect, but McCarthy establishes and develops the form across entire novels.

Nearing the Texas border, John Grady continues his circumnavigation of the Coahuila section of the Basin and Range, bringing us near the conclusion of the novel:

> He rode on, the two horses following, riding doves up out of the pools of standing water and the sun descending out of the dark discolored overcast to the west where its redness ran down the narrow band of sky above the mountains like blood falling through water and the

> desert fresh from the rain turning gold in the evening light and then deepening to dark, a slow inkening over of the bajada and the rising hills and the stark stone length of the cordilleras darkening far to the south in Mexico . . . and there was just the stillness and the silence and the sound of the horses breathing and the sound of their hooves clopping in the dark. (285–86)

The sentences here are magnificent in the way that they create grammatical equivalency between the protagonist, the horses, startled doves, fading sunlight, ridgelines extending to the horizon, the gravel dragged by erstwhile floodwaters, foxes, and sounds and light. Clauses rise and fall like the Basin and Range itself, with rows of coordinating grammar adjoining one to the next, connected by time and proximity to create a textual environment that replicates and materializes; it does not merely describe.

There is more to McCarthy's style than a writing about the places he sets his novels. Certainly, the border country is described in beautiful and compelling detail, and *All the Pretty Horses* waxes nostalgic for this wide-open and untrammeled landscape, nearly as lost as the cowboy days that Lacey Rawlings and John Grady Cole have gone adventuring after. A significant movement within ecologically minded literary theory and criticism over the past decade or so has sought to expand our notions beyond what we typically think of as "nature writing," to encourage writers and readers and critics to be mindful of the ways in which literary form itself, the *graphia* and not just the *choros*, is a site of our thinking environmentally. Cormac McCarthy's work, among its many accomplishments, takes part in motivating and developing how we might explore forms—literary forms, lifeforms, landforms, artforms—and how we might think more ecologically, embracing the paratactic bonds between the "things *we* lay among."

Note

1. See Morris and Trenker in Works Cited.

Works Cited

Bell, Madison Smartt. "The Man Who Understood Horses." Review of *All the Pretty Horses,* by Cormac McCarthy. *The New York Times*, 17 May 1992, p. 9, www.nytimes.com/1992/05/17/books/all-the-pretty-horses.html.

Dillman, Richard H. "Thoreau's Philosophy of Style." *The Bucknell Review*, vol. 31, no. 2, 1988, pp. 86–96.

Estes, Andrew Keller. *Cormac McCarthy and the Writing of American Spaces*. Rodopi, 2013.

Fletcher, Angus. *A New Theory for American Poetry: Democracy, the Environment, and the Future of Imagination*. Harvard UP, 2004.

Frye, Steven, editor. *The Cambridge Companion to Cormac McCarthy*. Cambridge UP, 2013.

McCarthy, Cormac. *All the Pretty Horses*. Alfred A. Knopf, 1992.

__________. *Blood Meridian, or The Evening Redness in the West*. Random House, 1985.

__________. *The Crossing*. Alfred A. Knopf, 1994.

__________. *The Road.* Alfred A. Knopf, 2006.

McPhee, John. *Basin and Range*, in *Annals of the Former World*. Farrar, Straus and Giroux, 2000, pp. 25–143.

Morris, Edward Parmelee. "Parataxis," *On Principles and Methods in Latin Syntax*. Charles Scribner's Sons, 1901, pp. 113–49.

Morton, Adam David. "The Warp of the World: Geographies of Space and Time in the *Border Trilogy* by Cormac McCarthy." *Environment and Planning: D. Society and Space*, vol. 33, no. 5, Oct. 2015, pp. 831–49.

Morton, Timothy. *Ecology without Nature: Rethinking Environmental Aesthetics*. Harvard UP, 2007.

__________. "Ecology as Text, Text as Ecology." *Oxford Literary Review*, vol. 32, no. 1, 2010, pp. 1–17. *JSTOR*, www.jstor.org/stable/44030819.

"parataxis, n." OED Online, Oxford UP, Mar. 2023, www.oed.com/view/Entry/137669.

"pleonastic, adj." OED Online, Oxford UP, Mar. 2023, www.oed.com/view/Entry/145717.

“polysyndeton, n.” OED Online, Oxford UP, Mar. 2023, www.oed.com/view/Entry/147397.

Thoreau, Henry David. *Journal of Henry David Thoreau.* Houghton Mifflin, 1949.

Trenker, S. “ARISTOTLE, ‘RHETORIC’ III, 12, 4.” *Proceedings of the Cambridge Philological Society*, vol. 182, no. 2, 1952, pp. 3–6. *JSTOR*, www.jstor.org/stable/44714935.

Weidie, Alfred Edward Jr, “The Stratigraphy and Structure of the Parras Basin, Coahuila and Nuevo Leon, Mexico.” LSU Historical Dissertations and Theses. 710. 1961, digitalcommons.lsu.edu/gradschool_disstheses/710.

Aldo Leopold's Land Ethic in McCarthy's *All the Pretty Horses*

Allison Harl

Conservationist and writer Aldo Leopold once said, "There are some who can live without wild things, and some who cannot" (vii). A requiem for the American frontier, Cormac McCarthy's *All the Pretty Horses* explores the moral responsibilities of a dispossessed cowboy in the modern mechanized West. Analyzing the novel through an ecocritical lens, this essay explores the characterization of John Grady Cole as a reflection of the fragmented and degraded American landscape. The last in a long line of family ranchers, John Grady questions his ethical obligations, seeking to adapt to a rapidly changing world defined by exploitation and violence. As his family, love, and future unravel, John Grady becomes increasingly disillusioned with no one to applaud his tenacious cowboy code of integrity or his proven abilities—only a judge to whom he offers his confession of culpability.

McCarthy's elegy echoes the values of Aldo Leopold, father of wildlife ecology, in his famous text *A Sand County Almanac,* published in 1949—the same year in which *All the Pretty Horses* is set. Having worked with the U.S. Forest Service for twenty years, Leopold pioneered a conservation movement concerned with the management of healthy ecosystems, particularly in the American southwest. In his reflections and critiques, Leopold defined a moral responsibility that derives from a conscious understanding of the interdependence of all creatures and the lands they inhabit. McCarthy's charged prose steeped in electrical imagery illuminates the inherent natural energy at play in this interdependent system of land and people.

In his essay "The Land Ethic," from the *Sand County Almanac*, Leopold advocates for a biocentric worldview, arguing that living organisms create symbioses, modes of co-operation that function not only biologically, but in larger societal systems of politics and economics (202). The complexities of the intricate ecosystem are ordered around seemingly chaotic events, and "its functioning depends on the cooperation and competition of its diverse parts" (215). Reiterating Leopold's treatise, McCarthy's narrative dramatizes the tensions in the "seeming chaos" among many "diverse parts" (Leopold 215) of environmental, political, and social hierarchies. The novel resists reductive binaries of nature/culture, which locate humans and their societies outside of the natural systems to which they belong. Rather, the author's southwestern borderlands function as the liminal space within this symbiotic interplay, the stage on which John Grady's character is developed in his coming-of-age journey. In *All the Pretty Horses*, the organic balance functions without sentimentality and often with violence. McCarthy's use of subtle metaphors depicts an enduring life force, a natural wildness inherent in the wounded terrain marred by mechanization.

McCarthy scholars have long recognized Leopold's influence on the *Border Trilogy* novels, the first of which is *All the Pretty Horses*. According to Michael Lynn Crews, in the marginal notes of his original drafts McCarthy made only two direct references to other writers, one of whom is Leopold. He wrote, "See A. Leopold" in his manuscript of *The Crossing,* the second novel of the trilogy (234–35). Lydia R. Cooper has also acknowledged the connection between the authors, observing, "McCarthy's project in the *Border Trilogy* in many ways reiterates Aldo Leopold's call for human recognition of the intrinsic value of the natural world, as a corrective vision to the utilitarian ethics that guides Western views of environmental policy through the lens of 'stewardship' rather than complex, adaptive symbiosis" (159). Due to the clear thematic influence of Leopold on *All the Pretty Horses*, this study attempts a more in-depth analysis of these connections than has yet been explored.

Ethics and American Progress

McCarthy frames *All the Pretty Horses* with questions regarding the ethics of America's imperialistic nation-building campaign. The novel begins and ends with allusions to the displacement of Indigenous peoples from their lands. The reader is first introduced to

John Grady as a disinherited American cowboy on his family ranch that once belonged to the Comanche. Leopold explained, "A land ethic, of course, cannot prevent the alteration, management, and use of these 'resources,' but it does affirm their right to continued existence in a natural state" (204). But like the Comanche who preceded him, John Grady has suddenly lost his land, his identity, and his place in the world: "Nation and ghost of nation passing in a soft chorale across that mineral waste to darkness bearing lost to all history and all remembrance like a grail the sum of their secular and transitory and violent lives" (5). His preference for riding his horse on the vanishing old Comanche road, described as a dream vision of the lost warrior nation, aligns his character with the old traditions and an Indigenous peoples' tragic journey into oblivion.

After John Grady attends the viewing of his grandfather's dead body, an oncoming train in the Texas landscape announces the death of his own future on the bygone frontier:

> It came boring out of the east . . . howling and bellowing in the distance and the long light of the headlamp running through the tangled mesquite brakes and creating out of the night the endless fenceline down the dead straight right of way and sucking it back again wire and post mile on mile into the darkness. (4)

The train's beastly "howling and bellowing" personify the deadening advance of modern transportation, which is presented in contrast to his horse—a living, breathing animal. The interminable fence stretches deeper into the dark night than John Grady can see. The cowboy cannot envision his future in such a mechanized country.

Leopold emphasizes the value of perception, the power of observation, in raising conscious awareness of western culture's obligation to a land ethic. In his chapter "Conservation Esthetic," he details the importance of influencing how one views natural resources:

> The outstanding characteristic of perception is that it entails no consumption and no dilution of any resource. The swoop of a hawk, for example, is perceived by one as the drama of evolution. To another

> it is only a threat to the full frying-pan. . . . To promote perception is the only truly creative part of recreational engineering. (173)

McCarthy's creative third person objective narrator promotes this perception through a transcendent lens that observes from a highly attuned consciousness of the environment. Christopher White examines the unique narrative style of *All the Pretty Horses,* explaining, "McCarthy's unconventional narrational and stylistic techniques give the effect of a narrator who envisions the story world rather than merely reporting on it. . . . The vision seems perennial but virtual—always potentially there to be seen if the right viewer is present" (129). The narrator thus filters John Grady's experiences in a manner that results in the readers' appreciation of the sensory details of the southwestern desert. For instance, John Grady "crossed a dry gypsum playa where the salt crust stove under the horse's hooves like trodden isinglass and he rode up through white gypsum hills like a cave floor uncovered to the light" (242).

The focus of John Grady's experience lies in the narrator's perception of the intricate details of his environment. His point of view does not filter the experience for the audience; rather, he is situated as an observer alongside the audience. Leopold argues, "Recreation, however, is not the outdoors but our reaction to it. Daniel Boone's reaction depended not only on the quality of what he saw, but on the quality of the mental eye with which he saw it" (173–74). Like Daniel Boone, John Grady appreciates the land and its interconnections within with a keen mental eye.

In his forward to *A Sand County Almanac*, Leopold summarizes the ecological dilemma facing American culture in modern times. He prefaces his land ethic by asking the reader to measure the cost of progress and technology at the expense of a healthy relationship between people and land. He explains,

> We abuse land because we regard it as a commodity belonging to us. When we see land as a community to which we belong, we may begin to use it with love and respect. There is no other way for land to survive the impact of mechanized man. (vii)

Leopold sees his perspective as one belonging to a diminishing minority. Also among "a diminishing minority," is John Grady, whose ethical code derives from a sense of obligation that defines his character and drives the plot. For instance, despite his best friend's uneasy feelings about traveling with the young Jimmy Blevins, John Grady decides to allow him to accompany the cowboys across the border into Mexico simply because he believes it is the right thing to do. John Grady suspects Blevins would be dependent on them for possibly survival. When Lacey Rawlins asks Blevins, "What in the hell would we want you with us for?" he replies, "Cause I'm an American" (45). Blevins follows John Grady and Rawlins like an American Jungian shadow. John Grady feels responsible for him while Rawlins consistently pushes him away. The corrupt lawman who imprisons the cowboys in the Mexican town of Encanta, The Captain, later tells John Grady that Blevins is not the innocent, good boy that John Grady believes he is, that he is, in fact, a thief and a murderer. Blevins may symbolize the unchecked American drive for material gain. He claims that the gun and horse belong to him just as the Americans have claimed lands that belonged to others. He seems to have convinced himself in the nationalist tradition that he is the rightful, justified owner. John Grady, and the reader by extension, never learn anything about the true identity of Blevins or the true owner of the horse. Even the name "Jimmy Blevins" proves questionable, which likely was appropriated from a Gospel radio show aired by a con artist (294–98). As the novel ends, finding out to whom Blevins's horse belongs still hangs "like a millstone" about his neck (293). If Blevins represents an American shadow, his horse symbolizes what America has stolen from the Comanche and Mexicans but can never give back. Moreover, the mechanized culture and developed land will never be returned to its wild, natural state in a country obsessed with progress and materialism. But due to his ethics, John Grady's perseverance and sense of obligation to America's wild, natural resources endures.

The Electrical Circuit

Leopold sums up his land ethic with a dynamic metaphor: "Land, then, is not merely soil; it is a fountain of energy flowing through a circuit" (216). This circuit portrays a universal energy, which Leopold explains flows upward through the food chain and downward into death and decay:

> "The circuit is not closed; some energy is dissipated in decay, some is added by absorption from the air, some is stored in soils, peats, and long-lived forests; but it is a sustained circuit, like a slowly augmented revolving fund of life." (216)

McCarthy adopts similar imagery to emphasize the shared energies that connect his characters to the natural world in which they belong. The theme of electricity is woven throughout the novel, associated with death, which is often violent; but also with life, which often throbs with energy.

One such example is lightning, which appears consistently throughout *All the Pretty Horses*, electrifying the landscape and plot with passion and danger. John Grady watches Alejandra from a distance with lightning falling around her as her beautiful image moves across the pristine pasturelands and lakes. When the thunderstorm catches up with her, the rain "shrouded her figure away in that wild summer landscape: real horse, real rider, real land and sky and yet a dream withal" (132). The electrical storm merges the vision of Alejandra with animal, land, and atmosphere, blending them all in the "wild summer landscape" (132). The scene foreshadows his loss of both Alejandra and the wild Mexican terrain.

Blevins's intense fear of lightning also ignites the narrative. His character functions like a circuit through which the energy of the plot is charged. Rawlins senses from their first meeting that allowing him to tag along would prove a ruinous mistake. Blevins details how many members of his family have suffered sudden, gruesome deaths by lightning. His grandfather was struck in a mine 180 feet deep—"fried em like bacon" (68), while his young cousin was partially paralyzed with his jaw fused shut by melted fillings. As an electrical storm overtakes the young cowboys, Blevins avoids being struck at the steep cost of losing everything: his clothes, his gun, and most importantly, his horse. The reclamation of the horse, likely stolen by Blevins as well, ignites the tragic events of the story.

The violent energy of this thunderstorm is highlighted in its aftermath through the description of a gruesome scene of birds impaled on cacti: "Gray nameless birds espaliered in attitudes of stillborn flight or hanging loosely in their feathers. Some of them were still alive and they twisted on their spines as the horses passed and raised their heads and cried out but the horsemen rode on" (73). These horrifying deaths inflicted by fierce natural forces are met with indifference and resignation. However, in the next lines, McCarthy layers this violent death scene with a contiguous poetic description of beauty and life:

> The sun rose up in the sky, and the country took on new color, green fire in the acacia and paloverde and green in the roadside run-off grass and fire in the ocotillo. As if the rain were electric, had grounded circuits that the electric might be. (73)

The passage reflects Leopold's ethic that death and violence regenerate into new life; energy is simply transposed through the circuit of the natural order. Moreover, McCarthy's reference to the charged "green fire in the acacia" (73) recalls to the reader Leopold's famous green fire in the eyes of a dying wolf.

In 1909, Leopold was working as a forester in the Apache National Forest of Arizona when he spotted a mother wolf with her pups. He explains in his essay "Thinking Like a Mountain" that he shot her because he saw her as a threat to the deer that hunters pursued. He then witnessed a fierce green fire dying in her eyes as she perished. "After seeing the green fire die, I sensed that neither the wolf nor the mountain agreed with such a view" (130). Leopold realized that without the wolves, the mountain would become overgrazed and eroded by the unchecked deer populations, and they too would starve. This canonical moment shaped the evolution of the ecological movement. Leopold's epiphany of the important dependence of predators in the natural energy balance shaped his eco-centric perspective.

In many stories, wolves symbolize the wild and undomesticated energy that has slowly been extinguished in the modern, mechanized world. The lamentation of their howls in the darkness seem to mourn this disappearance. Leopold argues that "every living thing (and perhaps many a dead one as well) pays heed to that call" (129). As John Grady and his two cowboy friends ride deeper into the wilds of Mexico in the late 1940s, they hear the howls of a wolf, a sound they have never heard before in America. John Grady lies in the darkness, "listening to the others breathing in their sleep while he contemplated the wildness about him, the wildness within" (60). The cowboys, the atmospheric storms, the wild animals, and the land interconnect in an electrified circuitry for both better and worse, in life and in death.

Bodies and Landscapes

The blurring of the wild energies within the characters and without in the natural world underscores Leopold's treatise that all natural beings in the greater biota function as diverse parts belonging to a greater organism. McCarthy's narrative casts the cowboys as just one of many diverse parts that make up the greater organic body of "mother" nature, a terrain enfleshed with corporeal imagery. The line separating John Grady's body from his land blurs through association. Having been dispossessed from his own land and the ranch that had been in his family for generations, John Grady is metaphorically *disembodied* as these ties are irrevocably severed.

James D. Lilley finds that "in McCarthy's texts, the boundaries that hold the body in its discrete, impenetrable place soon begin to distend and reconfigure themselves, transforming the site of interface—the frontier of the body—into a fluid, hybrid borderland" (149–50). What is most essential, as Leopold emphasizes, is awareness of this fluidity within the biotic system. For example, John Grady's heightened sensitivity to his environment is demonstrated as he and Rawlins sit at a fire discussing the prospect of Alejandra:

> "He slowly turned dead center to the world, all of it taut and trembling and moving enormous and alive under his hands" (119).

Personified as a large, living animal, the land is portrayed as an energetic field that John Grady plugs into and connects with through his own body. The imagery of the world as flesh, "taut and trembling," connects back to the wild horses he has recently broken, the horse's bodies frenetic beneath his firm, taming clutch. This imagery simultaneously foreshadows the surrender of Alejandra's young body, which will move in the same ways beneath his subduing hands in their future lovemaking. Cooper discusses the erotic languages used in the scene in which John Grady proves what she calls "his cowboy 'machismo'" (175) when in only four days he breaks sixteen wild horses. She believes, "The textual splicing of his erotic gaze and his yearning for horses is no accident" (175). However, while he will exert his authority by taming several wild horses, none will belong to him. Even though he will win Alejandra's love, he will not succeed in convincing her to deny her family to stay with him. Through his impressive abilities taming wild horses and women, John Grady may have proven himself the great stallion worthy of breeding with Alejandra, the superior mare, but the sixteen-year-old must learn the harsh reality that the wild Mexican frontier does not operate according to his idealistic moral principles. Roosevelt's American promise of reward for individual merit, of rising up by the bootstraps through grit and resilience, holds little sway in a country rooted in hierarchies based in tradition and family allegiances.

As John Grady crosses the border from innocence to experience, he is stripped of what he feels is rightfully his—first in the dispossession of his own land then in the dispossession of Alejandra. Later, being sent to prison, he and Rawlins are dispossessed of even their own horses, as was Jimmy Blevins. John Grady's innocence and idealism guide his illusion that the wild bodies and lands are his for the taking and shaping. However, the American myth of the frontier as a site of progress and opportunity proves a fragile illusory dream, crumbling quickly as innocence gives way after WWII. This infantile national consciousness echoes in the title *All the Pretty*

Horses, which alludes to a centuries-old lullaby John A. and Allen Lomax believe to be of unknown origin: "Hush-a-bye, don't you cry/Go to sleep, my little baby/When you wake, you shall have/All the pretty little horses" (Lomax 304). As he crosses the border into Mexico, John Grady leaves this childhood behind, entering a world of experience that reveals the harsh realities that define his own identity and that of the violent national consciousness of modern mid-century America.

The Mother Earth trope emphasizes a relationship of dependence on the greater ecological force that doles out both life and death despite the integrity or high ideals held by a cowboy with strong notions of what is morally just. All beings submit to the ecological force that shapes and balances the greater biotic system. The dispossession of John Grady's land and his beloved Alejandra both were enacted by foils of matriarchal authority under whom he proved powerless. These women echo an uncompromising feminine force, a symbolic extension of an indifferent Mother Nature whom John Grady cannot subdue.

First, his mother's decision to sell the family property was firm. His father had no influence, having been stripped of emotional and legal power through the divorce. Absent most of his life, John Grady's mother is referred to as only as "she," suggesting her son's desire to deescalate her power by not naming her. As she denies him his request to lease his grandfather's land, she effectively emasculates him by denying him of his inherited opportunity to prove his masculinity. "You're sixteen years old. You cant run a ranch" (15). He looks to her one last time for maternal guidance by attending a play in which she performs, but her script has nothing to offer him. "He'd the notion that there would be something in the story itself to tell him about the way the world was becoming but there was not. There was nothing in it at all" (21). The mother paradigm has failed him, so he must create his own narrative, his own rite of passage for becoming a man in the strange new world.

Before he leaves Texas, John Grady runs into his ex-girlfriend, who had left him for an older eighteen-year-old with his own car. Like his mother, the ex-girlfriend is referred to mainly as "she" and "her." Rawlins tells him, "She aint worth it. None of em are," but John Grady responds after a long pause, "Yes they are" (10). Later, Rawlins warns him not to pursue Alejandra, predicting nothing but heartache and ruin. Rawlins argues, "This one of course she probably dates guys got their own airplanes let alone cars" (119). Even though John Grady says he is probably right, he confesses that "it dont help nothin though, does it?" (119). Rawlins suggests that John Grady, a traditional cowboy with a simple horse, cannot compete with his male rivals who are deemed more eligible through possession of cars and airplanes. These modern men are associated with the "progress" of modern mechanization. Ultimately, John Grady realizes he has little control over the feminine forces that drive him—even when he is aware they are not in his best interest. His experiences of desertion by the women in his life reflect the feminine natural forces to which he is attracted but nevertheless denied access.

Likewise immovable, Dueña Alfonsa refuses to provide her permission for the relationship with Alejandra. Again, John Grady must appeal to the matriarch rather than to Alejandra's father, Don Héctor. But John Grady's idealistic notions of the world are rejected by Dueña Alfonsa, who explains to the young cowboy, "I'm not sure you can understand what I am telling you. I was seventeen and this country to me was like a rare vase being carried about by a child. There was an electricity in the air. Everything seemed possible" (233). She goes on to elaborate how her energetic optimism was destroyed with the violent death of her idealistic lover, how the harsh realities of humanity will always persevere. John Grady's good intentions and ethical values fail to convince Alfonsa; in fact, his idealism works against him in her assessment of his eligibility to contend as a potential match for Alejandra. Just as Alfonsa's own youthful idealism as a revolutionary in the Mexican Civil War was crushed by the ignoble assassination of her heroic lover, John Grady's romanticized perceptions of the wilderness frontier of Mexico dissolve into disillusionment as well.

One woman alone does not deny John Grady, but unfortunately, she does not survive long in the modernized world. The novel concludes with the funeral of Abuela, Louisa's mother, the beloved grandmother figure to John Grady. This final death pronounces the end of the old country, of any residual land ethic—a time before deflowering of the virgin land. John Grady says a teary goodbye in Spanish to this matriarch who had cared for him and his family for half a century. The Mexican grandmother tied him to the feminine forces that he desperately craves, to the Indigenous traditions and connections to the land before it was appropriated and developed by masculine conquest. The women in his life have all disappeared, leaving him dispossessed emotionally in a land where he no longer feels connected.

McCarthy's frontier landscape as embodied organism is wounded and fractured by the development of fences and roads. Fences crisscross the bygone American frontier, foreshadowing the stitches across John Grady's wounded body after the knife fight in prison:

> "To the west a mile away ran a wire fence strung from pole to pole like a bad suture across the gray grasslands and beyond." (38)

As a consequence of a series of decisions, which Rawlins warns him against throughout, the young Texan finds himself trapped in a foreign federal prison system without any political muscle. In the climactic scene of the knife fight, he prevails through his foresight and skill, but not without serious injury as he is cut deeply across his torso. John Grady's sixteen-year-old body, torn and stitched, represents the young American landscape that has been fragmented and compromised, limiting the free expanse. The fence wires, like stitches, "strung from pole to pole" seem endless and confining. The fences symbolize John Grady's perception of Texas—and America by extension—as a place denying access, restricting and stunting his growth into his manhood, a place in which he has lost his inheritance and opportunity to prove himself a real cowboy. In their homeland, Rawlins complains as they have to maneuver through fences, "How the hell do they expect a man to ride a horse in this country?" John Grady responds, "They dont." (31)

Only motorized vehicles are accommodated on the paved roads. In stark contrast, no fences spoil the great expanse across the border to corrupt the anatomy of the pristine utopia. Crossing the Rio Grande River into Mexico like a baptismal rebirth, John Grady seeks the paradisal open lands, the La Purísima ranch that stretches close to 11,000 hectares, or more than 27,000 acres (97). The expansive Mexican frontier as promised land with all its opportunity serves exactly what John Grady seeks in his idealism. "La Purísima" translates to "The Purest," a virgin land untouched and undefiled. The ranch "was well watered with natural springs and clear streams and dotted with marshes or shallow lakes or lagunas. In the lakes and in the streams were species of fish not known elsewhere on earth and birds and lizards and other forms of life as well all long relic here for the desert stretched away on every side" (97). However, through John Grady's rite of passage into manhood, he soon realizes that his dream of a utopia is, in fact, just that.

Alejandra's body belongs to her father just as his land, La Purísima, does. Leopold proclaimed, "Land, like Odysseus' slave-girls, is still property. The land relation is still strictly economic, entailing privileges but not obligations" (202–03). He argued that though philosophical ethics abound in politics and economics, no ethic has yet been established regarding the land (203). Alfonsa emphasizes to John Grady that in Mexico a woman's reputation is all she has. Alejandra explains that her mistake was that she did not realize her father could stop loving her, a fate she cannot abide because she cannot image herself independent of him. She affirms that her body, like La Purísima, belongs to her father. John Grady is once again exiled from the land and simultaneously broken by a woman.

Even though he resigns to repeated feminine wounding, submitting to his powerlessness, John Grady enacts his masculinity through the ability to regenerate and persevere. Historian Richard Slotkin finds that in frontier literature, a "regeneration through violence" (5) often provides a means for masculine self-renewal. Before crossing the border again on his return to America, John Grady retrieves his and his friends' stolen horses, a symbolic reclamation of his identity won through his difficult experiences. As he risks his life to do so, he is shot by the horse thieves. With his own hands, he sears the wound that rips through his leg using a fire-branded pistol. In doing so, he enacts Richard Slotkin's myth of regeneration through violence on the borderlands of American consciousness. Only after this regeneration does John Grady cross the border back into Texas, returning as a proven man and authentic cowboy, despite, or rather because of, his losses. Alfonsa had earlier explained,

> [N]othing can be proven except that it be made to bleed. Virgins, bulls, men. Ultimately, God himself . . . (McCarthy 230).

John Grady becomes a man not by being stabbed, shot, and broken-hearted, but through his convalescence after enduring these bloody experiences. Like Theodore Roosevelt's man in the arena, John Grady ultimately transcends his brokenness through sheer resilience, as do all wild things so that they might survive.

In addition to the violent rite of passage into manhood before he crosses the border back into America, John Grady's new identity is confirmed through a perception of himself as indistinct from the interconnected natural world. He experiences a subtle epiphany when he shoots a small doe for meat, again recalling Leopold's witness of the dying green fire in the wolf's eyes:

> When he reached her she lay in her blood in the grass and he knelt with the rifle and put his hand on her neck and she looked at him and her eyes were warm and wet and there was no fear in them and then she died. He sat watching her for a long time. (282)

He thinks about the likely death of the Captain, Blevins's execution, and finally Alejandra among the flora and fauna of her Edenic Mexican homeplace. Even though Alejandra does not suffer a violent death like the others, John Grady's hope to claim her love does. These reflections are transposed onto his observations of the dying deer:

> In the dying light a cold blue cast had turned the doe's eyes to but one thing more of things she lay among in that darkening landscape (282).

On the other side of the energy of fiery green life is the cold blue of death. John Grady's thoughts then shift to the land, also integrated into the grand biota of people and animals:

> Grass and blood. Blood and stone. . . . He thought that in the beauty of the world were hid a secret. He thought the world's heart beat at some terrible cost and that the world's pain and its beauty moved in a relationship of diverging equity and that in this headlong deficit the blood of multitudes might ultimately be exacted for the vision of a single flower. (282)

John Grady's individuality and humanity is checked against a greater ecological backdrop that can only humble him in its expansiveness. Through his journey, his rite of passage crossing the border and then back again, he changes from a young sixteen-year-old into a man. McCarthy's cowboy now submits willingly and vulnerably to an indifferent natural world to which he is inextricably bound—a world infused in violence and death as well as beauty and life.

Ethics and the Ecological Dilemma

Perhaps the most significant demonstration of John Grady's ethic occurs in his conversation with the judge after he returns to America. John Grady's choices are put forth for public scrutiny and are weighed by the American institution of law and justice as the judge probes a detailed account of his actions. Not only does the judge find John Grady innocent, but he also praises him as an ideal American citizen. This patriarchal validation of his character occurs in the absence of his own father's authentication or even that of God. However, John Grady never acts for the sake of approval, obedience to law, or religious instruction. His quiet integrity is private and self-substantiated.

In "Wildlife in American Culture" Leopold describes virtues of the hunter in a way that directly correlate to John Grady's character:

"A peculiar virtue in wildlife ethics is that the hunter ordinarily has no gallery to applaud or disapprove of his conduct. Whatever his acts, they are dictated by his own conscience, rather than by a mob of onlookers. It is difficult to exaggerate the importance of this fact" (178). John Grady turns up at the judge's house after the trial because his conscience is bothered that he was pronounced innocent. He offers a kind of confession due to the guilt for violating his own ethical code, explaining that he does not feel "justified" (290). First, he acknowledges that he violated the trust of Don Héctor, Alejandra's father, for his illicit relationship with his daughter, declaring,

> I worked for that man and I respected him and he never had no complaints about the work I done for him and he was awful good to me (291).

He explains that Don Héctor likely had considered shooting him, "and I was the one that brought it about. Nobody but me" (291). Despite his best intentions and love for Alejandra, he realizes his youthful notions of love and American self-entitlement were misguided. John Grady's identity is bound inextricably to the history of a colonizing America, and he eventually comes to realize the full extent of his ethical obligations.

The second confession John Grady gives to the judge is murder: he killed a boy in the Mexican prison, and he wanted to kill the captain who shot Blevins. Even though he knows he had no choice in the knife fight if he wanted to survive, he seeks to be exonerated from guilt. He then explains that he wanted to kill the captain, too, "because I stood there and let him walk that boy out in the trees and shoot him and I never said nothin" (293). Even though he is aware it would not have made any difference, he argues, "But that dont make it right" (293). John Grady feels a tension between his obligation for survival as an individual and his obligation to the survival of the interdependent community to which he belongs.

Leopold defines a similar predicament: "All ethics so far evolved rest upon a single premise: that the individual is a member of a community of interdependent parts. His instincts prompt him to compete for his place in that community, but his ethics prompt him also to co-operate (perhaps in order that there may be a place to compete for)" (204). John Grady wants to do the right thing by both himself and the larger community. He will not leave the young Blevins on his own to travel into the wilds of Mexico. He will not give in to Perez, the powerful prison leader. He will not go back to America without retrieving the stolen horses. John Grady would sooner die than compromise his personal ethical code, even if this code is all but extinct in the new world, reduced to an idealistic American dream.

In the end, much has been sacrificed, yet John Grady's return to America with the three stolen horses symbolizes the reclamation of his masculinity and the attempt to fulfill an ethical obligation—whether or not it proves futile. The young John Grady grows into an experienced man capable of survival in a land no longer his own. McCarthy frames the narrative in the final passage of the novel with a satirical cliché of the cowboy riding into the proverbial sunset. Again, John Grady follows the literal and figurative path of the ghostly Comanche who in the late 1940s still camped on the western plains. They looked at him with nothing to say, "as if they knew all that they needed to know" (301). A dispossessed American cowboy, John Grady rides the same road. He shares the same fate of the vanishing Indigenous peoples exiled from their lands. As Jacqueline Scoones notes, John Grady belongs to a broader narrative that he "only partially recognize[s] and understand[s], narratives of history, of politics, of laws, and their construction of the borderlands as sites" (139–40). He exemplifies the quixotic American cowboy who wakes from the American dream, the dream of a country still in its infancy.

McCarthy's *Border Trilogy* reiterates Leopold's land ethic, a sounded alarm that still rings three quarters of a century later. Leopold explained, "these wild things, I admit, had little human value until mechanization assured us of a good breakfast, and until science disclosed the drama of where they come from and how they live. The whole conflict thus boils down to a question of degree. We of the minority see a law of diminishing returns in progress; our opponents do not" (vii). John Grady Cole may identify with and love wild territories, but he takes with him a personal and national shadow inextricably linked to exploitation, violence, and mechanization. In a post-WWII society, the fragmentation of paradigms that promoted notions of superiority distillated into not only national reconstructions of power but prompted economic and ecological reimagining as well. Environmental and cultural ethics took a back seat to capitalist expansion, and preservation of the natural gave way to "alteration" and "management," without consideration of the interconnections of people and land. John Grady's unflinching integrity is contrasted against the corrupt postwar world in which he perseveres. The authentic cowboy is an anachronism, a dying breed of the past. Possessing a rare tenacity of moral responsibility, he demonstrates a lost code of the American cowboy. He values the wild, natural land resources that have been spoiled with industrial progress and materialism. Unfortunately, the rapid changes in John Grady's new environment leave him estranged and homeless, unable to adapt to or thrive in the old myths of the frontier.

Works Cited

Cooper, Lydia R. *Cormac McCarthy: A Complexity Theory of Literature.* Manchester UP, 2021, *EBSCOhost,* search.ebscohost.com/login.aspx?direct=true&db=mlf&AN=202122515163&site=eds-live.

Crews, Michael Lynn. "The Crossing." *Books Are Made Out of Books: A Guide to Cormac McCarthy's Literary Influences*, U of Texas P, 2017, pp. 232–35. *JSTOR*, www.jstor.org/stable/10.7560/313480.13.

Leopold, Aldo. *A Sand County Almanac and Sketches Here and There.* Oxford UP, 1949.

Lilley, James D. "Of Whales and Men: The Dynamics of Cormac McCarthy's Environmental Imagination." *The Southern Quarterly: A Journal of the Arts in the South*, vol. 38, no. 2, 2000, pp. 111–22. EBSCOhost, search.ebscohost.com/login.aspx?direct=true&db=mlf&AN=2001530052&site=eds-live.

Lomax, John A., and Alan Lomax. *American Ballads and Folksongs.* Dover Publications, *1994.*

McCarthy, Cormac. *All the Pretty Horses.* Vintage Books, 1992.

Scoones, Jacqueline. "The World on Fire: Ethics and Evolution in Cormac McCarthy's *Border Trilogy*." *Southern Quarterly*, vol. 38, no. 3, Spring 2000, p. 99. EBSCOhost, search.ebscohost.com/login.aspx?direct=true&db=hlh&AN=9984693&site=eds-live.

Slotkin, Richard. *Regeneration Through Violence: The Mythology of the American Frontier, 1600–1860.* 1st edition. Wesleyan UP, 1973.

White, Christopher T. "Dreaming the *Border Trilogy* : Cormac McCarthy and Narrative Creativity." *The Cormac McCarthy Journal*, vol. 13, no. 1, Sept. 2015, pp. 121–42. EBSCOhost, doi-org.ezproxy.ferrum.edu/10.5325/cormmccaj.13.1.0121.

The Use of Polysyndeton and Cinematic Montage in Faulkner's *As I Lay Dying* and McCarthy's *All the Pretty Horses*

Rosa Parker

Cormac McCarthy's use of rhythmic language is often revisited in literary criticism. The successful publication of *All the Pretty Horses* is seen to have revitalized academic interest in his use of language (Brewton 121). Revisits to McCarthy's novels are bringing forth new conclusions, with recent criticism reiterating the influence of William Faulkner on McCarthy's writing style. Cinematic montage appears in *All the Pretty Horses* and Faulkner's *As I Lay Dying* (1930), and attention to McCarthy's frequent use of *they rode on* and previously neglected sequences of horses in motion reward comparisons with Faulkner's cinematic language and Soviet filmmaker Sergei Eisenstein's early use of montage. Through the comparative analysis of montage, linguistic and cinematic attention to McCarthy's literature establishes his place in interdisciplinary criticism on film and novels.

McCarthy, Faulkner, and the Literary Canon

Lee Clark Mitchell's "A Book 'Made Out of Books': The Humanizing Violence of Style in *Blood Meridian*" cites an "ostensible debt" to Faulkner and argues that McCarthy wants us to pay close attention to his own use of "prose rhythms" (259–60). By "prose rhythms," Mitchell is referring to the different repetitions and patterns that can be found in McCarthy's style of writing, patterns that create a certain beat and pace. Such analysis establishes McCarthy's works within a "distinguished canon"; McCarthy's intriguing uses of rhythm makes him one of the great American novelists of the late twentieth century (Mitchell 260). In his 2011 essay, "Cormac McCarthy and the Aesthetics of Exhaustion" in *The Road*, Andrew Hoberek supports this reading, although he suggests that McCarthy holds a "central role in the contemporary transformation of what counts as serious fiction" (486). Here, Hoberek argues that McCarthy, whose writing style is often easy to follow, is transforming prior ideas that "serious" literary canons cannot include accessible works such as McCarthy's (486). As a modernist, William Faulkner is part of a literary canon which praises experimentation in novels, such as subverting traditional notions of plot by adopting a nonlinear structure, using excessive descriptive language, and establishing many different narrators. Such experimentation is considered a part of High Modernism or a "Faulknerian high style" (Hoberek 487). Although Hoberek agrees that McCarthy often adopts a "Faulknerian high style," he juxtaposes this with *The Road*, which has a more minimalist tone (487). Hoberek suggests that, in *The Road*, while McCarthy seems to be adopting an accessible tone, he still alludes to other styles and genres (486). Hoberek sees both novels as a "conflation" of genre-fiction, arguing that this distances McCarthy from his modernist influences, who favored art "for its own sake" (247; 487). Hoberek thus links McCarthy's use of a Faulknerian "excessive" language to Ernest Hemingway's stripped-down style (486), highlighting McCarthy's awareness of two approaches to Modernism, further establishing his works within modernist literary traditions (486).

Examining McCarthy's imitation of Faulknerian style is a rewarding engagement, particularly with attention to polysyndeton and cinematic montage. Polysyndeton is defined in *The Oxford Companion to English Literature* as "the repetition of conjunctions in close succession for rhetorical effect," and from Greek, it translates as "using many connectives," such as the use of *and* (Birch 792). McCarthy's use of a*nd* in long sentences appears repeatedly in *All the Pretty Horses*, often after *they rode on*, which creates sequences of movement—and of montage. McCarthy's echoing of Faulkner's cinematic style in *As I Lay Dying*, further highlights the author's position in established literary canon.

Early Montage, Eisenstein, and Intellectual Montage

In *Faulkner and Film*, Bruce F. Kawin dubs William Faulkner "the most cinematic of novelists" due to his use of cinematic montage (5). Meanwhile, the cinematic in McCarthy has previously been considered, but often in relation to the film versions of his texts, such as *No Country for Old Men*, and how true they are to the source materials (Bayless and Redmon 6). Both draw from an untraditional mode of montage, known as intellectual montage, used by Eisenstein in his 1920s experimental films.

How can we define traditional cinematic montage? How does this differ from intellectual montage used in Eisenstein's films, and how does it appear in the novels? Put simply, traditional montage is pieces of individual film edited together to make a sequence. One of the early uses of montage in film was by Eadweard Muybridge, an English photographer. His iconic image of the galloping horse Annie G in 1878 was one of the first depictions of movement through still image (Traisnel 153). *All the Pretty Horses* draws from this early cinematic history; McCarthy depicts time passing through the descriptions of advancing horses seen, for example, in this description: "it rained in the night and the rain hissed in the fire and the horses came in out of the darkness and stood with their red eyes shifting and blinking and in the morning it was cold and gray and the sun a long time coming" (93). Although the horses are moving slowly here, it is with their slow movement that the night passes quickly and it becomes day again, with the imagery of the sun struggling to break through the clouds contrasting with the darkness of the night. Through his descriptions of horses moving, McCarthy is working within the most established traditions of moviemaking. However, McCarthy's more experimental use of montage, such as using juxtaposing imagery, is comparable with Eisenstein's montage style seen later in cinema history.

Eisenstein's use of montage developed as a part of an avant-garde cinema movement during the early 1920s, a time in which Vladimir Lenin nationalized cinema in Russia (Parkinson 71). This made experimenting in film more difficult but also more invigorating for filmmakers like Eisenstein. As David Bordwell summarizes,

1920s avant-garde Soviet cinema emerges out of Russian Futurism, which was a pre-revolutionary movement crucially concerned with creating a new kind of art "appropriate to the machine age" (9). Eisenstein's "radical montage" thus emerges in response to concerns surrounding modernity, revolution, machinery, and what such changes could mean for everyday life (Bordwell 9). The radical montage style, as it has become known, creates a narrative "by formulating an artificial time and space," using edited sequences to guide the viewer, rather than creating plot through title cards or sound (Bordwell 9). Five different types of montage are found in Eisenstein's films: metric, rhythmic, tonal, overall, and intellectual. These types focus on different elements and produce different effects. Intellectual montage is most relevant for comparisons with McCarthy and Faulkner, but a summary of the first four modes and how they function will demonstrate how intellectual montage works differently.

In David Parkinson's *History of Film*, he defines metric montage as determining "the tempo of editing" (73). Metric montage focuses on the length of shots, rather than on their contents, working together with Rhythmic montage, which focuses on how the shots work together to create "sequences of sustained tension" (Parkinson 73). These types determine how the shots are edited in length and how they are ordered to create plot. Tonal montage can be summarized as "the textual feel" of running shots; it is most focused on the effect of one shot edited with another, to create the same tone throughout (Parkinson 73). Overall montage is a combination of the first three montages, assessing their success in creating appealing and tonally effective sequences within the entire film (Parkinson 73). The fifth montage, intellectual montage, is the most important in Eisenstein's films. Jerry L. Salvaggio argues that it is the only montage to develop intellectual thinking (295). It often interrupts or challenges the first four modes, as these function in more traditional ways, such as generating consistent tone and plot, while intellectual montage is often working *against* plot. Parkinson defines intellectual montage as "the linkage of contrasting shots to make ideological statements or express abstract ideas" (73). Intellectual montage is where individual images are juxtaposed, sometimes contradicting the original narrative plot, to generate further and often political meanings in certain scenes.

To analyze intellectual montage as it appears within the novels, we can draw from examples in Eisenstein's pioneering films, *Strike!* and *Battleship Potemkin*, which were both released in 1925. *Strike!* follows the events of an unsuccessful workers' strike in a factory in pre-revolutionary Russia. The film opens with a montage sequence, with each shot seemingly unassociated with the next. The workers appear collectively most of the time, so there is no sense of a main character. However, when later imagery from this montage reappears throughout the film, this gives certain visuals a greater emphasis and meaning. For example, the rapid but repeated running shots of workers standing in front of fences or barbed windows creates a sense of feeling trapped (Eisenstein 00:31:34). With little of the traditional markers of linear filmmaking, such as a plot or identifiable protagonist, the suspense Eisenstein generates with this imagery of entrapment becomes the central focus for the viewer. It is an example of intellectual montage, especially when considered with the later images of slaughtered cattle. As Julia Vassilieva argues, this use of montage "combines strikingly composed shots, visual metaphors, and rapid editing with a dense set of intertextual allusions" (113). If we unpack this scene and Vassilieva's analysis, we find that the shots of the dead animals are juxtaposed with the massacred workers during the scenes of the revolution. The sequence generates a connection between the powerless animals and the powerless humans, foregrounding a wider political meaning within the montage: the revolution is needed because we are like animals for slaughter. This sequence is an example of intellectual montage because it provokes a wider meaning beyond the basic plot.

Another example of intellectual montage occurs within Eisenstein's *Battleship Potemkin*. During the turning point in the film, when civilians are killed by revolting workers, there is a shot of an angel statue, followed by the explosion of a building, and concluding with three rapid and changing shots of a lion statue (00:54:40). The angel statue moves as though watching the violence unfold, while the lion is awoken from its slumber (00:54:50). If we were to consider this sequence in terms of the film's plot, the images might suggest that Eisenstein is against revolution, especially as the revolting workers have attacked innocent people. However, if we consider this sequence as an example of intellectual montage, new and subtle meanings appear within the editing of the scenes. These shots, edited together, formulate a statement on pre-Revolutionary Russia; Eisenstein implies that the civilians should develop a class consciousness and, like the lion statue, wake up to the injustices around them. It is this use of intellectual montage as a deviation from plot in Eisenstein's films that is echoed within *As I Lay Dying* and *All the Pretty Horses*.

They rode on: Horses, Montage, and Hiatus in *As I Lay Dying* and *All the Pretty Horses*

Like Eisenstein, Faulkner and McCarthy push the boundaries of traditional plot expectations. For example, Faulkner is known for rarely adopting a chronological structure and in *As I Lay Dying*, he de-emphasizes the importance of plot. He creates a seemingly linear storyline of the Bundren family's journey to bury their mother, but presents this through the eyes of multiple, contrasting narrative voices. While Hyatt H. Waggoner views these different narrators as representing a "hiatus," in which a reader must try to "discern its pattern," it is not necessarily the "pattern" that is interesting but the montage that occurs within the moments of paused plot (63). Moreover, as R. W. Franklin argues, in *As I Lay Dying*, "the points of narration and action are simultaneous. . . . Each of the minds is its own persona telling its part of the story" (58). It is through these conflicting narrative accounts, which collide with one another, that experimental montage becomes central to *As I Lay Dying*. These collisions, and the imagery Faulkner creates through these collisions, mirror the intellectual montage we have seen in Eisenstein's films.

According to Waggoner, Addie Bundren's son, Darl, is the narrator who "sees the most, and sees the most objectively," arguing that "what Darl sees is true" (63). However, this is not always the case. Darl eventually "splits" into two people, which, as Kawin notes, seems to be a result of the multiple narrators (147). The confusing nonlinear structure of the text culminates in one of the narrators losing their sense of narrative—and their sense of self. Even before this split, Darl complicates the notion of what he is really seeing. In one of his first narrations, he likens his brother, Jewel, to the movements of the horse he is riding. McCarthy mirrors this in *All the Pretty Horses*; John Grady "breathes in rhythm with the horse as if some part of the horse were within him breathing" (222). In *As I Lay Dying*, this imagery of man meshed with horse generates a sense of unreality, with Darl first insinuating that he cannot see Jewel, instead envisioning him "down there fooling with that horse" (8). He assumes that Jewel "will go on through the barn, into the pasture" but when he appears "the horse will not be in sight" (8). This guesswork is quickly replaced with Darl's apparent certainty that the horse is now in sight: "the horse comes dropping down the slope . . . stiff-legged, his ears cocking and flicking, his mis-matched eyes rolling" (9). The sudden imagery of the horse jars with his narrative claim that Darl will only be able to see Jewel, not the horse. Darl's later descriptions of the horse further connect Jewel with the animal: "they are rigid, motionless, terrific . . . they stand in rigid terrific hiatus. . . . He flows upward in a stooping swirl like the lash of a whip, his body in midair shaped to the horse" (9). The imagery of Jewel and the horse becomes unnatural, jarring with Darl's initial belief that he would not be able to see the horse when he arrives; as if Jewel has always been one with the horses.

In a later section, Darl refers again to Jewel and the horses: "Back tunneled between the two sets of bobbing mule ears, the road vanishes beneath the wagon as though it were a ribbon, and the front axle were a spool. . . . 'Do you know she is going to die, Jewel?'" (33). Darl returns to the imagery of the horse and later, the repetition of "Jewel, I say" after Addie has already died, comparing to McCarthy's repeated use of *they rode on* (33). When thinking of his mother before and after she has died, Darl returns to the image of the horse and his brother, complicating our understanding of what is occurring in the plot. Is Addie dead or alive when Jewel arrives? Did Jewel make it home in time for Addie's passing?

Erin Edwards claims that Darl rearranges what he is seeing as a revenge against Jewel because Addie favored Jewel (741). However, Faulkner places emphasis on the act of Darl's rearranging and repeating, rather than on a plot-point of the brothers' feuding. Eisenstein is known for "rapid cutting" in his montage. Through Darl, Faulkner mirrors this technique, creating "collisions" of imagery building to and from Addie's death, producing a sense of unreality furthered by Darl's descriptions of Jewel and his horse (Kawin 142). Even after Darl proclaims that "she is dead, Jewel. Addie Bundren is dead," he later speaks of her in the present, complicating our understanding of when she died (46). Here, Faulkner uses intellectual montage, juxtaposing Jewel and his horses with Addie's death, and rearranging the order of isolated events to portray the confusion and entrapment Darl feels. The montage-like sequence then shows how grief confuses our sense of time passing.

Like Faulkner, McCarthy also favors isolated events and the phrase *they rode on* evidences McCarthy's "disposal" of traditional plot (Mitchell 260). Grady and Rawlins are constantly on the move, journeying from San Angelo, Texas, and over the border to Mexico. *They rode,* which appears over eighty times in the text, is frequently followed by long sentences, creating a steady rhythm that mirrors their travels and advances the narrative along in lieu of a detailed plot. Bernard A. Schopen argues that McCarthy's characters are looking out for the next "haunting" event (179). However, *All the Pretty Horses* is more concerned with continuous movement, an interrupted journey rather than a clear destination. In the early chapters, physical movement is central and the consistent rhythm to McCarthy's language is rarely broken. Action and events appear as an inconvenience to the characters and to the rhythm of their journey, creating an unnatural break from *they rode on.* In other words, later plot points, such as Grady and Rawlins's arrest in Mexico, interrupts their journey, therefore, interrupting the continuous motion and, in turn, interrupting the polysyndeton. It is this polysyndeton and the later interruptions that imitates Faulkner's collisions of imagery, with both authors mirroring the juxtaposition and rapid editing seen in Eisenstein's intellectual montage.

The following is an example of polysyndeton through the use of *and*. In relation to the moving bodies of Grady, Rawlins, and their horses it becomes an example of intellectual montage:

> They rode out on the high prairie. . . . They heard somewhere in that tenantless night a bell that tolled and ceased where no bell was and they rode out on the round dais of the earth which alone was dark and no light to it and which carried their figures and bore them up into the swarming stars so that they rode not under but among them and they rode at once jaunty and circumspect, like thieves newly loosed in that dark electric, like young thieves in a glowing orchard . . . and ten thousand worlds for the choosing. (30)

The use of *and* here produces many images, occurring in a fast sequence. The moment where "somewhere in the tenantless night a bell that tolled ceased and where no bell was" highlights the speed in which the men are journeying. As they race along the plain, their surroundings flash in and out of light in a montage sequence. Moreover, the individual imagery of light, and stars, and the bell tolling are fleeting and do not follow from one another in a narrative sense. The frequent bursts of light and changing setting confuse our sense of where they are and where they are going, with the men like "thieves" at once in a "dark electric" and in "a glowing orchard" (McCarthy 30). The "ten thousand worlds" indicates many opportunities for these young men at this early stage. Yet, the imagery of a bell that appears and disappears, and a light that is never visible in the darkness for long, seems to undercut this sense of endless possibilities. The men are racing along, and so, the scenery around them is changing; however, the amount of ground they are covering is not clear. The sense that they are at once in several places generates a sense of unreality to the text, an unreality comparable with *As I Lay Dying*.

McCarthy furthers this unreality when Grady becomes romantically involved with Alejandra. Even in moments of calm, there is constant movement in Grady's thoughts:

> Leading the horses by hand out through the gate into the road and mounting up and riding the horses side by side up the Cienega road with the moon in the west . . . and him closing the gate and turning and holding his cupped hands for her to step into and lifting her onto the black horse's naked back and then untying the stallion from the gate and stepping once onto the gate slat and mounting up all in one motion and turning the horse and them riding side by side up the Cienega road with the moon in the west like a moon of white linen hung from wires and some dogs barking. (140)

Again, polysyndeton is used, connecting these passing moments, and highlighting that Grady's time with Alejandra is precious. The repetition of *and* at once slows down and speeds up the rhythm. Within this rhythmic sentence, McCarthy uses intellectual montage, rearranging the visuals and emphasizing certain moments, giving this exchange between the young lovers a wider meaning within the narrative. For example, the repetition of "riding side by side" and "the moon in the west" draws the reader to this phrasing. Grady and Alejandra appear to be stopping and starting constantly under the moonlight, "mounting up" at the beginning and at the end, as if "all in one motion." At the same time, Grady ensures that they are secure, checks that the horses are safe, and observes the beauty of "the moon in the west," all the while "riding side by side" with Alejandra. How can this be taking place at once? Why does this intimate moment feel so tense? The use of *and* in this section slows down the narrative; we are forced to pause and contemplate each individual moment even as they race by within the sentence. The visuals are stacking up on top of one another, "all in one motion," generating the same perpetual rhythm and sense of unreality we have seen through the moments that follow *they rode on*.

The use of *they rode on* and *and* in *All the Pretty Horses* thus becomes comparative with Eisenstein's intellectual montage, which, as we have seen, deliberately contrasts one shot with another to create new meaning. Returning briefly to *Potemkin*, in the infamous scene in which the Cossacks murder civilians on the Odessa steps, Eisenstein contrasts quick, individual shots of people running and screaming, with long shots of the seemingly never-ending steps and people desperately trying to flee (00:48:34). These shots occur before we see any of the soldiers firing. A woman and her child dying on the steps is shown last and is the longest running shot: the end focus of the scene. Here, Eisenstein uses intellectual montage, with the people enjoying the arrival of the sailors contrasting with their terror moments later as they flee from the soldiers. The rearranged visuals mean we cannot see the soldiers, with a new message emerging: who is the real threat? Perhaps a threat we cannot see.

Marilyn Fabe sees this onslaught of the civilians on the steps as Eisenstein conveying "the subjective reality of what it would feel like to be trapped in a traumatic situation that seemingly goes on forever" (32). In this way, *Potemkin* compares to *Strike!* as the workers are trapped like helpless animals. Such helplessness is then comparable with the effect of McCarthy's use of *they rode on.* Grady and Rawlins's reality is subjective too; they are also caught up in a seemingly never-ending moment. Although they choose to keep going, riding through the night like "thieves," there is a sense that the outside world will eventually catch up with them. Even in the moments where Grady seems to want to settle down, seen in his brief but intense tryst with Alejandra, the persistent use of *they rode on* and *and* implies that the young men do not have control over the rhythm of the narrative, They, too, are helpless, like the men in Eisenstein's films, the montage sequences pushing them onwards.

The idea that Grady can only find peace when with his friend or amongst the horses is further shown within his dreams: "That night he dreamt of horses in a field on a high plain where the spring rains had brought up the grass and the wild-flowers out of the ground and the flowers ran all blue and yellow far as the eye could see and in the dream he was among the horses running and in the dream he himself could run with the horses" (161). The repetition of *and* in this dream sequence is another example of polysyndeton. Even in his sleep, Grady is moving, a further use of intellectual montage, with contrasting imagery of Grady "running with the horses" and "he himself" running with the horses (161). At first, this appears to be the same description twice, with Grady delighted by his ability to run with the horses. However, McCarthy deliberately repeats this notion of "himself" and "running with the horses" to complicate the imagery of Grady's dreams. Just as Darl splits into two at the end of Faulkner's narrative, Grady is shown to be split into two here, with one version "running with the horses" and the other becoming "himself," as if conflicted: does he truly know who "himself" is?

When Rawlins and Grady part ways within the story, the rhythm is broken, and Grady becomes more conflicted. "He rode," in reference to Grady only, does not generate the same fast-paced movement: "the desert he rode was red. . . . [T]he small dust that powdered the legs of the horse he rode, the horse he led" (301). In this example, *and* is used only once to extend the sentence, with the commas creating more of a pause, a break in the movement, rather than a continuation. Previously, hiatus from the plot was used by both McCarthy and Faulkner to juxtapose different images and insert further meaning. Here, there is reference only to the horse Grady rode and to the dust they kick up. There are no endless possibilities, unlike what we have seen earlier in the text, and perhaps no room for further interpretation or cinematic visuals. The sense of freedom that pervades the beginning of the text is lost after the young men part ways.

Endings and Beginnings

McCarthy and Faulkner mirror Eisenstein's use of intellectual montage to create constant movement even within moments of hiatus. In their narratives, visuals of grief and loneliness emerge through the reordering of events and the use of *and,* rather than through traditional signifiers of plot. *All the Pretty Horses* presents McCarthy's debt to Faulkner, but also highlights McCarthy's strengths as a cinematic writer. Towards the end of the text, Grady "breathes in rhythm with the horse as if some part of the horse were within him breathing" (222). Grady appears to revitalize an earlier sense of freedom by becoming one with the horse, comparable with Jewel's attachment to his horse. However, at the end of the text, the sentences become shorter, and Grady becomes more and more despairing: "Nothing for their struggles, nothing for their names. Nothing for the living or the dead" (301). The novel ends with

Grady losing all links to his family. We do not know how his story ends, although we can speculate, like a projector still whirring after a film reel has concluded. As the young man journeys on in pursuit of wider meaning in *All the Pretty Horses*, we, too, can continue to discern new meanings hidden within the cinematic language of McCarthy's oeuvre.

Works Cited

Battleship Potemkin. Directed by Sergei Eisenstein, Mosfilm, 1925.

Bayless, Ryan S., and Allen H. Redmon. "'Just Call It': Identifying Competing Narratives in the Coens' *No Country for Old Men*." *Literature/Film Quarterly*, vol. 41, no. 1, 2013, pp. 6–18.

Bordwell, David, et al. *The Classical Hollywood Cinema: Film Style and Mode Production to 1960.* 2nd edition. Routledge, 1988.

Brewton, Vince. "The Changing Landscape of Violence in Cormac McCarthy's Early Novels and the *Border Trilogy*." *The Southern Literary Journal*, vol. 37, no. 1, 2004, pp. 121–43.

Edwards, Erin E. "Extremities of the Body: The Anoptic Corporeality of *As I Lay Dying*." *Modern Fiction Studies*, vol. 55, no. 4, 2009, pp. 739–64.

Fabe, Marilyn. "The Art of Montage: Sergei Einstein's *Battleship Potemkin*," *Closely Watched Films Book: An Introduction to the Art of Narrative Film Technique*. U of California P, 2014, pp. 19–36.

Faulkner, William. *As I Lay Dying*. Vintage Classics, 2004.

Franklin R. W., "Narrative Management in 'As I Lay Dying.'" *Modern Fiction Studies*, vol. 13, no. 1, pp. 57–65.

Hoberek, Andrew. "Cormac McCarthy and the Aesthetics of Exhaustion." *American Literary History*, vol. 23, no. 3, 2011, pp. 483–99.

Kawin, Bruce F. *Faulkner and Film*. Frederick Ungar, 1977.

McCarthy, Cormac. *All the Pretty Horses*. Picador, 2010.

Mitchell, Lee Clark. "A Book 'Made Out of Books': The Humanizing Violence of Style in *Blood Meridian*." *Texas Studies in Literature and Language*, vol. 57, no. 3, 2015, pp. 259–81.

The Oxford Companion to English Literature. Edited by Dinah Birch. 7th Edition. Oxford UP, 2009.

Parkinson, David. *History of Film*. Thames and Hudson, 2012.

Salvaggio, Jerry L. "Between Formalism and Semiotics: Eisenstein's Film Language." *Dispositio*, vol. 4, no. 12, 1979, pp. 289–97.

Schopen, Bernard A. "'They Rode On': *Blood Meridian* and the Art of Narrative." *Western American Literature*, vol. 30, no. 2, 1995, pp. 179–94.

Strike! Directed by Sergei Eisenstein, Goskino Proletkult, 1925.

Traisnel, Antoine. "The Stock Image (Muybridge)." *Capture: American Pursuits and the Making of a New Animal Condition*. U of Minnesota P, 2020, pp. 153–90.

Vassilieva, Julia. "Montage Einstein: Mind the Gap." *Film as Philosophy*. Edited by Bernd Herzogenrath. U of Minnesota P, 2017, pp. 111–31.

Waggoner, Hyatt H. *William Faulkner: From Jefferson to the World.* UP of Kentucky, 1959.

The Landscape of Grief: Dispossession and Self-Discovery in McCarthy's *All the Pretty Horses* and Woolf's *To the Lighthouse*

Elissa Greenwald

Both Cormac McCarthy in *All the Pretty Horses* and Virginia Woolf in *To the Lighthouse* set young characters on a journey of self-discovery following an important death in the family: McCarthy's protagonist John Grady Cole loses his grandfather; Woolf's character Cam Ramsay loses her mother. For both characters, Nature becomes not just a backdrop for their quests but at different times an antagonist and a guide. In contrasting settings—the desert in McCarthy, the seashore in Woolf—the teenage adventurers experience the wildness of Nature as a way to both express and tame the wildness in themselves.

Style as Emotional Expression

Many critics have noted the resemblance between the works of Cormac McCarthy and those of Ernest Hemingway (Cutchins). Their works share the "masculine" code of the seemingly laconic and inexpressive hero who pursues dangerous missions yet manifests hidden depths of emotion. Despite their similar subjects, McCarthy and Hemingway differ in style. Not only does McCarthy's hero in *All the Pretty Horses* express his feelings more frequently and articulately than a typical Hemingway hero—John Grady is far more loquacious than Robert Jordan in *For Whom the Bell Tolls*, for example—but McCarthy's style is lyrical and fluid as opposed to Hemingway's sparseness.

An unexpected stylistic predecessor of McCarthy is Virginia Woolf, whose use of polysyndeton (repeating conjunctions to pile up phrases) may be seen, for example, in a famous passage from *Mrs. Dalloway* capturing the chaotic energy of a great city: "in the swing, tramp, and trudge; in the bellow and the uproar; the carriages, motor cars, omnibuses, vans . . ; in the triumph and the jingle and the strange high singing of some aeroplane overhead was what she loved; life; London; this moment of June" (5). McCarthy also uses polysyndeton and repetition, for example in the last paragraph of *All the Pretty Horses.* The vivid language, especially the repetition of "red," enables McCarthy to project the emotions of his protagonist onto the landscape:

> The desert he rode was red and red the dust he raised, the small dust that powdered the legs of the horse he rode, the horse he led. In the evening a wind came up and reddened all the sky before him. There were few cattle in that country because it was barren country indeed yet he came at evening upon a solitary bull rolling in the dust against the bloodred sunset like an animal in sacrificial torment. The bloodred dust blew down out of the sun. He touched the horse with his heels and rode on. He rode with the sun coppering his face and the red wind blowing out of the west across the evening land and the small desert birds flew chittering among the dry bracken and horse and rider and horse passed on and their long shadows passed in tandem like the shadow of a single being. Passed and paled into the darkening land, the world to come. (302)

Repeated phrases and omitted punctuation: for Woolf it is a way to get inside the characters' heads in stream of consciousness (Gliserman 58) and becomes in McCarthy's hands a way to capture a seemingly infinite and infinitely changeable Nature. The bull writhing in "sacrificial torment" and the "bloodred" landscape mirror the injuries the protagonist John Grady Cole has sustained. The use of "bloodred" in this passage echoes and completes the red imagery near the novel's beginning: "The grasslands lay in a deep violet haze and to the west thin flights of waterfowl were moving north before the sunset in the deep red galleries under the cloudbanks like schoolfish in a burning sea" (93). Here the sufferings of human beings are foreshadowed and reflected in the restless energy, the "burning sea," of Nature.

Grief as Incitement to Action

The depth of John Grady's grief at the opening of *All the Pretty Horses* is hard to fathom. He has lost his beloved grandfather, and his parents are long separated. His mother seems uninterested in her son when they meet briefly, whereas his father's attempts to connect with John Grady are halting and incomplete. The father seems irreparably harmed, physically and psychologically, by his experience as a prisoner of war in World War II. John Grady has no siblings, so, after his grandfather's death, he is no more tied to the family home than a piece of tumbleweed. He soon heads to Mexico with his best friend, Rawlins; no one seems to know, or care, where they have gone.

Although the opening section of *To the Lighthouse* presents a picture of family unity, the ongoing thwarting of the joint desire of Mrs. Ramsay and her youngest son, James, to make a voyage to the lighthouse by the realistic but harsh Mr. Ramsay suggests incipient fissures in the family. A different kind of loss and anonymity than John Grady's is suffered by Cam Ramsay, a middle child surrounded by so many siblings and summer guests that she gets little attention from her parents or from any adult. As her willfulness matures into a sense of purpose in the last section of the novel, she stops dashing around madly as she does in the first section, taming her energy to the pursuit of a familial and social goal: steering a boat to bring clothes to the son of the lighthouse keeper. Cam and John Grady are not so much dispossessed as temporarily exiled from families and homes they never truly possessed.

Growth through Self-Discovery

John Grady's breaking of horses on the vast hacienda of Don Héctor is a demonstration of mastery. John Grady's mastery, like that of his friend Rawlins with a rifle, is seemingly inexplicable, although he grew up on a ranch and avows having studied a book on horses.

The act of breaking horses consists of a strange mixture of domination and comforting by the person who does the breaking. In a culture where we now celebrate horse whisperers, who soothe damaged horses, more than horsebreakers, breaking seems savage.

It involves hobbling horses with ropes around their legs and mouths, a spectacle that attracts up to 100 spectators as John Grady performs it over a series of four days. Then he cradles the horse's heads, as in a Pietà, an intimate gesture that only makes the breaking seem more cruel: "he cupped his hand over the horse's eyes and stroked them and he did not stop talking to the horse at all, speaking in a low steady voice and telling it all that he intended to do and cupping the animal's eyes and stroking the terror out" (103–04).

Yet, the effect of breaking, strangely, is to give the horses greater individuality. In the aftermath of the breaking, they are seen "coming to reckon slowly with the remorselessness of this rendering of their fluid and collective selves into that condition of separate and helpless paralysis which seemed to be among them like a creeping plague" (105). Is individuation, then, dependent on breaking, for humans and horses alike? Does the "training" of children by parents and teachers destroy children's essential wildness? Or is it a necessary taming that both enables children to live in society, just as the horses become useful to herd cattle, and encourages them to break away from the herd into individuals?

The answer is unclear because none of the major characters in McCarthy's book achieves adulthood unscarred. After thirteen-year-old Blevins is arrested for killing a man while stealing back his own horse, he is killed by the minions of a corrupt police captain. At sixteen, John Grady suffers the loss of a love who is distinguished by her ability to ride horses, Alejandra, after they give way to their natural impulses despite the explicit and implicit opposition of her grand-aunt Alfonsa and her father, the hacienda owner Don Héctor. Don Héctor, rather than Blevins as Cole first surmises, is responsible for John Grady's arrest. John Grady, along with Rawlins, suffer nearly fatal knife wounds from a hired assassin in prison. He is also injured by a gunshot through his leg in the last part of the book, when he goes on the second part of his quest, this time not for discovery but for revenge or justice. McCarthy suggests that being "broken" by human laws and customs, for humans as well as horses, means losing the vitality that makes us part of nature.

In the more domestic setting of *To the Lighthouse*, Cam Ramsay, unlike John Grady, is constantly in the presence of her family. Like John Grady, Cam Ramsay is also described as "wild," a "wild villain" (83). In the first part of the novel, "The Window," she dashes through rooms like an animal, so quickly that we barely glimpse her.

Though her behavior is typical of someone her age–she is about seven at that point–Cam seems especially restless, perhaps oppressed by the closeness of her large family, symbolized by the matriarchal triangle of her mother and younger brother, as well as the constant presence of guests in their seashore home, depriving her of privacy. She has tremendous physical energy but, unlike John Grady, Rawlins, and Blevins, little opportunity to express it amidst the constraints of a late Victorian home and the expectation of girls at that time to be passive.

In the last section of the book, "The Lighthouse," after her mother has died and ten years have passed, Cam is finally able to express and channel her energy. The rough waves off the shore of Cornwall, England, which impede the progress of Cam, her father, and her younger brother as they row to the lighthouse, symbolize her emotions. At first, the waves are tumultuous and seem to fight with each other: "the water was sliced sharply and fell away in green cascades, in bubbles, in cataracts" (246). When Cam, James, and her father, after years of conflict following Mrs. Ramsay's death, finally act together by rowing to the lighthouse, the waves suddenly reflect their harmony. First "from her hand, ice cold, held deep in the sea, spurted up a fountain of joy . . . at the adventure" (280). Soon "they were sailing swiftly, buoyantly, on long rocking waves which handed them on from one to another with an extraordinary lilt and exhilaration" (306). Cam accepts her father's authority when she cooperates by joining the journey to the lighthouse he undertakes as a belated tribute to his late wife. By acquiescing to a joint familial goal, Cam also becomes mature, an individual adult. For Cam, this is breaking of a sort, reflected in the harmony of the previously agitated waves.

Nature as 'Vale of Soul-Making'

The poet John Keats speaks of the world as "the vale of soul-making," after describing life as a "vale of tears" (Keats). The infinite scale of the natural world provides refuge, challenge, and ultimately growth for McCarthy's and Woolf's youthful protagonists. In some places in McCarthy's novel, a haunted Nature seems to reflect human emotions. Soon after the teenage protagonists John Grady and Rawlins set off together, following the death of Cody's grandfather, "they could hear the rain coming down the road behind them like some phantom migration," (69) as if the ghost of the grandfather inhabits the rain. In the middle section of *To the Lighthouse*, after Mrs. Ramsay dies and the house sits deserted for a decade, the house becomes haunted. Nature, represented by the wind, becomes a source of chaos, breaking apart the order Mrs. Ramsay attempted to impose on her children, her guests, her home, her life, but which she achieves only in passing moments, like the dinner around which the opening section centers.

In McCarthy, Nature presents dramatic tensions of its own, indifferent to human action and understanding. John Grady and Rawlins are frequently surprised by sudden turns in weather, despite being lifelong residents of the border area between Texas and Mexico. The vastness of the landscape dwarves human activity. Even the hacienda of Don Héctor, covering a vast number of acres, seems infinitesimal compared to the limitless natural landscape. That landscape creates a sense of wonder from the beginning of the novel, when Rawlins and John Grady leave their home: "They rode out on the high prairie where they slowed the horses to a walk and the stars swarmed around them out of the blackness. They heard somewhere in that tenantless night a bell which tolled and ceased where no bell was and they rode out on the round dais of the earth which alone was dark" (30). McCarthy sets the landscape as a stage for a quest.

McCarthy's painterly descriptions of landscape are rich in visual, auditory, and tactile imagery: "the last of the day's light fanned slowly upon the plain behind him and withdrew again down the edges of the world in a cooling blue of shadow and dusk and chill and a few last chitterings of birds sequestered in the dark and wiry brush" (6). Similarly, much of *To the Lighthouse* is filtered through the eye of an artist, Lily Briscoe, who is painting a landscape incorporating the Ramsays' house that is both abstract—reducing Mrs. Ramsay reading with her son James to a triangle—and realistic, reproducing the blues, greens, and yellows of a summer day at the seashore (Bell 171; Guth 233). The color must be delicate but the underlying truth of the painting inexorable, Lily reflects: "Beautiful and bright it should be on the surface, one colour melting into another like the colours on a butterfly's wing; but beneath the fabric must be clamped together with bolts of iron" (255). This could also describe Woolf's novel, which under the seemingly free alternation of points of view has a fairly strict tripartite structure, in which the third section continuously echoes the first.

The author's perspective in *All the Pretty Horses* and the artistic perspective of Lily in *To the Lighthouse* are not directly available to the protagonists of the two novels. Rather, landscape acts on the characters beyond their conscious recognition (Lanser 108; Smythe 65; White 121). Within the natural world, as in the human one, aspects of strife and division appear: "a long rolling crack of thunder went pealing down the sky to the north. The ground shuddered" (70). The rhythms of reconciliation in Nature–sunlight after rain, for example–foreshadow healing in the emotional realm of humanity. The brilliant sunsets that conclude several sections of McCarthy's work, the seascapes dotted throughout Woolf's, remind us of the power, unpredictability, and uniqueness of the natural world. Those are also qualities of individuals that must be adapted to the world around them, social as well as natural, for the individual to grow and thrive.

The horses in McCarthy's book become individuals through taming. A similar process happens to John Grady and Cam Ramsay. In their cases, Nature is their school. By learning how to survive in and adapt to Nature, they learn much: how to adjust to the inevitable passage of time, how to accommodate themselves to challenging circumstances, and how to undergo deprivation with the understanding that plenitude will recur.

For both protagonists, Nature becomes a mother, as it was for the romantic poet William Wordsworth, who lost his mother at the age of eight. For Wordsworth, Nature is "the anchor of my purest thoughts, the nurse, / The guide, the guardian of my heart, and soul / Of all my moral being" ("Tintern Abbey," ll. 109–11). The waves in *To the Lighthouse*, when Cam rows through them, take on the preternatural calm and harmonizing influence of her late mother. For John Grady, who barely knows his mother, Nature is where he tests and proves himself against a reality he cannot control. He learns that loss and death are inevitable but that love is worth the price of loss.

Both novels contain elements of the hero's quest defined by Joseph Campbell ("Monomyth: Hero's Journey"), where the hero sets off from home to experience adventures and returns transformed. In Woolf's and McCarthy's works, descriptive language translates feelings of abandonment and alienation into reconciliation with Nature and human nature. Their protagonists' identities are formed by weather, waves, and wind as much as any human influence.

Trials by Fire and Water

Both books have a three-part structure, emphasized in *To the Lighthouse* by separate sections: "The Window," a portrait from multiple perspectives of family harmony at a seashore home; "Time Passes," in which a decade elapses as the family and house decay, told from the perspective of no human being; "The Lighthouse," in which a mature Cam returns to the home of her childhood memories and, along with her brother and father, fulfills her mother's goal of voyaging to the lighthouse.

Like *To the Lighthouse*, *All the Pretty Horses* begins and ends in the protagonist's family home, the ranch that is sold at the end of the book. Woolf presents an idyllic time of innocence in "The Window" section of *To the Lighthouse*, when the Ramsay children are young, and their mother protects them as well as her husband and their guests. McCarthy's John Grady Cole, by contrast, is thrust out of his childhood home as a teenager near the beginning of the book after his grandfather's death, his family's financial destitution, his father's illness, and his mother's maintenance of distance from her son. By the end of the book's first chapter, he is wandering through Mexico with his friend Rawlins and the mysterious Blevins.

The second chapter, set on the La Purísima ranch, represents a recovery of innocence for John Grady in his Edenic romance with Alejandra, daughter of Héctor, the owner of the ranch. An air of foreboding hangs over this section, though, and the forbidden love concludes with John Grady's ejection from this earthly Paradise. In the third chapter, John Grady descends into the hell of prison because of his love of Alejandra and his link to Blevins. In the fourth and final chapter, his return first to the La Purísima ranch and ultimately to his original home does not result in the healing reconciliation with which *To the Lighthouse* concludes. Rather, John Grady comes home to learn that his father has died. The healing touch of a decade of Time, which dismantles everything so that a new reality can be built in "Time Passes," the middle section of *To the Lighthouse*, is not present in *All the Pretty Horses*, as the entire novel transpires within about two years. The rhythm of innocence lost and regained that Woolf creates in her novel is in McCarthy rather a sequence of repeated, ever more tragic losses.

After the initial scenes of loss and family fracture in *All the Pretty Horses*, John Grady Cole sets off on a journey of discovery deep into Mexico. He encounters helpers like his friend Rawlins and scoundrels like the mysterious Blevins, who joins the two friends for awhile. In the desert, Cole learns how to live with Nature with few or no resources; he later learns to live in plenitude at the paradisiacal hacienda "La Purísima." There he exercises to the fullest his skills in horse-breaking and consummates his love for Alejandra, daughter of the hacienda's owner, after an Edenic scene in which they bathe naked in a stream.

John Grady Cole remains innocent until he is taken into custody, along with Rawlins, and imprisoned with Blevins in La Encantada, where Blevins originally lost and regained his horse, the big bay. Then John Grady learns, as the captain who arrested him warns, what human beings are capable of: he, Rawlins, and Blevins are subjected to constant, indiscriminate violence. The people in prison are like horses, broken in order to be initiated into society. But while

John Grady breaks horses with strange compassion, stroking their heads and talking to them, in the prison there is no compassion, no governance, no God (Spurgeon 29). It is a place where "Evil . . . goes about on its own legs" (194–95). It is impossible to see the violence there as rehabilitation; rather, in this prison human life is reduced to survival of the fittest, governed by power and money rather than justice.

When Cole and Rawlins are ransomed by Alejandra's grand-aunt Alfonsa, with the stunning condition that Cole relinquish his love for Alejandra, after one night more with Alejandra, Cole goes on a second quest. His goal now is not to explore the countryside but to restore justice to the world that has victimized him and many other courageous people, including leaders of Mexico such as the Madero brothers, in the account of history Alfonsa gives Cole (Hamilton 42). Cole's loyalty to brave people is unwavering, as expressed at the book's outset: "all his reverence and all his fondness and all the leanings of his life were for the ardenthearted and they would always be so and never be otherwise" (56). Cole's personal code gets him into trouble when he pursues a romance with Alejandra and stays loyal to Blevins, but also enables him to survive. His determination to bring justice for Rawlins and Blevins brings him into dangerous situations but gives him strength to survive.

Cole's quest to restore his and Rawlins's self-respect and right the wrong of Blevins's murder centers on recovering their horses–a La Purísima horse Alfonsa gives him, Rawlins's lost horse, and Blevins's big bay, which Cole steals back. The cost of that theft, inflicted by one of the men who stole the bay horse, is symbolic castration, a gunshot wound in his thigh that John Grady self-cauterizes with a pistol he heats in a fire. Later, a cleansing rain completes his mythic transformation into an adult, confirmed by the statement of a judge who exonerates him of wrongdoing. As John Grady says to the judge in defense of his actions–killing a man in self-defense in prison, stealing back the horses, kidnapping and nearly killing the corrupt police captain—, he wanted to set right the senseless killing of Blevins: "The reason I wanted to kill him was because I stood there and let him walk that boy out in the trees and shoot him and I never said nothin" (293). Unlike many people he has encountered for whom acquiring power is the ultimate motive, for John Grady loyalty is the most important principle. John Grady may see in Blevins a younger version of himself; by redeeming Blevins's death, John Grady gives meaning to his own life.

The judge tells John Grady that the judge's own zeal to promote justice was not always satisfied: he torments himself with the case of a young offender he once sentenced to death. Growing up means accepting that the world is beyond human control: Time and Nature are implacable entities. As if to demonstrate that principle, John Grady returns home to learn that the event imminent from the beginning of the novel—his father's death, expected after a long illness—has occurred. At the end of the book, John Grady Cole, like Huckleberry Finn, sets off again into the natural world, knowing that family, for him, is an illusion and that human life has no permanence (Herlihy-Mera 485). His second departure from home is witnessed by a group of Native Americans: "They stood and watched him pass and watched him vanish upon that landscape solely because he was passing. Solely because he would vanish" (301).

Virginia Woolf also illustrates the force of Time in the middle section of *To the Lighthouse*, "Time Passes." There, the multiple perspectives of people in the first section vanish, giving way to a perspective apart from human consciousness. Nature, Time's handmaiden, destroys all that humanity constructs: a home, a shelter, memory itself. The home that was the family's foundation decays without human inhabitants. Meanwhile, in interspersed events told in parentheses, the family falls apart along with the world: a Ramsay son dies in World War I, a Ramsay daughter in childbirth. The only human being who acts in this section is the cleaner, Mrs. McNab, whose efforts to hold the house together are futile. Real agency is exercised by Nature in the form of the wind, personified as the new inhabiting force of the house. The memory of humanity disappears as does the presence of God: "no image with semblance of serving and divine promptitude comes readily to hand bringing the night to order and making the world reflect the compass of the soul" (193).

Nature is no "mirror" to humanity, as "with equal complacence she saw his misery . . . and acquiesced in his torture" (202).

For Cam, the last section of the book is a trial by water and fire. Her brother's anger against their father is incendiary, as he envisions killing their father, while the waves pose a potentially life-threatening challenge. Woolf says of her young heroine that, like John Grady Cole, "of all human qualities she reverenced justice most" (251). As in *All the Pretty Horses*, where the survival skills John Grady has learned through his experiences in Nature enable him to achieve his notion of justice, Cam unites her mother's emotional skills and her father's intellectual ones to help forge a new, delicate family unity. Most importantly, like John Grady Cole, Cam Ramsay has a kind heart; her compassion for others enables her to forgive and cooperate with them. The tamed impulse is also a natural one: the desire to live in harmony with others and one's own moral code.

Whereas Cam Ramsay enjoys being reintegrated into her family, the scarred and traumatized John Grady Cole, bearing the marks of his experience on his body, ends without family, friends, or romantic love. Yet, like Cam Ramsay, he can take pride in the discovery of his own identity and integrity. Both characters derive their identity and ethics from Nature's ceaseless change amid continuity, in their different settings of the desert and the ocean. Growing up in those environments shapes these young heroes into defenders of fidelity to themselves and others.

Works Cited

Bell, Ilona. "'Haunted by Great Ghosts': Virginia Woolf and 'To the Lighthouse.'" *Biography*, vol. 9, no. 2, 1986, pp. 150–75. *JSTOR*, jstor.org/stable/23539308.

Campbell, Joseph. "Monomyth: Hero's Journey." *University of California Berkeley Office of Resources for International and Area Studies*, 2000, orias.berkeley.edu/resources-teachers/monomyth-heros-journey-project.

Cutchins, Dennis. "All the Pretty Horses: Cormac McCarthy's Reading of 'For Whom the Bell Tolls.'" *Western American Literature*, vol. 41, no. 3, 2006, pp. 266–99. *JSTOR*, jstor.org/stable/43022482.

Gliserman, Martin. "Virginia Woolf's 'To the Lighthouse': Syntax and the Female Center." *American Imago*, vol. 40, no. 1, 1983, pp. 51–101. *JSTOR*, jstor.org/stable/26303727.

Guth, Deborah. "Virginia Woolf: Myth and 'To the Lighthouse.'" *College Literature*, vol. 11, no. 3, 1984, pp. 233–49. *JSTOR*, jstor.org/stable/25111615.

Hamilton, Patrick L. "Recuperation and Re-Imagination: Frontier Space in Cormac McCarthy's 'All the Pretty Horses' and Alfredo Véa's 'The Silver Cloud Café.'" *Interdisciplinary Literary Studies*, vol. 9, no. 2, 2008, pp. 29–44. *JSTOR*, jstor.org/stable/41210293.

Herlihy-Mera, Jeffrey. "'Mojado-Reverso' or, A Reverse Wetback: On John Grady Cole's Mexican Ancestry in Cormac McCarthy's 'All the Pretty Horses." *Modern Fiction Studies*, vol. 61, no. 3, 2015, pp. 469–92. *JSTOR*, jstor.org/stable/26421901.

Keats, John. "Letter to George and Georgiana Keats," 21 Apr. 1819. In *The Letters of John Keats*. Edited by Hyder E. Rollins, vol. 2, p. 102. Harvard UP, 1958.

Lanser, Susan Sniader. "Fictions of Absence: Feminism, Modernism, Virginia Woolf." *Fictions of Authority: Women Writers and Narrative Voice*, Cornell UP, 1992, pp. 102–19. *JSTOR*, jstor.org/stable/10.7591/j.ctt207g6vm.9.

McCarthy, Cormac. *All the Pretty Horses*. Vintage, 1992.

Smythe, Karen. "Virginia Woolf's Elegiac Enterprise." *NOVEL: A Forum on Fiction*, vol. 26, no. 1, 1992, pp. 64–79. *JSTOR*, doi.org/10.2307/1345605.

Spurgeon, Sara L. "'Pledged in Blood': Truth and Redemption in Cormac McCarthy's 'All the Pretty Horses.'" *Western American Literature*, vol. 34, no. 1, 1999, pp. 24–44. *JSTOR*, jstor.org/stable/43024973.

White, Christopher T. "Dreaming the *Border Trilogy*: Cormac McCarthy and Narrative Creativity." *The Cormac McCarthy Journal*, vol. 13, no. 1, 2015, pp. 121–42. *JSTOR*, doi.org/10.5325/cormmccaj.13.1.0121.

Woolf, Virginia. *Mrs. Dalloway*. Harcourt, 1925.

__________. *To the Lighthouse*. Harcourt, 1927.

Wordsworth, William. "Lines Composed a Few Miles above Tintern Abbey." *Selected Poems and Prefaces by William Wordsworth*. Edited by Jack Stillinger. Houghton Mifflin, 1965.

Under the Influence: Melville, Bloodlines, and McCarthy's *All the Pretty Horses*

Stephen Daly

Recognizing the influence of Faulkner and Melville, Cormac McCarthy has said, "The novel depends for its life on the novels that have been written" (qtd. in Woodward). While commentators have noted the confluence between *Moby Dick* and McCarthy's *Border Trilogy*, there also exists a convergence between Melville's novel and McCarthy's *All the Pretty Horses.* From the opening paragraph of McCarthy's novel, which alludes to the "glass, darkly" of Corinthians, there is a pronounced privileging of vision over other senses. The visual is also central to Melville not only because his narrators are conduits of pictorialism but because visuality forms part of the nexus of the exploratory apparatus of colonialism and its cultural offshoots—travel writing, the guidebook, and anthropology. A scopophilia, or erotic pleasure derived from looking, gives rise to a libidinal, masculinist vision of the world. Critics have pointed to a propensity of the colonial mindset to feminizing the Other as an absence or negation, a *terra nullius* to be claimed and controlled. John Grady Cole, the putative hero of McCarthy's novel, is a conduit for these colonial discourses. However, he is also a victim, deprived of agency by these master discourses. McCarthy's treatment of him, and the use of the trope of the sublime—with its turn to paradox, inefficacy, and silence— suggest an ethics of representation.

From the outset of *All the Pretty Horses,* there is an emphasis on the visual, indicated by the doubled image of the "candleflame and the image of the candleflame caught in the pierglass" that "twisted and righted" upon the reader's entrance of the vestibule or threshold of this novel (3). This is also a liminal moment, marking the ambiguous position between oppositions of inside and outside, light and dark, absence and presence, life and death. In its emphasis on the visual and the duality of light and dark, the opening alludes to the "glass, darkly" of Paul's letter to the Corinthians, a missive that outlines a system of governance for the early church and compares the imperfect knowledge of our world with the perfect wisdom of God, foregrounding epistemology—the nature of knowledge and understanding—and the binary of subjectivity versus objectivity. The King James version of 1 Corinthians 13:12 states: "For now we see through a glass, darkly; but then face to face: now I know in part; but then shall I know even as also I am known" (*King James Bible Online*). Significantly, this passage is preceded by a major theme of McCarthy's *bildungsroman*—the renunciation of youthful delusion: "When I was a child, I spake as a child, I understood as a child, I thought as a child: but when I became a man, I put away childish things" (1 Cor. 13:11). Paul was also a missionary and evangelist, and an archetype that informs the actions of Grady; just one of Grady's "forebears only dimly known to him all framed in glass and dimly lit" in the hallway (3). Indeed, it is a novel that is concerned, even if obliquely or "dimly," with its own genealogical structure. This attitude reflects the underlying reality of literature, since as McCarthy himself put it, acknowledging a debt to his forebears, "The ugly fact is books are made out of books. The novel depends for its life on the novels that have been written" (qtd. in Woodward).

This is a concern shared with Melville's flagship novel, *Moby Dick*. Melville's novel begins properly, not with the invocation to address the narrator by a potential pseudonym "Ishmael," but in the Etymology and Extracts sections that also form a kind of vestibule to the novel. Both sections exhibit a concern with, in the Etymology section, the etymological ancestry of the word "whale," with the Extracts section also focusing on the literary pedigree of Melville's putative topic. This reflects the contemporaneous concern for origins that would result in Darwin's *On the Origin of Species*, published eight years after Melville's novel. The Extracts section represents a wide-ranging collection of "views" on the whale from multifarious disciplines, offering a "bird's-eye view of what has been promiscuously said, thought, fancied, and sung of Leviathan" (xlii). These panoramic vistas or discourses on the whale trace a lineage or genealogy—an ethos shared by the dominant paradigm of the age, natural history. It is also thereby a paradoxical one, based on an impulse derived—as indicated by Melville's use of Genesis—from the foundational book of the Bible, which is suffused in a binary mode of division and an Adamic principle of naming. These multifarious discourses form a kaleidoscopic, agonistic structure underlying the novel, forming as the "pale Usher" of the Etymology section reminds the reader, part of the "old grammars" or underlying structures (xl).

Moby Dick, in common with many novels of exploration, exhibits a pronounced ocularcentrism, often defined as a perceptual and epistemological bias ranking vision over other senses in Western cultures. The "bird's-eye view" suggested by the Usher introducing the Extracts is reiterated later by the trope of the panorama, an invention of the late eighteenth century that proposed to give hyperrealist renditions of a scene in 360-degree verisimilitude:

> For in the mere act of penning my thoughts of this Leviathan, they weary me, and make me faint with their outreaching comprehensiveness of sweep, as if to include the whole circle of the sciences, and all the generations of whales, and men, and mastodons, past, present, and to come, with all the revolving panoramas of empire on earth, and throughout the whole universe, not excluding its suburbs. (406)

The panorama's view approximates a god-like perspective, and is shorthand for the empirical, objective viewpoint of exploration and its cultural offshoots: travel writing, the guidebook, natural history, and anthropology. If Melville is immersed in this visual mode, he is also implicated in the imperialistic ideology of exploration as exemplary of the "seeing man" or simply, "the male imperial European subject" who "possesses as he looks" (Pratt 7). Ishmael is also a conduit and representative of the objectifying gaze of the natural historian. He admits whilst surveying Queequeg that he "was guilty of great rudeness: staring at him from the bed, and watching all his toilette motions, for the time my curiosity getting the better of my breeding" (25). Nevertheless, reiterating Queequeg's anthropological value, Ishmael states that "he and his ways were well worth unusual regarding" (25). Underscoring this underlying structure of visuality, Pip the cabin boy is washed overboard towards the novel's end, "carried down alive to the wondrous depths of the unwarped primal world" and upon returning can only monotonously repeat the structural grammar of the depths: "I look, you look, he looks, we look, ye look, they look" (388).

The centrality of vision can be traced from Melville's earliest novels, *Typee* and *Omoo,* which illustrate the overarching culture of the explorer as imperialist vanguard. Throughout these novels, Melville's narrators are swayed, indeed governed by multiple discourses that, in turn, determine agency and behavior: generic conventions, codes, archetypes and paradigms that underlie and dictate thought, behavior and expression. The concern with and interplay between visuality, agency and governing structures reaches an apex in *Moby Dick.* Visuality is understood as a proxy for understanding, and Ishmael, confirming his role as interpreter between the visual and verbal (in his role as verbal painter), confirms to the reader that he aims to "paint to you as well as one can without canvas something like the true form of the whale" (236). In objectifying Linnaean terms, Ishmael promises, a "systematized exhibition of the whale in his broad genera" (116), availing of the language of the museum that Timothy Mitchell calls the "exhibitionary order." In Mitchell's schema the Other to the rational, objective West is a series of absences (reason, order, meaning, and so on), with the world set up as a picture to be consumed; as a curiosity to be investigated, controlled and comprehended by the European gaze. This sense of the world is presented as an "enframed totality, something that forms a structure or system" (304). The point of view from which the object or exhibit is ascertained is set apart and outside it, akin to Jeremy Bentham's panopticon where one could see and yet not be seen. For Mitchell, the detachment of objectivity similarly seeks to eliminate the presence of the observer. In a self-reflexive act of the awareness of his own cultural composition and the ideological underpinnings of the novel of exploration, Melville avails in an ironic manner of the sublime and its trope of ineffability, subscribing to an ethical silence. Of the whale, Ishmael states "it is in vain to attempt a clear classification of the Leviathan" (122), and concludes, "Leviathan is that one creature in the world which must remain unpainted to the last" (240). Melville embraces silence, ambivalence, and paradox as an aesthetic choice: "I promise nothing complete; because any human thing supposed to be complete, must for that very reason infallibly be faulty" (117). The adoption of antinomy—of contradiction or paradox—highlights Melville's purpose in the use of ambivalence since it represents an interstitial (or in-between) viewpoint, between polar oppositions, a contrast to the singular, totalizing and deity-like position of the panorama. It is a stereoscopic attitude, one synonymous with that of the whale, which is more "subtle than man's that he can at the same moment of time attentively examine two distinct prospects, one on one side of him, and the other in an exactly opposite direction" (297).

The opening of McCarthy's novel acknowledges this binocular mode and is replete with uncanny echoes of its exploratory heritage. It begins with a rupture, as John Grady Cole attempts to come to terms with the revolutionizing forces of modernity—symbolized by the relentless controlled violence of the steam train—that threaten extinction for him and his ilk. This opening echoes obliquely with associations of exploration. The reference in Spanish, for example, to the light of "la vela" (4), an ostensible synonym for candle, also signifies when capitalized "the sail" in Latin, and the name of a former part of the Argo Navis constellation, representing in mythical terms the *Argo,* and the quest for the golden fleece. It, thus, registers simultaneously as the first of multiple references to stars (with their compound associations of navigation and fate), the first of many uncanny echoes of McCarthy's knowing genealogical construction, and a reflexive acknowledgement of his "forebears." This is echoed again in the early landscape descriptions—of "a thin grey reef beginning along the eastern rim of the world" (3), or of the sun, "elliptic under the reefs of bloodred cloud" (5), or of the stars, "Orion and Capella and the signature of Cassiopeia all rising up through the phosphorous dark like a sea-net" (60). The antinomy or paradox of "phosphorous dark" like that of the "dark electric" (30) betokens the interplay of oppositions, such as past and present, presence and absence, life and death. From the opening pages of the novel in which Grady rides along the "old Comanche road"—an image betokening the taking of well-worn (historical/discursive/literary) paths—resonances of "nation and ghost of nation" (5) create an uncanny cognitive dissonance that foreground a fundamental ambivalence, pointing to an unknowable cognitive centre at the heart of the novel. Later, of the rationale for Don Héctor's decision to hand Rawlins and Grady over to the authorities, the boys conclude: "If he did it was because of some lie. Or some truth" (155). McCarthy plays with presence and absence: "They heard somewhere in that tenantless night a bell that tolled and ceased where no bell was" (30). This interplay of binary oppositions echoes the stereoscopic vision of Melville's whale. This attitude is thereby also an interstitial one—as Melville writes of the whale's doubled vision—that encourages "[d]oubts of all things earthly, and intuitions of some things heavenly; [and that] combination makes neither believer nor infidel, but makes a man who regards them both with equal eye" (335).

The emphasis on vision evident in Melville's work is also fundamental to the navigation and knowledge of the territory of *All the Pretty Horses*. The ocularcentrism or scopophilia demonstrated by Melville's characters is replicated by Grady when pressed for a rationale as to his presence in Mexico: "I just wanted to see the country, I reckon" (114). It is a masculine, libidinal mode, a confluence of the male gaze and the imperialistic desire for possession. The erotic spark enflamed by the Americans' first meeting with Alejandra, the hacienda owner's daughter, is directly equated with Mexico and territorial desire:

> You reckon that was his daughter?
> I'd say it was.
> This is some country, ain't it? (96)

The psychosexual association between landscape and sexual possession arises again when Rawlins questions Grady's interest in Alejandra: "You got eyes for the spread?" (138) It is also a mode that is equated with the investigative, analytical attitudes of the likes of

Humboldt and Darwin. Of the landscape surrounding La Purísima (one translation of which is "The Virgin") is written, "In the lakes and in the streams were species of fish not known elsewhere on earth and birds and lizards and other forms of life as well all long relict" (97), a prelapsarian landscape that simultaneously conjures resonances of Melville's Edenic South Pacific. Rawlins echoes the historical motivations of western explorers in the aside, "Where do you reckon that paradise is at?" (59) as well as resonances of conquistadors of old when Rawlins asks, "What's them lights?" to which Grady responds, "I'd make it Eldorado" (32). The visual mode is the primary means of comprehension, and mapping of the territory corresponds to knowledge of it. Johannes Fabian writes that "the ability to 'visualize' a culture or society . . . became synonymous for understanding it" (106). Furthermore, according to Susan Bassnet, mapping is heavily linked to the history of travel writing, exploration, and colonialism, since "[n]aming the new and labelling it became a means of marking ownership, in both physical and intellectual terms" (231). Moreover, "the early history of colonialism is one in which new territories were metaphorized as female, as virgin lands waiting to be penetrated, ploughed, and husbanded by male explorers" (231). The unexplored realms, the mirror Other to the developed civilization of the United States is defined as absence:

> It was an oil company roadmap that Rawlins had picked up at the cafe and he looked at it and he looked south toward the gap in the low hills. There were roads and rivers and towns on the American side of the map as far south as the Rio Grande and beyond that all was white. It dont show nothing down there, does it? said Rawlins. (34)

Consequently, the landscape as refracted through the eyes of the American duo is one of absence and deficit. McCarthy reports: "There was nothing along the road save the country it traversed and there was nothing in the country at all" (57). When John Grady spies Alejandra for the first time, as she passes, Grady "was still looking down the road where she'd gone. There was nothing there to see but he was looking anyway" (95). As she and Grady consummate their relationship, Alejandra's skin is synonymous with the whiteness and emptiness of the map: "[H]e watched across the still black surface to where she stood on the shore with the horse and he watched where she stepped from her pooled clothing so pale, so pale" (141).

Alejandra's association with horses is both a symbol of sexual relationships and colonial domination. As Rawlins states, "A good lookin horse is like a good lookin woman" (89). The horses broken by John Grady represent how Indigenous populations become subjugated and the rhetoric through which evangelical discourse dominates populations (the Hacienda La Purísima coincides with the name of a Franciscan mission in California, La Mission Purísima, founded in 1787, to convert Indigenous populations). On the improbability of breaking in wild horses in such a short time, Grady claims, "I'll make em believe, he said. You'll see," to which Rawlins replies, "I'm goin to tell you right now, cousin. This is a heathenish bunch" (103). Grady's evangelical discipline is "like the voice of some god come to inhabit them" (105). He exhibits the prototypical modus operandi of the missionary, speaking the native language to better facilitate his message, creating subordination and dependence in the subject: "[H]e spoke constantly to it in spanish in phrases almost biblical repeating again and again the strictures of a yet untabled law. Soy comandante de las yeguas, he would say, yo y yo solo. Sin la caridad de estas manos no tengas nada. Ni comida ni agua ni hijos" ("I am the commander of the mares . . . I and I only. Without the care of these hands you have nothing. Neither food nor water nor offspring"; 128). Later, Grady will be thus characterized: "As if he were some personage bearing news for the countryside. As if he were some newfound evangelical being conveyed down out of the mountains" (217). Conversion, as shown by the fate of the horses, is simultaneously incarceration.

Yet this is also a fate shared by Grady Cole, who endures a literal incarceration. This is shown to be directly related to Grady's quasi-colonial libidinal desire but is also an important thematic parallel with Melville. The amorous lakeside scene with Alejandra marks a liminal, pivotal point in the narrative, where events, "like a chrysalis emerging" careen away from Grady, and the subjugation he had practiced in horse-breaking is inverted and imposed upon him. McCarthy plays with the ambiguity in Alejandra's phrase "Me quieres?" (which can mean both "Do you love me?" and "Do you want me?") signaling Grady's accession to the greater authority underlining his behavior: "God yes, he said," the invocation wittily recalling earlier conversations between Grady and Rawlins concerning the nature of free will, fate, and divine providence (141). Thereafter, Grady becomes subject to Alejandra's desire when she forcefully imposes her presence in his bed "nine nights running" (142). The relationship between desire and incarceration is playfully indicated later when the jailer orders Grady's handcuffs removed: "Las esposas, he said," punning on the singular *la esposa*, or wife (157). This is underlined when McCarthy writes of Grady and Alejandra's last day together spent in the (ironically termed) "Jardín Independencia" whereupon Grady purchases strawberries in "a paper alcatraz," and where a stone angel displays wrists from which "dangled the broken chains of the manacles she wore" (253). This is a radical subversion of the masculine, epic hero's agency. A closer inspection of McCarthy's putative hero shows that this agency is challenged from the beginning, a paradoxical antinomy of choice and compulsion evident even in his choice to leave the homestead in a westward direction: "He rode where he would always choose to ride" (5). He is a man already chosen in a predetermined fashion by fate for extinction, "like a man come to the end of something" (5). This concern with agency is one McCarthy shares with Melville, Ishmael's decision to take the whaler *Pequod* announced satirically as part of the "grand programme of Providence"; a pawn of "the Fates, who has the constant surveillance of me, and secretly dogs me, and influences me in some unaccountable way" (5). This is a situation Melville states reflects all humanity: "Who ain't a slave? Tell me that" (4). It is a predicament that is embodied and symbolized by the whale: "All men live enveloped in whale-lines. All are born with halters around their necks" (254).

As Gail Moore Morrison points out, Grady Cole meets a number of instructors on his journey, befitting a novel structured as a *bildungsroman.* In this it follows Melville's epic, Ishmael relating how the "whale-ship was my Yale College and my Harvard" (99). The most significant of these instructors is the Dueña Alfonsa, who "looked like the schoolteacher she in fact had been" (133). At their second encounter she rejects the rational mode and the contemporaneous search for "the origins of things," seeing "nothing of the kind" (231). Instead, addressing the issue of agency, the world is a "puppet show" of unknowability, for "when one looks behind the curtain and traces the strings upwards he finds they terminate in the hands of yet other puppets, themselves with their own strings which trace upward in turn" (231). The agency deficit implicit in the imagery of marionette strings is significant in that the Dueña points to her own subjugation, relating how societies are "largely machines for the suppression of women" (230). Importantly, she does not disavow the idea of "fate" or governing structure, but rather "its nomination," a phrase with important implications for the novel's thematic structure (241). Furthermore, the process by which meaning is generated is questioned by the Dueña in a manner that suggests the underlying purpose of McCarthy's aesthetic: "If there is a pattern there it will not shape itself to anything these eyes can recognize. Because the question for me was always whether that shape we see in our lives was there from the beginning or whether these random events are only called a pattern after the fact. Because otherwise we are nothing" (230). Her statement questions the basis for not only the construction of history but reflexively, the basis of Grady's narrative and the process by which meaning itself is constructed.

McCarthy shares this scepticism towards the structures that generate meaning. Indeed, he shows a pronounced skepticism towards representation itself. When John Grady attends his mother's performance, he views it with the "notion that there would be something in the story itself to tell him about the way the world was or was becoming but there was not. There was nothing in it at all" (21). McCarthy directly addresses the representational heritage of the cowboy genre, specifically that of the late nineteenth/early twentieth century author, Owen Wister (and his collaborations with the sculptor and painter Frederic Remington), whose writings such as *The Virginian*, according to John Jennings, romanticized more than any other the impending disappearance of the cowboy. Representations, such as an "oilpainting of horses" in the homestead, which had been "copied out of a book," are thus dismissed as "picturebook horses" (16). McCarthy gestures playfully to the inefficacy of his own representation, at times reflexively parodying it as performative and one-dimensional. A young Mexican girl, for example "reading a comic book" offers a wry critique of Grady and Rawlins when they walk into a small store, and she appears to question their similitude—"[S]he looked up at them and looked at the comicbook and then looked up again" (49). A farmhand, McCarthy comments reflexively, "looked like an extra in a stageplay reciting his only lines" (261).

If Grady is a scion of the evangelical ethos and conduit for colonial discourses based on visuality as a root metaphor, McCarthy's turn to the sublime and its trope of inefficacy represents both a submission to the demands of the genre and an ethics of representation. McCarthy, turning away from what the Dueña regards as the world's "nomination," instead embraces deficit, absence, and silence—as denoted by the repeated iteration of "nothing" throughout—and a species of confusion created by a paradoxical, antinomian viewpoint. This paradoxical position is one imbued by the whale, as noted by Ahab: "Thy silence then; *that* voices thee" (146). The whale itself is also a paradoxical, interstitial being, "an anomalous creature" (330), that evades classification, forming an honorary part of what Linnaeus termed, in his first editions of *Systema Naturae,* "Animalia Paradoxa" or contradictory animals, which included such mythical creatures as the phoenix and dragon. Melville duly recalls the "famous story of St. George and the Dragon; which dragon I maintain to have been a whale; for in many old chronicles whales and dragons are strangely jumbled together, and often stand for each other" (325). It is an interstitial position, between binary oppositions; one that enables a view of the world that is as the Dueña puts it, "between the dream and the reality" (238). This attitude also embraces the sense of deficit in her pronouncement that "there is little that can be truly known" (238).

McCarthy undermines the link between seeing and knowing, and accordingly the act of bearing witness, the basis of judgement, and the empirical ethos. John Grady's account in the courtroom is just another re-telling of the narrative, each iteration changed in subtle ways to suit its audience. His narrative, thus, becomes subject to suspicion as less an act of verisimilitude and more an act of self-justification, the latter acknowledged by Grady himself when he admits to the judge, "I don't feel justified" (290). The act of bearing witness and the authority of proof that underpins judgement is satirized and undermined when the judge asks Grady to show the court his bullet holes, so that Grady "unbuckled his belt and dropped his trousers to his knees and turned his right leg to the judge" (289). The psychosexual dimension of visuality, and the link between the libidinal and knowledge here is evident when compared to a similar scene in *Moby Dick* that emphasizes the interplay between carnality and visuality in the construction of empirical knowledge of the whale: "But to a large and thorough sweeping comprehension of him, it behoves me now to unbutton him still further, and untrussing the points of his hose, unbuckling his garters, and casting loose the hooks and eyes of the joints of his innermost bones, set him before you in his ultimatum" (400). Indeed, even the judge and the base structures of judgement are prey to the same deficit of agency permeating the novel, as is revealed in the decision to become a judge: "I think I just didnt have any choice. Just didnt have any choice" (292).

Nevertheless, deficit and loss, in McCarthy's schema, also suggest ethical possibilities. Grady's newfound sense of loss and absence, which is also the experience of being othered, follows him across the border, where he enters the present from the anthropological/ethnographic past of colonial exploration, like "some apparition out of the vanished past" (287). He is aligned with colonial subjects and figures previously marked for extinction and indeed, defined by the absence that was previously imposed on the Other. McCarthy places the final viewpoint in the eyes of the displaced natives, with Grady the object of their gaze: "They stood and watched him pass and watched him vanish upon that landscape solely because he was passing. Solely because he would vanish" (301). This newfound sense of reality leads Grady to a new sense of identity now shared with the subjects of colonial subjugation, one that is interstitial, and notably without "nomination": "He found that he was breathing in rhythm with the horse as if some part of the horse were within him breathing and then he descended into some deeper collusion for which he had not a name" (266). Melville's Ishmael, in the urge to understand Queequeg, and, apprehending this "joint-stock world," relinquishes his "Presbyterian form of worship" (a form of Protestantism highly active in Pacific evangelism, with an emphasis on the confessional and authority of biblical scripture as a form of governance) and vows to "turn idolator" (47). Grady, by the close of McCarthy's novel, becomes, in parallel, an apostate figure:

> Where is your country? he said.
> I don't know, said John Grady. I don't know where it is. I don't know what happens to country. (299)

Grady is no longer able to navigate the territory and is unable to see or verify that which is before him. This sense of deficit and loss is suggestive of Grady's own father's: "Looking over the country with those sunken eyes as if the world out there had been altered or made suspect by what he'd seen of it elsewhere. As if he might never see it again or worse did see it right at last" (23). The instructive ethos of the *bildungsroman* operates here in a circular way, returning to an earlier narrative point, at once fulfilling the traditional structure of the epic, but also notably defying linear progression—what John Samson calls the "Christian pattern of history" and the "ideology of exploration as subsumed by the idea of progress" (7). Grady begins the novel as a scion or conduit for colonial modes of thought and being, but in his subjection to the result of his quasi-colonial desire sustains all the loss, pain, and captivity of the colonial subject. In this fundamental sense of loss, he becomes a double to Ishmael—a fellow apostate—who at the close of Melville's novel is to be found isolated, alone, "an orphan" (508). Bereft of patriarchal modes of governance, and stateless, Grady loses the ground of his being and his means of orientation, yet in this loss he becomes a vehicle, as Mary Louise Pratt writes, for "imagining what a decolonization of self might mean" (224).

A comparison between *Moby Dick* and McCarthy's novel suggests ways in which *All the Pretty Horses* engages reflexively with the forebears of its literary ancestry. As Melville's epic novel gestures in the opening sections to the ways in which it is discursively composed—through various modes of thought compelling certain behaviors and attitudes—so McCarthy in an analogous way calls attention to the ways in which not only are his characters ideologically composed and thus deficient in agency, but reflexively, how narrative itself, through precedents of genre, convention, and literary history is necessarily ideologically imbued. Caught within the confines of these constitutive discourses, McCarthy's response is to avail himself of the trope of the sublime to suggest an ethics of representation or means of seeing "otherwise." The viewpoint of antinomy, or inner contradiction composed of opposing terms, recalls the white whale and its stereoscopic vision with its ability to appraise two opposing viewpoints at the same time. This vista encourages an interstitial position, one that is composed of doubt, and thus an antidote to the systems of objectivity derived from historical colonial ventures.

Works Cited

Bassnett, Susan. "Travel Writing and Gender." *The Cambridge Companion to Travel Writing.* Edited by Peter Hulme and Tim Youngs. 8th edition. Cambridge UP, 2013, pp. 225–41.

Fabian, Johannes. *Time and the Other: How Anthropology Makes Its Object.* Columbia UP, 1983.

Jennings, John. "The Cowboy Legend: Owen Wister's Virginian and the Canadian-American Frontier." West series, 7. U of Calgary P, 2015.

King James Bible Online, www.kingjamesbibleonline.org/.

McCarthy, Cormac. *All the Pretty Horses*. Alfred A. Knopf, 1993.

Melville, Herman. *Moby Dick.* Oxford UP, 2008.

Mitchell, Timothy. "Orientalism and the Exhibitionary Order." *Colonialism and Culture*. Edited by Nicholas B. Dirks. U of Michigan P, 1992, pp. 289–318.

Moore Morrison, Gail. "*All the Pretty Horses:* John Grady Cole's Expulsion from Paradise." *Perspectives on Cormac McCarthy*. Edited by Edwin T. Arnold and Dianne C Luce. U of Mississippi P, 1999, pp. 175–94.

Pratt, Mary Louise. *Imperial Eyes: Travel Writing and Transculturation.* Routledge, 1992.

Samson, John. *White Lies: Melville's Narratives of Facts.* Cornell UP, 1989.

Woodward, Richard B. "Cormac McCarthy's Venomous Fiction." *The New York Times Magazine*, 19 Apr. 1992, nytimes.com/1992/04/19/magazine/cormac-mccarthy-s-venomous-fiction.html.

The Cowboy and the American Dream: Charting the Binaries of the West in McCarthy's *All the Pretty Horses*

Shubham Singh

Cormac McCarthy's *All the Pretty Horses* is the most acclaimed novel of his *Border Trilogy*, each of which is synthesized by the repetition of the act of crossing of a physical frontier: the Mexican American border. The individual/s crossing these limitations traverse not just physical boundaries but several ideological binaries as well. The cowboys in the narrative set out to chase the promising American dream, however, the binaries in the text work to undermine the myth. In the narrative, the North, which is representative of America, is privileged over the South, implying the Mexican countryside. But the distinction transforms from visual to the ideological, with America's value for civilization conflicted with Mexico's underdeveloped topography. The protagonist—the cowboy caught up in the midst of the clash—struggles to get past the binaries desiring to move to the uncharted Western territory, for the cherished ideals of civilization and industrialization in the American society challenge his own existence. Violence and death color the world of the novel since the very beginning where his grandfather dies, and his father returns from war injured. Suffering inherent in existence is a major theme running through the novel. The inaptitude to distinguish the grandfather from the ranch and his horses lies at the base of the narrative. His passing symbolizes the passing of the old West that creates a conflict for the baffled cowboy to find his own place to belong: "the burial of John Grady's grandfather occasions a local loss of medial space between domesticity and wilderness" (Ellis 202). Thus, the binary of space comes into play with the very onset of the novel. The horses play a unifying role in the novel in multiple ways, principally on the level of space and charting the boundaries between the North and South. Horses represent the glory of a past when human beings had a deeper association with the natural landscape, and they become the link connecting all the characters. The horses also stand as symbols of constancy amid the transience of life. They connect the present to the past apart from serving the work function. This essay considers the novel in terms of its dramatization of the conflict between competing binaries and the crossing of the physical and philosophical boundaries that lead to coming of age of the protagonist, and also to re-evaluate the novel in the contemporary contexts.

The myth of the frontier or of the West is one of the long-established and surviving myths of the American culture. Several writers, critics, and historians have contributed to the forging of the myth of the frontier as a vast and lush uncharted territory at the edge of the civilized society waiting to be explored by the adventurous and spirited men. For centuries, the European Americans conquered the natives living in the western frontier and colonized the territory leading to expansion into North America. This became romanticized and glorified in literature to create a myth that overshadowed the violent realities of the expansion and the exploitation of the natural region as well as the Native Indians. In 1893, Frederick Jackson Turner promoted his thesis of the frontier as the "meeting point between savagery and civilization" (3), claiming that American pioneers had moved to the West in waves, and they were transformed through their interaction with the Native Americans and the wilderness of the western frontier to become self-willed individuals who cherished their dearly earned freedom. Another renowned scholar of the frontier myth, Richard Slotkin devoted his career to studying the several dimensions of the myth that he condensed in three trilogies where he begins with a general understanding of the myth of the frontier implying America to be a land of limitless opportunity, moving on to the capitalist exploitation of the natural landscape as America became an industrialized nation, to its being an agent of cultural ideology in contemporary popular culture. To put the matter plainly, there are two perspectives of the West, one being the historical west where farmers, ranchers, and certain outlaws followed their individual happiness, and the other being the mythical west that is glorified in popular narratives to take a solid shape in the common American imagination. As they were one of the prime frontiersmen in the Wild West, the cowboys and the ranchers were idealized in the beliefs of the people through the mass media and the earlier perception regarding the cowboys as meritless idlers rapidly transformed into the celebration of their prized individuality and masculinity. McCarthy takes a revisionist approach to the myth of the frontier in his *Border Trilogy*.

In *All the Pretty Horses*, the binaries of the West find a full expression as well, as they co-exist in the region creating a kind of identity crisis for the protagonists. Mexico is an idealized frontier in the world of the novel and is depicted as untouched by the impact of modernization. It is the only available alternative to cowboys like John Grady Cole and Lacey Rawlins who are perplexed as they witness the passing of the Old West that they so readily associate with. The narrative replaces the conventional movement toward the West with a southward movement in which the cowboys cross the Mexican border to find a place to belong. Mexico entails the promised freedom of the West as well as the opportunity for flowering of that individualism that is denied to them back home. John Grady Cole comes face-to-face with the realities of the New West as the narrative works to deflate the idealism of the Old West. He is unable to belong to the Mexican territory owing both to the cultural differences that alienate him creating a crisis of identity as well as the unrealistic cowboy myth that does not hold ground.

The celebrated notions regarding cowboys with their rugged individualism, oneness with the natural landscape, and a conquering masculinity are, in fact, hollow mythical conceptions whereas in reality the ordinary cowboy was a young man driven to desperation by the rapidly altering ways of life that made his survival quite difficult. Wallace Stegner's comment in this regard is pertinent: "the cowboy in practice was and is an overworked, underpaid hireling, almost as homeless and dispossessed as a modern crop worker, and his fabled independence was and is chiefly the privilege of quitting his job in order to go looking for another just as bad. That or go outside the law, as some did" (69). When the events of the novel are assessed, this is found to be certainly true. The novel commences in Texas with a funeral scene, and we learn that John's grandfather has passed. The ranch that his grandfather owned is being sold by his mother and despite his sincere efforts he is unable to persuade her not to sell it. His father, a World War II veteran, had money at one time, but he wasted it all away and was estranged from John's mother for seven years. Left with no other option, John Grady attempts to look for help from a lawyer named Franklin who affirms what his mother said about the ranch being unprofitable. In his naivety, John Grady also expresses hope that the ranch could once again be lucrative but is dismissed soon enough.

John Grady's entire existence is under threat of extinction, and this causes him to take the drastic step of escaping his current predicament. The horses that have been his companions all through his years as a cowboy become the instrument of his escape as well. The hope of a better livelihood takes him and Lacey Rawlins on horsebacks to a large, landed estate in Mexico. On the way they come across a young boy named Jimmy Blevins who stole a horse and was running off to Langtry to escape his pursuers. The horse he carried was a fine one, and they did not believe that it belonged to him. Even though they had their suspicion about the boy, they let him accompany them on the ride. Their journey is full of camping and struggling to find food and water to survive. When a storm comes and Blevins tries to outrun it, he is separated from the boys. The next morning, they find him naked wearing only his underpants and his horse and pistol have gone. They decide to retrieve the horse from the villagers who have taken it, and in the process, they are again separated as Blevins runs off to lead the pursuers away asking them to meet him down the road. Later, the cowboys reach a beautiful hacienda where they are hired. The Mexicans refer to them as "caballero," which is the highest designation for cowboys, and it derives from the word *gentleman*. Here John Grady Cole is noted by Don Héctor, the manager, for his understanding and special skill with horses. He is given his own room in the barn where he could oversee the breeding of the horses. He finally has a place to belong where his skills as a cowboy are valued and rewarded. He becomes fascinated with Alejandra, the daughter of Héctor, who too, reciprocates likewise. As she returns after riding through the rain one day, she appears both real and dreamy to John: "real horse, real rider, real land and sky and yet a dream withal" (132). His relationship with Alejandra, too, is colored by the binaries of the North and South. Even though the feelings they have for each other are quite genuine, the differences between them, particularly the obstructions created by her grand-aunt and father owing to cultural sanctity make their fulfilment appear to be a dream rather than an objective reality.

The novel itself is about endings. It begins with the death of John's grandfather, emblematic of the passing of the Old West, and it ends with the death of an old Mexican woman known as "Abuela" or grandmother in Spanish, who played a key role in raising John. At the heart, the novel is about the culmination of America's mythical and historical narrative of cowboys and the world of ranches. Although John Grady Cole is based on a myth that probably never existed in reality, his determination to not let go of the old order and his desperate search for a place to belong, along with a genuine love for the ranch, the horses, and the independence it entails, imbue him with the characteristic heroic charm that surrounds so much of the traditional cowboy myth. In other words, John Grady recreates that mythic West with his determination to find a place where his skills as a cowboy are both appreciated and put to use. He finds it in Mexico, and for some time he lives the adventurous life with all the connotations of honor and thrill that it promises. He falls passionately in love with Alejandra and refuses to give up and almost decides to fight for his love if it comes to that. At the end of the novel, he still moves toward the West and rides off into the sunset, still signaling his optimism to locate the place he idealizes somewhere far off in the western territory. The novel is also equally a complex clash between the binaries of romanticism and reality. Whereas John's doomed romanticism is the primary force fighting off the advance of dismal realities throughout the narrative space of the novel with his assertion of independence and his nascence of manhood that he reflects in both his protestation for saving his grandfather's ranch as well as defending his love for Alejandra, the brutal invasion of the physical as well as the psychological region is clearly perceptible in the chapters that show them in prison with some of the worst facets of humanity: "McCarthy illustrates further in the novel that there is no place for the mythic cowboy dream in Mexico, a territory where John Grady, after facing several tests of endurance, can only aspire to mere survival" (Raigadas 197). When they are taken to Encantada jail, they find Blevins there who as it happens went back to retrieve his gun and in the skirmish chase that followed, killed one of his pursuers and taken in custody. Rawlins is taken away by a local police captain and forced by physical torture into acknowledging to crimes he did not actually commit. Rawlins also has his tiffs with a prisoner and gets injured. Perez, one of the influential prisoners, claims that there is only one kind of moral code in the world and that is realism. He ridicules Americans to be romantics who fail to see things as they are and rather believe what they choose to be real. Evil is a constant presence and a lived reality and going by strict moral standards and being meek would get them killed in this brutal territory. Eventually as they are moved to an abandoned farm, Blevins is forcibly taken to a grove where he is executed while the two cowboys watch the gruesome act. Later, even John Grady gets into a bloody quarrel with a fellow prisoner who tries to kill him but ultimately John Grady is able to kill him, although he gets gravely wounded. It is sheer luck that he and Rawlins are bailed out of prison by Alejandra's grand-aunt on the condition that he is never to meet Alejandra again. To her, greed and lust for blood are deeply rooted in essential human nature, and it is foolishness to be stubborn in following one's dreams and passions against better judgement. But the dichotomy of her worldview highlights the competing binaries within herself. She is known to have been a libertine and also a rebel but her failure to secure her dreams transforms her into a bitter woman who despises the individuality and freedom that John Grady and Alejandra have and hence resolves to thwart their relationship.

Through a lot of suffering, both physical and psychological, John Grady attains maturity. In the closing chapter of the novel, he displays a charismatic rugged individualism that is famed of the traditional cowboys as he holds captain and the charro who killed Blevins at gunpoint to retrieve the horses that the men had wrongly captured. As he leaves the ranch, he is shot in the leg and drags the wounded captain along with him. Later he heats up a pistol barrel to cauterize his wound and goes through intense physical suffering and pain. When he ultimately crosses the border to reach Texas, he is informed about his father's death, and this shatters him to the core as he begins to weep inconsolably for the first time in the narrative. Later when he is given the charge of Blevins's horse, he approaches the judge who ruled in his favor and narrates his guilty conscience at having killed an assassin in the Mexican jail and almost killing the captain. Even though he acted under compulsion, his sound heart does not let him rejoice at the act of eliminating evil to some degree. Rather, he is tormented by the fact that he had to kill another human being in order to save himself. The novel closes with him being forced to acknowledge his rootlessness as the ranch he grew up in is sold, his father has died, and eventually Abuela is dying too. With the deaths and the gloominess that surround him he is left uncertain if this is where he belongs and confesses to Rawlins that "it aint my country" (250). Lamenting on the grave of Louisa's aunt he realizes that the world has gone mad with its frenzied pace of modernization, and people have almost become mechanical toward the people who were so crucial to their growth, people like Abuela who have been forgotten: "nothing for their struggles, nothing for their names. Nothing for the living or the dead" (251). But even till the final page of the novel, his horse is with him, and it is the one true companion who has not forsaken him till the very end. His horse proves to be an instrument of hope, riding, as he moves ahead to seek "the world to come" (252). Even though the romanticism he swears by and the way of life he had known hitherto are perishing, he still harbors optimism for the future, and his search continues. The American dream of a land with plenty of opportunities for the daring ones has been exposed to be hollow, and the several competing binaries in the text highlight the contradictions in the ease of things that the dream promises.

It is crucial to note that the novel takes its title from one of the popular children's lullabies that offers a promise of "all the pretty horses" but John Grady's experiences through the novel offer "anything but the fulfilled promises or the dreamy satisfaction of wishes and desires promised by lullabies" (Tatum 27). Rawlins, being the cynical and practical of the two, vents his frustration claiming that they had to go through all their suffering just because of a horse, but John Grady, being the idealist and sensitive young man, states that "horses had nothin to do with it" (185). Although the events in the novel serve to suggest that, indeed, it is the horses and the worldview they symbolize that define the plot. The novel's main concern is with the selling of the ranch because of the increasing industrialization of the American West, and horses with their mobility become the source of escape as well as hope for the cowboys in their longing for their oldworld order. Not just this, all the incidents in the story revolve around horses, and whether it be the cowboys or the ones who capture them, the characters in the novel still hold dearly to the passing way of life at the ranches. Whereas Blevins is caught and brutally shot for possession of a magnificent horse, presumably, too, beyond his station in life, the boys have to go through a lot of ordeals just in order to find a place to call home and to prove worthy. Even in Mexico, the idealized world of the ranch and the horses is preserved from external intervention so much so that the manager who prized John Grady for his exceptional skill and knowledge about the horses, gets him and Rawlins apprehended when he finds that his daughter has taken a liking to the young man, and this threatens to corrupt the cultural sanctity that he hopes to maintain.

At some instances in the narrative, the resolution of the binaries is also witnessed as in the case of spatial negotiations. John Grady approaches the estate of a landowner in Mexico, and the place is kind of a "medial space" between "domestic places and wilderness spaces" (Ellis 203). He leaves the ranch because of the rapidly modifying world around him in which he does not quite feel at home. His fascination for Alejandra and the desire for union with her reflect on the lack that defines his life, a lack of domesticity at his own home where his mother and father have been estranged from each other for several years. He desires a domestic life above all, and life at ranch offers him opportunity to be his most real self where he could also feel productive. However, the modernization of his homeland leads to generation of a feeling of alienation, and the cultural differences in Mexico cause him to be seen as an outsider corrupting the so-called purity of the Indigenous culture. Therefore, at the core of the narrative is the binary of the self and the other where the cowboys recognize the onslaught of industrialism and the purchasers of the ranch as the other. Whereas the manager of the ranch in Mexico view John Grady and Lacey Rawlins as the "other" and is unable to tolerate the affair between his daughter and the foreigner. This binary becomes the source of much physical and mental agony for the cowboys who receive excruciating torture for pursuance of the American dream and their movement far West. This is co-related to the binary of America/Mexico that forms the bedrock of the entire *Border Trilogy*. Industrialization of America gives rise to further sub-dimensions of this binary where America with its fascination for development is seen as "civilized" whereas Mexico with its underdeveloped and "wild" topography is considered "savage." However, it is this supposed inferiority of the Mexican landscape that John Grady desires for the values that the developed region of America celebrates, such as civilization and industry, serve to destroy his worth within the Western. The binaries in the novel serve to debunk the conception of the American dream by exposing how attempts at civilization have come to overshadow and negate the freedom of the American countryside. The culmination of the novel leaves the reader with an ambiguous ending that brings them face-to-face with the "mystery of existence" (Cremean 15). The characters and the occurrences in the novel serve to establish this mystery. Thus, even though the connotations of defying independence and spirited individualism paint an ideal picture of the humble cowboy as an explorer into uncharted western terrain, the hollowness of such an imaginary conjecture is revealed in the harsh realities that depict the plight of the cowboys who face a rapid encroachment of their homeland by the forces of mechanization and are left with no choice other than the compulsion of forever being on the move to secure their desired country to belong.

Works Cited

Cremean, David N. "On Cormac McCarthy." *Critical Insights: Cormac McCarthy*. Edited by David N. Cremean. Salem Press, 2012, pp. 3–17.

Ellis, Jay. *No Place for Home: Spatial Constraint and Character Flight in the Novels of Cormac McCarthy*. Routledge, 2006.

McCarthy, Cormac. *All the Pretty Horses*. Alfred A. Knopf, 1992.

Raigadas, David Rio. "Cormac McCarthy's Borderlands: A Challenge to a Mythic Construct of the American West." *ES*, no.25, 2003–04, pp. 193–202. *1library,* 1library.co/document/4yrg138q-cormac-mccarthy-borderlands-challenge-mythic-construct-american-west.html.

Slotkin, Richard. *Regeneration Through Violence: The Mythology of the American Frontier, 1600–1860*. Wesleyan UP, 1973.

__________. *Gunfighter Nation: The Myth of the Frontier in Twentieth-Century America*. Macmillan, 1992.

Stegner, Wallace. *The American West as Living Space*. The U of Michigan P, 1987.

Tatum, Stephen. *Cormac McCarthy's All the Pretty Horses: A Reader's Guide*. Continuum, 2002.

Turner, Frederick Jackson. "The Significance of the Frontier in American History." Madison State Historical Society of Wisconsin, 1894.

John Grady Cole as an Example of (Non) Traditional Western Masculinity in McCarthy's *All the Pretty Horses*

Amanda Zastrow

Scholars of the American West largely equate a cowboy's masculinity with his physical exterior; a cowboy is a masculine man because of the way that he looks and is perceived visually by others, because of his actions, and because of his silence. Lee Clark Mitchell, for example, argues that a cowboy's masculine presence is often related to the costume that he wears. In *Westerns: Making the Man in Fiction and Film*, Mitchell states that "clothing properly worn conveys a personal, highly gendered meaning" (164). The way a man looks and the clothing he wears "delineat[es] masculinity" (156), and it "permits the eye to roam across the male body without seeming to focus on that body as flesh" (165). Cowboys are watched; their masculinity is viewed. Violence as well, according to Mitchell, is another qualifier related to a man's appearance that signifies masculinity. Violence in Westerns, Mitchell states, "is less a matter of violating another" than it is "of constituting one's physical self as a male." Even though violence often destroys the male body, the occasion creates a highly visual scene that allows a man to appear especially manly, and the concomitant scene of the cowboy's female love interest nursing the cowboy back to health reinforces this masculinity and trumps any potential destruction that occurs (169). A cowboy is often seen as strong for recovering from his beating and bruises, and in turn, he then has the attention of a beautiful female: "the woman's gaze is both reminder and promise," Mitchell argues, "evoking the developmental moment when manhood's violence first emerged even as it ensures the hero's reaccession to full masculinity" (178–79). Jane Tompkins argues in agreement with Mitchell's assessment of a traditional cowboy's masculinity. In *West of Everything: The Inner Life of Westerns*, Tompkins, like Mitchell, claims that a cowboy's masculinity is defined by what can be *seen* of him, not *heard*. Tompkins argues that it is neither by language skills nor verbal communication that a cowboy's masculinity is revealed; rather, the silent type, a man who is not well-spoken or obviously learned, is the image that most often conveys masculinity in a Western. As Tompkins states, "Western's heroes don't have the large vocabularies an expensive education can buy. They don't have to read that many books. Westerns distrust language" (51).

As both of these critics argue that the Western genre regards cowboys as masculine through their *visual* depictions, this argument begs the question of whether or not this traditional masculine cowboy is still found in literature today. As Tompkins has found, classic Westerns such as Owen Wister's *The Virginian,* written in 1902, stress the physically strong and mentally stoic type (62–66), but what of literature written more recently? Are more recent authors still committed to this classic trope? Cormac McCarthy, for example, in *All the Pretty Horses* certainly offers John Grady Cole as a cowboy figure. John Grady is one in a long line of Texas ranchers, and he has spent his life among horses. But is John Grady Cole really a traditional masculine cowboy, one whose masculinity is painted in regard to his visual characteristics and descriptions? Through an analysis of McCarthy's 1992 novel, I suggest that McCarthy reveals John Grady to be, seemingly, a character who *wants* to fit the role of a traditional masculine cowboy, but that through moments that culminate in his deep love for Alejandra Rocha, John Grady Cole emerges, rather, as a character who, on his path to coming of age, dismisses this traditional type of masculinity and adopts instead a feminized perspective of what it means to be a cowboy.

The Progression of John Grady as a Masculine Cowboy

At the beginning of the novel, John Grady Cole is only sixteen years old, and thus, it makes sense that early depictions of the text's main character describe him as not yet a traditionally masculine cowboy but rather as a boy who is longing to gain this time-honored status. McCarthy's novel begins with a funeral for John Grady's grandfather. Here, the text immediately lacks developed dialogue, a stark indicator of Tompkins's traditional masculine cowboy;

however, by next focusing on the land instead of on John Grady's actions and movements, McCarthy makes it clear that John Grady is not yet the cowboy that he perhaps wants to be. John Grady "saddled his horse and rode out west from the house. The wind was much abated and it was very cold and the sun sat blood red and elliptic under the reefs of bloodred clouds before him" (5). Here, McCarthy chooses to highlight John Grady's surroundings rather than John Grady himself. John Grady is drastically young after all, especially in comparison to "the shadows [that] were long and the ancient road [that] was shaped before him" (5). Though only a "dream," McCarthy writes, John Grady can picture the "riders of that lost nation" on this "old Comanche road" and how these "warriors" keep riding "on in that darkness" (5–6). John Grady, however, "must turn the pony up onto the plain and homeward." The land reminds John Grady of his youth as there are years of experience that separate him from these venerable men. He has yet to gain "stone-age tools of war" like those grasped by the apparitions on horseback, but he has hope, as McCarthy in this section as well signals a coming transition for his main character (6). The novel *will* delve into John Grady's future masculine cowboy-hood, but a change of scenery is necessary, as McCarthy foreshadows the novel's main plot point, a trip, through John Grady looking toward the south, toward Mexico, before he heads home.

John Grady "turned south along the old war trail and he rode out to the crest of a low rise and dismounted and dropped the reins and walked out and stood like a man come to the end of something" (5). Through this depiction of John Grady on "the old war trail," at "the end of something," his childhood, McCarthy insinuates that a new part to John Grady's life will soon begin. He will soon be participating in more action, as is suggested by the name of the trail—the "war trail," war, obviously suggesting a period of action and violence, as both terms are commonly associated with traditional masculine cowboys—and because of John Grady's impatience to begin his journey south (He says to Rawlins, "Well let's go" when Rawlins remarks that he is early, that "it ain't even four yet"), readers can assume that John Grady is eager to grow up and become the masculine cowboy that Mitchell and Tompkins have discussed as traditional and as recurring in Western texts (30).

As the plot of the novel moves forward, McCarthy begins to mold John Grady more and more into the archetype of a masculine cowboy. For example, right before John Grady leaves for his adventure on the path to Mexico with Rawlins, he sees his mother one last time. Though a female character, John Grady's mother is not the typical female love interest found in most Westerns. She does not help to cement into place the cowboy masculinity that John Grady is attempting to emulate; rather, John Grady's mother represents his inability to be a man. She has refused his wishes to keep the farm, a farm that had the potential to lend John Grady status and respectability, and therefore, in his quest to be viewed as a traditional masculine cowboy, he must expunge his life of this relationship. Traveling south to Mexico can be viewed as John Grady searching for manhood as well as John Grady escaping unhelpful, unmanly memories and relationships from his past. In his final scene with his mother, the beginning of John Grady's traditional cowboy masculinity is seen as McCarthy utilizes Mitchell's theory: after saying their good-byes, "He [John Grady] stood back and touched the brim of his hat and turned and went on up the street. He didn't look back but he could see her in the windows of the Federal Building across the street standing there and she was still standing there when he reached the corner and stepped out of the glass forever" (29). McCarthy stresses that John Grady, having "come to the end of something," having "stepped out of the glass forever," is on his way to procuring his coveted cowboy masculinity, and here, McCarthy expresses this emerging masculinity through the concept of John Grady being *viewed* by his mother as he walks away from her, down the street.

He can see her in the windows as he retreats from their meeting, and he knows that she is still watching him until the very last moment when he is out of her sight. As Mitchell argues, a man is known as a man because people *look* at him, and here, on the cusp of his traditional cowboy manhood, John Grady is not only being *viewed* but being viewed by the very character whom he is fleeing due to the emasculation that he found in her earlier actions. As his mother watches him, she gives back John Grady some of the masculinity that she had before taken; by the very act of her watching him walk away, Mitchell's argument states that John Grady, being looked at, is passively acting in such a way that defines him as a masculine cowboy.

John Grady's progressing traditional cowboy masculinity becomes more defined as he and Rawlins advance on their trip south. McCarthy shows this progression throughout the boys' journey by focusing his text not on the landscape, as was exemplified earlier in the text, but on the actions of John Grady and Rawlins; in doing this, McCarthy does not treat the boys' dialogue as the focal point of his words. His prose is reminiscent of Tompkins's masculine cowboy qualifications as, broken up by small bits of dialogue, each page of text contains sentences that most often begin with the boys' actions: "They crossed the river. . . . They rode up out of the river among the willows and rode single file upstream through the shallows onto a long gravel beach where they took off their hats and turned and looked back at the country they'd left. No one spoke" (45). Josef Benson as well addresses this lack of dialogue as he finds that it "shows the boys' desire to act like cultural cowboys." They "strictly adher[e] to the cowboy code of brevity" as they try to exhibit what they have been taught a cowboy is (32). This reticence is a part of their heritage as John Grady attempts to join the ranks of his father and grandfather; these men in his mind encompass this "culture" that Benson mentions, and John Grady wishes to be like these men. He wishes to be a part of their culture.

During these early moments of their trip, cowboy appearance also comes into play as McCarthy describes the boys' clothing. Crossing the water, McCarthy writes, "They'd stuffed their boots upside down into their jeans and stuffed their shirts and jackets after along with their warbags of shaving gear and ammunition and they belted the jeans shut at the waist and tied the legs loosely about their necks and dressed only in their hats" (45). Here, the boys' outward appearance is described, but McCarthy goes beyond simple description as his prose insinuates that John Grady and Rawlins are rather innovative. The two boys have figured out how to best traverse the river without ruining their belongings, belongings that are related to their appearances, and thus, it is implied that if they wish to be masculine cowboys, to appear as such, they must keep their things safe. McCarthy also implies cowboy masculinity as he writes of Blevins's gun: "It was an old Colt Bisley with guttapercha grips worn smooth of their checkering" (47). The boys' knowledge of the gun, how to "[flip] open the gate with his thumb and put the hammer at halfcock," as well as the idea that the gun is weathered—it is not a virgin gun—suggests that the boys are not virgins either when it comes to manly topics like riding horses over rivers and shooting things (47). McCarthy, through his various descriptions relating to the boys' appearances, begins to build his argument that John Grady is becoming more and more a traditionally masculine cowboy.

As the story moves on, the boys are hired by vaqueros, Mexican cowboys, an event that leads to the epitome of John Grady's traditional masculinity. Having encountered the vaqueros by chance while riding and camping in the hills, John Grady is again described by McCarthy as a potentially traditional cowboy as the vaqueros invite John Grady and Rawlins to their boss's house based solely on the two boys' appearances and actions. Immediately upon meeting them, "the vaqueros knew them by the way they sat their horses and they called them caballero and exchanged smoking materials with them and told them about the country" (93). Though the vaqueros know nothing about John Grady and Rawlins, they refer to them as "horsemen" out of respect, simply because they *look* like horsemen; thus, in tune with Mitchell's assessment of a traditional masculine cowboy, the boys are regarded as men based solely on the way that they look and the way that they handle their gear. It is shortly thereafter that John Grady and Rawlins are accepted into Rocha's ranch where they begin breaking horses. John Grady says to Rawlins, "You think you and me could break all of em in four days?" (100). In terms of horses, John Grady exudes confidence, and no sooner have the boys broken eight horses, but the "entire complement of vaqueros had come from the bunkhouse to watch"

(105). Here, John Grady is again *viewed* by others, but beyond being viewed, John Grady is *admired*.

He is recognized by the men for his special way with horses, and thus, the descriptions of John Grady's horse become another way for McCarthy to characterize John Grady's masculinity. As earlier John Grady had stated that his feelings for horses matched his feelings for men, or humans, McCarthy, too, defines John Grady, a man, in relation to his horse. John Grady "lifted the blanket and placed it on the animal's back and smoothed it and stood stroking the animal and talking to it and then he bent and picked up the saddle and lifted it with the cinches strapped up and the off stirrup hung over the horn" (106). Here, John Grady takes care in dressing his horse, and thus, just as John Grady's masculinity has been defined thus far by his looks, he, too, gains masculinity through the physical descriptions of his horse. He also talks to his horse as he dresses him.

Though Tompkins argues that verbal communication is not traditionally a sign of masculinity, John Grady speaks to the horse while surrounded by elements of masculine appearance, and thus, both the dressing of the horse and the secret words that they share enhance his cowboy status. He has repurposed language to fit within this masculine bubble that he has created. At this point in the novel, John Grady is enveloped with characteristics relating to Mitchell and Tompkins's traditional masculine cowboy. McCarthy has taken John Grady from a position in which something has just ended for him, his childhood, and brought him, through a journey, to a new location of manhood. John Grady has been recognized as an emerging manly man by his actions, by his clothes, and by his silence (or by his use of an identifiably masculine language), and now, at Rocha's ranch, he has been visually recognized by other cowboys for his success with horses, a trait that literally defines a cowboy, someone who works with horses. McCarthy, through John Grady's journey to escape childhood and the emasculation that he felt from it, depicts John Grady as a cowboy characterized by the traditional masculine traits of past Westerns.

The Entrance of Alejandra, a Different Sort of Cowboy

Although John Grady has worked to become a traditionally masculine cowboy, McCarthy, at this point in the novel, introduces a new character who causes John Grady to second guess his commitment to the traditional ways of cowboys before him. The character of Alejandra Rocha, through her very first mention in the novel, works to dismantle John Grady's traditional manhood. In the scene that follows, John Grady and Rawlins have just interacted with the Rocha vaqueros for the first time, and it is here that McCarthy depicts John Grady's inceptive attraction to Alejandra, the ranch owner's daughter. McCarthy writes:

> [A] young girl came riding down the road and passed them and they ceased talking. She wore english riding boots and jodhpurs and a blue twill hacking jacket and she carried a ridingcrop and the horse she rode was a black Arabian saddlehorse. She'd been riding the horse in the river or in the cienagas because the horse was wet to its belly and the leather fenders of the saddle were dark at the lower edges and her boots as well. She wore a flatcrowned hat of black felt with a wide brim and her black hair was loose under it and fell halfway to her waist and as she rode past she turned and smiled and touched the brim of the hat with her crop and the vaqueros touched their hatbrims one by one down to the last of those who'd pretended not even to see her as she passed. Then she pushed the horse into a gaited rack and disappeared down the road. (94)

Here in his description of Alejandra, McCarthy uses several of the same strategies that he uses to describe John Grady as a traditional masculine cowboy. First, immediately, Alejandra is visually observed, or stared at, by the men as she rides past on horseback. Every single vaquero, "down to the last," sees her, and they all acknowledge her, touching the brims of their hats out of respect. Though this is not unusual, as women are often the object of the male gaze in Western texts, here, it is not Alejandra's body, her beauty, nor her sexuality that is being remarked on; rather, in accordance with Mitchell's philosophy, McCarthy's details of how Alejandra is viewed pertain specifically to Alejandra's equestrian clothing, her gear, and her actions. She rides by with ease; she is certainly not sedentary; and thus, Alejandra's opening scene is somewhat of a mirror of earlier scenes in which John Grady and Rawlins ride throughout the Mexican countryside.

Alejandra, in fact, has been riding through water just as John Grady and Rawlins previously were, when they had expertly saved their belongings. Her clothing, her physical appearance, specifically marks this feat as her boots and horse are wet, and thus, readers can see that Alejandra has completed masculine endeavors just as the novel's main males have. Alejandra wears a hat just as they wear a hat, and she does this all with a smile on her face. One can just picture the slight surprise in John Grady's eyes; who is this woman who disappears as quickly as she has arrived? This would be said internally, of course, as along the lines of Tompkins, Alejandra is silent as she passes the men, and they as well "ceas[e] talking" in regard to her presence. She does not utter verbal conversation, as is traditional for female characters in Westerns, and her body is not sexualized for its femininity either. In all ways, Alejandra meets Mitchell and Tompkins's qualifying traditional characteristics of a masculine cowboy. The one exception to this, of course, is that she is not a man; she is a woman.

Despite this, however, it is significant that McCarthy introduces Alejandra in such a manner at the onset of John Grady's relationship with the vaqueros and the Rocha ranch. Just before John Grady "officially" becomes a man due to his successful breaking of Rocha's horses, McCarthy, in turn, describes Alejandra in terms that equal in many ways John Grady's masculinity. As Allen Berry reminds, "the 'cowboy and the senorita' is a familiar trope in the Western genre," but McCarthy's characters of John Grady and Alejandra attack this familiar theme through a different angle (27). "She is his equal," Berry states, but she also has the upper hand (30).[1] As Alejandra disappears from view, McCarthy presents this concept as John Grady is "still looking down the road where she'd gone. There was nothing there to see but he was looking anyway" (94). In a scene reminiscent of his farewell to his mother, it is John Grady this time who stares stationary at the retreating figure, that of Alejandra.

Alejandra is not watching John Grady, and thus, here, McCarthy shows that Alejandra, though not even a male, is beginning to *succeed* John Grady in terms of traditional masculinity. A foreshadowing of future occasions, McCarthy's depiction of John Grady staring into her dust alludes to the important presence of Alejandra; McCarthy suggests that John Grady will continue "looking anyway" toward this new woman in his life. Being looked at, as Mitchell has asserted, is an indicator of masculinity, and thus, John Grady's looking has reduced his own manhood, and it will also cause him to look to Alejandra for validation rather than to his earlier desire for cowboy masculinity.

McCarthy, in the scenes following John Grady and Alejandra's introductory meeting, begins to describe John Grady less and less in terms of masculinity and more in terms of the passionate love that he develops for Alejandra. Alejandra herself is recounted in such masculine terms that John Grady seems to ignore the openings for his own masculine behavior, and as was foreshadowed earlier, he looks toward Alejandra rather than to his previous goal of traditional masculinity. For example, upon having been rebuked by Alejandra's grand-aunt, the Dueña Alfonsa, John Grady is visited by an unsettled Alejandra who does not appreciate her grand-aunt having spoken to John Grady about her. Alejandra says to John Grady, "I wont be treated in such a manner," which causes John Grady to respond, "Tell me what to do. . . . I'll do anything you say" (140). Even after having been talked to by Alejandra's father and warned by Rawlins that "I hope you know what you're doin," John Grady only views the situation from Alejandra's eyes (148). Because she does not see the reasoning in Alfonsa's argument that, "There is no forgiveness. For women," John Grady ignores the advice that he is given by those who know better than he does and follows the initiative of Alejandra, his love (137).

In doing so, John Grady ultimately gives up the very thing that had made his cowboy masculinity complete: his job at the ranch. By following Alejandra, a masculine figure in her own right, John Grady gives up his own masculinity, but for cowboy defying tradition, McCarthy shows that there are consequences: John Grady and Rawlins are arrested. According to Benson, the reason for this unfortunate turn of events is that John Grady's "central flaw" is that he "refuses to acknowledge Mexican customs and propriety" (40). I argue, however, that John Grady and Alejandra's relationship has less to do with John Grady's lack of knowledge regarding Alejandra's culture and more to do with his incredibly strong feelings for Alejandra; as Berry notes, "John Grady, despite the potential hazards brought on by pursuing his employer's daughter, follows the desires of his heart" (31). This is not actually unusual for John Grady. McCarthy warns us at the very beginning of the story that the "ardenthearted," whether they be horses or humans, have John Grady's devotion; this "would always be so and [would] never be otherwise," McCarthy writes (6).

Thus, John Grady is blinded by his love for Alejandra. She is his "ardenthearted" individual, and he feels comfortable believing in her views and opinions of their relationship. She exerts a masculine, aggressive, or passionate demeanor, and he, therefore, is not harshly refusing her culture; he is just too much in love to worry himself about the problems they may be forced to face. John Grady, here, is expressing emotions unusual to the traditional cowboy that Tompkins has identified. Tompkins looks to Peter Schwenger, author of *Phallic Critiques*, for his view on the topic: "It is by putting words to an emotion that it becomes feminized," Schwenger states, and thus, McCarthy is feminizing the character of John Grady as John Grady professes his fidelity to Alejandra (56).

Within the couple's last encounter together, McCarthy continues to reduce the fragile masculinity that cowboy John Grady at one point maintained. Though John Grady convinces Alejandra to meet with him in an effort to convince her that they should be together, McCarthy persists in his Mitchell/Tompkins-esque descriptions of Alejandra. Alejandra is given the power, and John Grady is relatively passive. He has lost the masculine designations that had earlier accompanied his character's descriptions; Alejandra, on the other hand, has acquired what John Grady has lost. For example, when Alejandra exits the train and meets John Grady on the platform, McCarthy composes a lengthy physical description of her. Within this description, McCarthy once again focuses on her costuming, and he denotes power in her clothing, rather than submission: "She was wearing a blue dress with a skirt almost to her ankles and a blue hat with a wide brim and she did not look like a schoolgirl either to him or to the other men on the platform" (248). Here, Alejandra has the eye of those around her, but rather than look like a girl, McCarthy has provided her with a commanding presence. She has "beauty," John Grady notes, but in a dress that covers her ankles and a wide brim hat that forbids mention of her waist-length hair, Alejandra's beauty is not feminized; in fact, she wears a hat that is a recurring piece of clothing from the novel, worn most notably by vaqueros and John Grady himself. Alejandra is also the one making the moves with John Grady. McCarthy stresses, "As *she* walked toward him her beauty seemed to him a thing altogether improbable. . . . *She* came toward him and *she* smiled at him sadly and *she* touched her fingers to the scar on his cheek and leaned and kissed it" (248, emphasis mine). To identify that Alejandra is the one with the power in the situation and that she is what would traditionally be the masculine figure, McCarthy identifies *her* as the executor of the actions, not John Grady. In their first face-to-face experience since John Grady was taken to jail, she is the one who is setting the tone and expectations for their meeting, even though John Grady had been the one to initiate it. Readers are given more details as later, after having dinner, McCarthy also writes that John Grady "told her everything. Then they sat in silence" (249). Tompkins, in her assessment of cowboy masculinity, does not allow for a cowboy to have the ability to speak well nor at length; however, John Grady does not simply tell Alejandra his story, he tells her *everything,* and following his address, *she* does not respond. She does not follow up with words of her own but rather, sits in silence; John Grady has become the "politicians and women" of McCarthy's Western (Benson 32). Through this description, McCarthy suggests again that Alejandra, though a woman, is not the traditional Western female character; instead, she is allocated masculine traits, which, in turn, diminish the traditional masculinity of John Grady, her counterpart. Gender is binary in typical Westerns; thus, John Grady's love for

Alejandra causes him to accept their reversal of roles, something which is not common for Western texts. His neglected traditional masculinity causes him to play the feminized role as John Grady attempts to convey his love for Alejandra.

Finally, Alejandra is the one whose actions end their relationship. McCarthy again emphasizes her actions and physical description in the following scene: "She came from the shower wrapped in a towel and she sat on the bed and took his hand and looked down at him. I cannot do what you ask, she said. I love you. But I cannot" (254). McCarthy, in this passage, writes of Alejandra taking John Grady's hand and looking down on him. Alejandra is the character who is active, masculine, while John Grady is passive; Alejandra even *looks down* on John Grady, as a traditional masculine cowboy would (both in action as well as in thought) toward his women. Juxtaposed with Alejandra's actions, McCarthy follows up her refusal with a focus on John Grady's emotions: John Grady, McCarthy writes, "saw very clearly how all his life led only to this moment and all after led nowhere at all. He felt something cold and soulless enter him like another being and he imagined that it smiled malignly and he had no reason to believe that it would ever leave" (254). The absence of love is a feeling that John Grady does not enjoy; however, nonetheless it is present within John Grady's heart, and his use of words for emotions explain that John Grady, here, has taken on femininity within their relationship.

Whereas Alejandra's actions and physical description gift her traditional masculinity, John Grady has given up his masculinity to be in love with Alejandra, to be able to express his feelings for her, and at the end of their love affair, McCarthy persists in his descriptions of Alejandra as the masculine female. John Grady is a male feminized while Alejandra's character depicts the opposite; she cuts off their relationship, and John Grady likely cannot return to his original goal of cowboy masculinity. He does not believe his feelings for her will "ever leave," and thus, he defies the qualifications Tompkins and Mitchell have outlined. He does not fit within the Western myth, but then again, neither does Alejandra, technically.

Cormac McCarthy's *All the Pretty Horses* is a novel that breaks down the traditional myth of the West, specifically the common aspects of cowboy masculinity argued by Lee Clark Mitchell and Jane Tompkins. John Grady, once a boy in search of his traditional manhood, finds cowboy masculinity only to watch it recede in light of his love, Alejandra's, own masculine traits. John Grady gives up his masculinity in an effort to embrace his powerful love for her; however, at the end of their relationship, John Grady is left without his cowboy masculinity and without his love. Alejandra's masculinity, however, remains intact. McCarthy has rewritten the classic cowboy trope in an arguably modern light, as what is traditional in terms of gender roles has become muddled.

Note

1. For more on John Grady's submission to Alejandra, see Berry 30: "Both John Grady and Alejandra ride the hacendado's prize stallion, without saddle and with equal skill, symbolizing the equality of the passions that burn within them. John Grady, like the horses he breaks for the hacendado, is brought into submission by Alejandra's will."

Works Cited

Benson, Josef. "A Hero by Default: John Grady Cole as Hypermasculine Heroic Failure in *All the Pretty Horses*." *Hypermasculinities in the Contemporary Novel: Cormac McCarthy, Toni Morrison, and James Baldwin*. Rowman and Littlefield, 2014, pp. 25–54.

Berry, Allen. "The Cross-Border Relationship Pastiche in Cormac McCarthy's *All the Pretty Horses*." *Journal of the American Studies Association of Texas*, Nov. 2014, pp. 27–40.

McCarthy, Cormac. *All the Pretty Horses*. Alfred A. Knopf, 1992.

Mitchell, Lee Clark. "A Man Being Beaten." *Westerns: Making the Man in Fiction and Film*. U of Chicago P, 1996, pp. 150–87.

Schwenger, Peter. *Phallic Critiques: Masculinity and Twentieth-Century Literature*. Routledge and Kegan Paul, 1984.

Tompkins, Jane P. "Women and the Language of Men." *West of Everything: The Inner Life of Westerns*. Oxford UP, 1992, pp. 47–67.

Wister, Owen. *The Virginian*. Macmillan, 1902.

The Quest for Romantic Love: The Role of Women in *All the Pretty Horses*

Elissa Greenwald

All the Pretty Horses begins with the hero's rejection by his enigmatic mother, who left his father and John Grady Cole long ago. When his grandfather dies in the novel's opening, John Grady is disenfranchised and made homeless, exiled from his grandfather's ranch where he grew up. The surrogate mother who raised him—Luisa, the family's cook—tries to comfort him, but John Grady is distraught with grief. The seemingly casual way in which his mother informs him that she is selling his birthright dispossesses him at once of home and family: "There's not any money. This place has barely paid expenses for twenty years" (15). For the rest of the novel, John Grady seeks a home and love. For a while, he finds such a home at the hacienda of Don Héctor and such a love with Héctor's adventurous daughter, Alejandra. Yet, the romantic idyll of Alejandra and John Grady at her father's hacienda is over almost as soon as it begins. As a result of nine nights of passion with Alejandra, John Grady is made into an outlaw. His brief reunion with Alejandra weeks later, staged and arranged by her grand-aunt Alfonsa, is ironic and tragic. The beautiful natural setting of the hacienda that was the background to their love affair gives way to a last romantic encounter in the city of Zacatecas.

Romantic love is the catalyst that makes John Grady seem real to himself and others for the first time in his life. Yet, in *All the Pretty Horses*, it is also the agent that undoes men. Alejandra's grand-aunt, trying to justify her actions to John Grady, explains her own history, which makes her feel that independence for women puts them in danger. But for John Grady, loss of love means being sentenced to an independence that seems less like freedom and more like imprisonment in the self against the empty spaces of the West.

Dispossession

The novel begins with a series of losses; John Grady Cole loses his beloved grandfather, his parents, and then his home, the ranch that his grandfather owned. His mother was lost to him long ago; as his father informs him shortly after the grandfather's death, she left the family from the time John Grady was five months old until he turned three. From an external perspective, the mother's desire to become an actress and to have "a little more social life than what she's had to get used to" (17), as her lawyer puts it, seem sympathetic. John Grady, however, interprets her actions as desertion of him, his father, and their home. Because the ranch is not a "payin proposition" (17), she plans to sell it.

John Grady's lack of sympathy for his mother is cemented when he tracks her to San Antonio, where she is performing in a play. He watches the play and then, without making his presence known to his mother, spies on her. He sees her descending the staircase at the hotel with a man who is not his father and learns that she has not registered under the name Mrs. Cole (22), Just beforehand, he learned for the first time, from his mother's lawyer, that his parents are divorced (17). Just afterwards, he learns from his father that his mother "was gone from the time you were six months old till you were about three" (25). This new knowledge changes John Grady forever.

Like Adam and Eve, John Grady, by acquiring knowledge of his mother's sexuality and independence, is expelled from the Eden of his original home. The opening of the novel echoes Milton's *Paradise Lost* and the Bible, as John Grady's forced expulsion from the family ranch after his grandfather's death resembles Milton's description of Adam and Eve leaving Eden at the end of his epic poem: "They hand in hand with wand'ring steps and slow, / Through Eden took their solitary way" (Book XII, lines 648–49). Unlike Milton's Adam and Eve, however, John Grady leaves alone, astride a horse. He says a desultory farewell to his former girlfriend, Mary Catherine, after which he "stepped out of the glass forever" (29). It is as if, on leaving his home, John Grady emerges into a different plane of being.

Vince Brewton discusses the myth of America itself as an Edenic garden (124). As he claims, when sent out of the paradise of his home, "Cole accepts this psychologically withering condition, however, without surrendering his fundamental will to live" (135). His way seems aimless, however; he sets off on a trip with his friend Lacey Rawlins, but they have no fixed destination or plan. They spend their days seeking shelter and food and trying to impress each other with their prowess, Rawlins with guns. Thus, they are vulnerable to being led astray by the young scoundrel Blevins, who leads them into danger, as Milton's Satan tempts Adam and Eve. Blevins's entanglement with a man who steals his horse has unexpected tragic consequences for all three young men.

In Paradise

For weeks, John Grady and Rawlins wander in the wilderness, where they endure many privations, lacking food, money, and supplies. They cross the border into Mexico, to places they have never traveled before, depending on people they meet to guide them, never knowing what reception they will get. As Meg King argues, at the novel's beginning, John Grady "seeks a pre-modern, patriarchal enclave as a sphere in which he may be valued as a laborer and therein recuperate masculinity" (70).

When the two friends reach the hacienda of Don Héctor Rocha y Villareal, the "Hacienda de Nuestra Señora de la Purísima Concepción," a "ranch of eleven thousand hectares" (97), echoes of Paradise abound (Morrison). The part of the country near the hacienda appears almost like a mirage, a Promised Land in the mostly dry part of Mexico near the border that they have been traversing:

> They climbed steadily into the deepening cool of the mountains until in the evening of that day from the crest of the cordilleras they saw below them the country of which they'd been told. The grasslands lay in a deep violet haze and to the west thin flights of waterfowl were moving north before the sunset in the deep red galleries under the cloudbanks like schoolfish in a burning sea and on the foreland

> plain they saw vaqueros driving cattle before them through a gauze of golden dust. (93)

On the hacienda, John Grady has the opportunity to exhibit his skill with horses, breaking them in a strangely tender way; "he cupped his hand over the horse's eyes and stroked them and he did not stop talking to the horse at all, speaking in a low steady voice and telling it all that he intended to do and cupping the animal's eyes and stroking the terror out" (103–04). Don Héctor promotes John Grady for his knowledge of horses, while Don Héctor's daughter Alejandra, a skilled horsewoman herself, is also attracted to John Grady for his skill. McCarthy implies that a gentle horse breaker would make a gentle lover or husband. Alejandra is as strong spirited as the horses her father owns. Unlike the horses, however, she refuses to be broken, to obey any restrictions set by her father or grand-aunt. For example, she insists that John Grady let her ride the expensive thoroughbred stallion that is her father's most precious possession bareback.

The parallel between the horses she rides and the young woman is clear from the moment John Grady catches his first glimpse of her, as the description of Alejandra with her long black hair echoes that of the horse she rides: "her black hair was loose . . . and fell halfway to her waist . . . " (94). Jennifer Reimer notes that "The repetition of 'black' emphasizes Alejandra's exotic beauty—her dark otherness—while also linking the young girl to the . . . stallion she rides" (425–26) In a vision John Grady has when he sees her on horseback, both Alejandra and the horse she rides seem dreamlike: ". . . the rain caught her up and shrouded her figure away in that wild summer landscape: real horse, real rider, real land and sky and yet a dream withal" (132). The spiritual quality that the horses represent—according to Luis, an old man who works on the hacienda, "the souls of horses mirror the souls of men" (111)—is also represented by Alejandra. Both symbolize a wholeness and fulfillment that John Grady has been seeking even before he set off from home.

The parallels between both young people and the horses go beyond appearance. The passion that must be tamed in the horses pulses as strongly in the veins of John Grady and Alejandra; John Grady thinks about Alexandra that there is "no caution to her at all" (142). John Grady is self-controlled and in command when he breaks horses with an assurance tempered by gentleness. At the height of his powers and his longing for Alexandra, he imagines he could tame the whole Earth just as he tamed the horses: "he put his hands on the ground at either side of him and pressed them against the earth and in that coldly burning canopy of black he slowly turned dead center to the world, all of it taut and trembling and moving enormous and alive under his hands" (119). He seems helpless and passive, however, before Alejandra's beauty (Morrison 181) and especially her "sorrow": "Tell me what to do he said. I'll do anything you say" (140). Later he remembers that she repeated the "selfsame words he'd said to her" (146).

For a while, Alejandra and John Grady enjoy a paradisiacal idyll in which they linger in parts of the enormous grounds of the hacienda as if in the Garden of Eden. They spend their time together swimming nude in glimmering pools and riding as far as they can. As they swim one night in the moonlight, her face appears to him "sweeter for the larceny of time and flesh, sweeter for the betrayal." The very sweetness of this interlude is shadowed by a sense that it is stolen, as time and reality loom over this seemingly timeless Edenic idyll.

The class difference that divides them ultimately makes John Grady the victim of the aftermath of these encounters. Even as he bends to Alejandra's will and makes love to her every night for nine nights, knowing that such behavior is prohibited by her father and grand-aunt, there is an impending sense of doom. That doom, like that of Romeo and Juliet, turns out to be more extreme than either of the teenage lovers could have guessed. Arrested by a corrupt police captain, John Grady assumes that the crime of which he is accused is related to the murder committed by his former companion, Blevins. In jail, John Grady is initiated into a world not just of dispossession, but one in which human beings are turned into savages. He is randomly attacked by a man with a knife for no reason. By the end of his imprisonment and the ordeals incurred when he sets out to achieve justice after his release from prison, including plunging the barrel of a burning-hot pistol into his own thigh to cauterize a wound, John Grady is thoroughly disillusioned with the human world. A world of men without women, like the ironically named Encantada prison, as McCarthy depicts it, is one of violence and injustice. In the prison, authorities do not regulate but incite and commit violence, as the police captain organizes the foray in which the police deliberately shoot and kill their prisoner, thirteen-year-old Blevins, within earshot of John Grady and Rawlins.

Paradise Regained?

When John Grady returns to the hacienda seven weeks after he was hauled away in handcuffs, he is summoned to the presence of Alejandra's grand-aunt Alfonsa, who informs him that she was the one responsible for his release from prison by paying the police a huge sum. The price she exacts is that John Grady never sees Alejandra again. Although Alfonsa does not accuse John Grady of being a criminal, admitting that "I'm prepared to believe that certain circumstances must have conspired against you," she believes "But what is done cannot be undone" (228).

The story of her life, which Alfonsa proceeds to tell John Grady, reveals that male subjugation to violence and female loss of independence are two sides of the same coin, indelibly inscribed in human history. Alfonsa states, "The societies to which I have been exposed seemed to me largely machines for the suppression of women" (230). Referring to fate as a master puppeteer, she avows, "In my own life I saw these strings whose origins were endless enact the deaths of great men in violence and madness. Enact the death of a nation. I will tell you how Mexico was. How it was and how it will be again. You will see that those things which disposed me in your favor were the very things which led me to decide against you in the end" (231).

Alfonsa's love was the real historical figure, Gustavo Madero. He taught her that "those who have endured some misfortune will always be set apart but . . . it is just that misfortune which is their gift and which is their strength and . . . they must make their way back into the common enterprise of man for without they do so it cannot go forward and they themselves will wither in bitterness" (235). Alfonsa concludes that, to be a "person of value" as she longs to be, "I had to ask myself how this could be possible if there were not something like a soul or like a spirit that is in the life of a person and which could endure any misfortune or disfigurement and yet be no less for it" (235).

Historically, the attempts of Gustavo Madero and his brother Francisco, who became the first democratically elected president of Mexico, to liberate the people of Mexico from poverty and tyranny, came to a tragic end. A coup led by three generals, including General Huerta, ended in the torture of Gustavo and murder of both Madero brothers.

As a result of the tragedy she experienced, Alfonsa, once as independent as Alejandra, wishes to protect her grandniece, paradoxically by restricting her independent nature so that Alejandra is not subjected to worse predations in the grand-aunt's view: ". . . I have seen the consequences [of idle gossip] in the real world and they can be very grave indeed. They can be consequences of a gravity not excluding bloodshed. Not excluding death. I saw this in my own family" (136).

Critic Natasha Mayne states that, in the *Border Trilogy*, women are "marginalised as mute, shadowy figures on the periphery of the narratives' visual . . . field" (6). In Alfonsa's 15-page-long monologue, however, a woman takes control of McCarthy's narrative (Woodson 26). Alfonsa, delineating distinct roles for men and women, earlier in the book drew an explicit parallel between herself and her grandniece: "she is much like me at that age and I seem at times to be struggling with my own past self" (135). In her monologue, she also draws an implicit parallel between her and John Grady. Both have been left bereft of their intended mates. Like John Grady, Alfonsa "refused to believe in a God who could permit such injustice as I saw in a world of his own making. I was very idealistic" (232).

Indeed, for Alfonsa, "John Grady is a sort of male version of her young and idealistic self" (Spurgeon 28). Alfonsa does not comment on the irony that she has been the cause of John Grady's disillusionment and despair, though he is keenly aware of that. He later learns that he was arrested at the behest of Don Héctor, Alejandra's father, who learned of the secret relationship and was determined to break it up. Once again, parental figures have betrayed John Grady to protect their property and, in the case of Alejandra's family, their propriety depends on strict rules of behavior that keep men and women in separate spheres.

John Grady's body and soul are permanently scarred by the time he encounters Alejandra again shortly after his conversation with her great-aunt. Nonetheless, he tries to convince Alejandra to marry him, but she has been tamed like the horses she once rode so blithely. Marrying John Grady Cole would entail giving up her relationship with her father and her grand-aunt as well as her home and her place in society.

The outcome of the last encounter between John Grady and Alejandra is reminiscent of that between Winston Smith and his love Julia at the end of George Orwell's dystopian novel *1984*, when desire has been tortured out of both of them. The government allows them to meet because now their bond is no threat to the state in asserting the selfhood that erotic desire affirms. After each has been induced to betray the other, no love remains between them.

There is still an erotic bond between John Grady and Alejandra when she visits him for one last night together in Zacatecas. The romanticism that so possessed John Grady Cole is rekindled when he sees her again as she steps off the train: "He looked into those blue eyes like a man seeking some vision of the increate future of the universe" (248). But when Alejandra refuses to marry John Grady Cole, the breakup strangely echoes the breakup of his parents. His father was incarcerated for years in a Japanese prisoner of war camp during World War II. The father blames his divorce on that experience: "It aint her fault. I aint the same as I was. I'd like to think I am. But I aint" (12). He believes that his suffering as a POW and his response to it are the reasons his wife left him temporarily when John Grady was young, then permanently. Similarly, John Grady has been so changed—physically, emotionally, and spiritually— by his ordeal in prison that he is no longer someone Alejandra can see as a lover. As she says to him after he relates his prison experiences to her, "How do I know who you are?" (249)

In a sad double bind, the risk of romantic passion John Grady took with Alejandra, which for the first time in his life made him feel fully alive and connected to another human being, led inexorably to his confinement in a world of violence from which women were entirely excluded. That experience, in turn, made him ineligible for further romantic fulfillment. Katherine Sugg refers to McCarthy's "refusal of both domestic spaces and state-sanctioned couplings of any kind" (126). Beyond even the polarized worlds of men and women, an estrangement between the self and others pervades this novel.

The Solitary Wanderer

By the end of the novel, with no attachments left after the deaths of his father and Abuela, his surrogate grandmother, John Grady is no longer an individual, as he seeks to blend in with the landscape. At Abuela's funeral, "no one looked at him" (300). For Gail Morrison, who also notes the tri-partite structure of the story as expulsion, idyll in Paradise, and return, by the end of the novel John Grady "does not fall prey to existential despair in an irrational and indifferent world" (190). Yet, the ending of the novel seems irredeemably bleak. As John Grady stands alone in the cemetery after Abuela's funeral, he "held out his hands as if to steady himself or as if to bless the ground there or perhaps as if to slow the world that was rushing away and seemed to care nothing for the old or the young or rich or poor or dark or pale or he or she. Nothing for their struggles, nothing for their names. Nothing for the living or the dead." As Tom Pilkington notes, "This epiphany—that the individual is alone in a cold, indifferent universe—appears to be the sum of John Grady's experiences . . . " (314). The romantic longing that led him out of his parents' home and to Alejandra remains unfulfilled. John Grady thus falls into what Vince Brewton describes as "the distinctive apartness common to McCarthy's characters as the price of maintaining their original humanity"(129).

John Grady strives to find a connection to the land when he no longer has a clear connection to any human being. He returns to a landscape where his presence is only ghostly, where he is watched by Native Americans whose ancestors were displaced long ago, as he has been more recently: "They had no curiosity about him at all. As if they knew all that they needed to know. They stood and watched him pass and watched him vanish upon that landscape solely because he was passing. Solely because he would vanish" (301).

At the end of the book, the earlier image of Alejandra on horseback silhouetted against the sky, seen as if in a vision, is echoed in the closing image of John Grady Cole, as if he, too, is becoming imaginary: ". . . horse and rider and horse passed on and their long shadows passed in tandem like the shadow of a single being. Passed and paled into the darkening land, the world to come" (302). According to Christopher White, the visions of the *Border Trilogy* arise not only from the characters' perspectives but from the perspective of an oracular narrator who speaks for the author. In these books we sense "the ghostly virtual presence of an ultimate dreamer figure, dreaming the various character-dreamers" (121). The dream of John Grady is not complete, however, as McCarthy continued his tale in the third and last volume of the *Border Trilogy*, *Cities of the Plain*. Whether John Grady Cole will find his way back to "the common enterprise of man," in Alfonsa's words, remains an open question. The figure of the young man seeking satisfaction for his soul hunger continued to haunt McCarthy, arguably to the end of his long career.

Works Cited

Brewton, Vince. "The Changing Landscape of Violence in Cormac McCarthy's Early Novels and the *Border Trilogy*." *The Southern Literary Journal*, vol. 37, no. 1, 2004, pp. 121–43. *JSTOR*, www.jstor.org/stable/20078400.

King, Meg. "'Where Is Your Country?': Locating White Masculinity in *All the Pretty Horses*." *The Cormac McCarthy Journal*, vol. 12, 2014, pp. 69–88. *JSTOR*, www.jstor.org/stable/10.5325/cormmccaj.12.69.

Mayne, Natasha. "As Far as the Eye Could See: Cormac McCarthy, Myth and Masculine Visions in the 'New' American West." *Australasian Journal of American Studies*, vol. 20, no. 2, 2001, pp. 1–12. *JSTOR*, www.jstor.org/stable/41053864.

McCarthy, Cormac. *All the Pretty Horses.* Vintage,1992.

Milton, John. "Paradise Lost." *John Milton: Complete Poems and Major Prose*. Edited by Merritt Y. *Hughes*. Bobbs-Merrill, 1957.

Morrison, Gail Moore. "All the Pretty Horses: John Grady Cole's Expulsion from Paradise." *Perspectives on Cormac McCarthy*. Edited by Edwin T. Arnold and Dianne C. Luce. Mississippi UP, 1999, pp. 175–94.

Orwell, George. *1984*. Signet, 1949.

Pilkington, Tom. "Fate and Free Will on the American Frontier: Cormac McCarthy's Western Fiction." *Western American Literature*, vol. 27, no. 4, 1993, pp. 311–22. *JSTOR*, www.jstor.org/stable/43021039.

Reimer, Jennifer A. "All the Pretty Mexican Girls: Whiteness and Racial Desire in Cormac McCarthy's 'All the Pretty Horses' and 'Cities of the Plain.'" *Western American Literature*, vol. 48, no. 4, 2014, pp. 422–42. *JSTOR*, www.jstor.org/stable/43025376.

Sugg, Katherine. "Multicultural Masculinities and the Border Romance in John Sayles's Lone Star and Cormac McCarthy's *Border Trilogy*." *CR: The New Centennial Review*, vol. 1, no. 3, 2001, pp. 117–54. *JSTOR*, www.jstor.org/stable/41949296.

White, Christopher T. "Dreaming the *Border Trilogy*: Cormac McCarthy and Narrative Creativity." *The Cormac McCarthy Journal*, vol. 13, no. 1, 2015, pp. 121–42. *JSTOR*, doi.org/10.5325/cormmccaj.13.1.0121.

Woodson, Linda. "'This Is Another Country': The Complex Feminine Presence in *All the Pretty Horses*." *Cormac McCarthy: All the Pretty Horses, No Country for Old Men, The Road*. Edited by Sara L. Spurgeon. Continuum, 2011, pp. 25–42.

Puppets Upon Puppets Upon Puppets: Forces at Play in the Mother's Construction in *All the Pretty Horses*

Amy Leshinsky

In discussions of Cormac McCarthy's female characters in the *Border Trilogy*, scholars continue to cite McCarthy's 2007 interview with Oprah Winfrey (June 5 2007) in which he shares, "Women are tough. They're tough. I don't pretend to understand women. I think men don't know much about women; they find them very mysterious." These lines continue to be pulled and analyzed because McCarthy gave few interviews; big ideas are gleaned from these small moments. As McCarthy suggests knowledge of women was not his strength, Richard B. Woodward, who interviewed McCarthy prior to the release of *All the Pretty Horses*, aligns McCarthy's writing with the male psyche, calling him a man's novelist. Early reviews of his works provided limited engagement with his female characters, citing instead his detailed knowledge of areas aligned with the western genre. Madison Smartt Bell, for example, shares in her early review of McCarthy's work, he is a man who understood horses. Despite proclamations about lacking knowledge of women, some scholars take him at his word, providing textual examinations that corroborate his failures to understand women, whereas others proclaim his knowledge is far deeper than he credits himself.

Male characters are the primary focus of Cormac McCarthy's *All the Pretty Horses*; however, from behind the scenes, McCarthy's female characters drive John Grady Cole's perceived sense of choice through their beliefs, actions, and decisions. The female desire for independence controls the trajectory of John Grady's quest for self-discovery. In Texas, John Grady decides to pursue life outside his hometown due, in part, to the actions of his estranged mother. Once John Grady crosses the border to Mexico, John Grady seeks respite in the home of Don Héctor where his daughter, Alejandra, and Dueña Alfonsa, Alejandra's grand-aunt, control John Grady's fate inside and outside their home. John Grady's release from prison is arranged by Dueña Alfonsa, and his decision to return to the home of Don Héctor occurs due to his feelings of hope inspired by Alejandra.

The reception of McCarthy's female characters shows critics have varying viewpoints that pave the way to understand challenges in evaluating the mother's role in the text. John Grady's mini-quest to observe his mother in San Antonio teaches him that he has no place in her life, so he embarks on a greater journey, where he will again face rejection by women he longs to have in his life. Dueña Alfonsa's resounding thoughts on the interconnectedness of humankind and the infinite tensions at play in one's actions and decisions contain implications for the relationship between John Grady and his mother. The juxtaposition of the mini-quest against the metaphor of the puppets shows the larger than life meaning behind the mother's characterization in *All the Pretty Horses*.

Contrasting Views of Women

Writings on McCarthy's female characters in *All the Pretty Horses* illustrate competing viewpoints. In the first lens, critics cite McCarthy's failure to develop well-rounded female characters and often note their absence. In building an argument, McCarthy's use of the frontier is used in a discussion of his exclusion of women, with critics citing the frontier's relationship with the desire for male escape and relationship with American values. In the second lens, critics cite the power of the female characters in McCarthy's work. Despite their absence, women are seen powering key movements of John Grady's journey and are essential to his development into manhood. Regarding his female characters, some critics cite the feminist values of the female characters and their ability to deviate from the traditional 1950 societal expectations.

Nell Sullivan discusses the absence of women in McCarthy's work. Sullivan penned, "Boys Will be Boys and Girls Will Be Gone: The Circuit of Male Desire in Cormac McCarthy's *Border Trilogy*," detailing McCarthy's pattern of expulsion and containment of women in the *Border Trilogy*. Patrick W. Shaw discussed a similar concern with the *Border Trilogy*, expressing that the female characters fail to "emerge from the androcentric narratives with attributes enough to define them as distinct personae" (258). In an effort to emphasize the waning role of women in the text, Shaw writes of John Grady's love interest, Mary Catherine Barnett, at the inception of the book, that her "name is disproportionate to the space committed to her actual appearance in the text" (258). In regard to the other females in the text—the mother, Dueña Alfonsa, and Alejandra Rocha—Shaw examines their nebulous roles and failure to emerge as fully rounded characters.

Writers often examine the setting in McCarthy's work to analyze the symbolism and limitations of the frontier, which is often aligned with the desire for male escape. In the work, *Reclaiming Nostalgia: Longing for Nature in American Literature*, Jennifer K. Ladino writes: "American nature narratives are often infused with nostalgia—for the western frontier, for unspoiled landscapes, for a preindustrial golden age, or for pastoral communities with close connections to their environments" (xiii). Thus, the concept of the West is often aligned with freedom and longing. Additionally, the interwoven relationship between the frontier and violence is part of the landscape's examination—both in reference to McCarthy's work as well as in history. Amy Kaplan wrote in *Cultures of United States Imperialism* that the frontier no longer constitutes an empty, vast wilderness, but represents "a bloody battlefield of conflict and conquest" (16). The frontier, Kaplan explains, reveals much in the realm of American studies where cultures clash, new cultures are produced, and power struggles are imposed and negotiated. Thus, the frontier as a place of freedom, violence, longing, and male discovery is not new to American readers.

Within a discussion of the frontier, a relationship is often established between the scarce female presence and the freedom of the American West. Michael Kimmel shares the escape of American men to, among other places, the frontier. In *The History of Men: Essays on the History of American and British Masculinities*, Kimmel opens his second chapter with a reference to John Bunyon's 1678 *Pilgrims Progress*, where a man abandoned his home, leaving his wife and children behind and "fled towards the middle of the

Plain" (3). In this description of a dream, the man "put his fingers in his Ears" as he cried for, "Life, Life, Eternal Life" (3). American men, Kimmel asserts, using a reference from the seventeenth century, have been working to escape women for the past 200 years. Escape takes a variety of forms, as "men have run away to join the army, been kidnapped or abandoned on desert islands, gone West, or, as today, run off to the woods for an all-male retreat" (19–20).

American West and masculinity is explored in other works of literature as well. For example, Ladino references Don DeLillo's *White Noise* wherein the main character, Jack Gladney "'retreats into essentialist conceptions of masculinity' in which maleness was most at home in a natural setting" (178). This concept has longevity in American literature and has been embedded in American literature for many centuries. Nearly 50 years ago, Larry Goodwyn wrote, "The Frontier Myth and Southwestern Literature," and references works like John Graves's *Goodbye to a River* and Tom Lea's written works and paintings of southwestern life. Although some paintings were published in *Life* magazine, Lea's 1956 oil on canvas work, "Southwest," resides at the Smithsonian American Art Museum. Not only does contemporary American literature consider the relationship between frontier and American values, but art depicts the importance of landscape to American life and values.

Additionally, the use of the frontier as a place of escape, a location for bloodshed, and masculine identity applies to *All the Pretty Horses* as well as other works of American literature. In Leslie Harper Worthington's *Cormac McCarthy and the Ghost of Huck Finn*, Worthington writes on the similarities between Mark Twain's *Adventures of Huckleberry Finn* and McCarthy's oeuvre. Among numerous similarities, Worthington notes that Huckleberry Finn's journey starts and ends with his need to escape women. Mark Twain writes of Huck's need to "light out for the Territory ahead of the rest, because Aunt Sally she's going to adopt me and sivilize me and I can't stand it" (262). Like Huck, John Grady seeks independence and growth that only the frontier can provide.

Other voices, like Ann Fisher-Wirth in "Abjection and 'the Feminine' in Outer Dark," examine complexities of McCarthy's female characters. Fisher-Wirth writes that while fully developed female characters do not exist, "paradoxically, McCarthy's female characters become more interesting the less he attempts to develop them, for their power is poetic, gestural" (127). Linda Woodson's work, "'This Is Another Country': The Complex Feminine Presence in *All the Pretty Horses*," writes that John Grady's actions are determined by women in the text. Woodson writes that John Grady's expulsion from La Purísima, his release from prison, and John Grady's ultimate return to Texas, are orchestrated by Alfonsa and Alejandra; however, Woodson juxtaposes the action in the text with John Grady's belief that he was the one propelling the action. Back in Texas, alone with a Judge, John Grady reflects on his journey, discussing his work in Mexico, his relationship with Alejandra, and the death of the boy he killed in jail. He assigns blame to himself, telling the judge, "Nobody but me" was responsible for his actions (291).

Critics often take a feminist view of the female characters in the text. Although some critics contend John Grady was abandoned by his mother, others highlight the mother's resolve to work outside the home at a time when women were encouraged to be caregivers within the home. Regarding John Grady's mother, John Blair writes, "His mother, female, different, modern, wanting more, represents both the way in which the world has advanced beyond John Grady's conception of self and the way in which self is determined by the desire for relevance" (302–03). The mother, Blair articulates, is given agency to establish the direction of her career, her relationships, and her future.

Despite contrasting views of women in the novel, John Grady's view of women is shared early in the text. In a conversation about women between Lacey Rawlins and John Grady, Rawlins tells John Grady, "She aint worth it. None of em are" (10); however, John Grady disagrees with his peer, replying that "Yes they are" (10). This moment of John Grady's introspection shows the depth of his character and potential for maturation. As he sets out on his journey into the frontier, he is armed with this belief system and willingness to further understand women despite experiencing childhood neglect and rejection by a girlfriend and his mother.

The Mother

Despite John Grady's avoidance of his mother—emotionally and physically—John Grady is much more like his mother than they both realize. Born into a family of adventurers, John Grady and his mother are descendants of a family whose grand adventures frequently resulted in death. McCarthy outlines the family history early on by sharing that "they seemed to fear only dying in bed" (7). Thus, John Grady's mother's desire for an adventurous life outside the home aligns with her family's history and prepares readers to better understand John Grady's journey as well. In her work, "*All the Pretty Horses*: John Grady Cole's Expulsion from Paradise," Gail Moore Morrison writes that within the episodic organization of McCarthy's novels, there are "metaphoric and literal journeys which bring their voyagers inevitably into a series of conflicts and confrontations within themselves as well as with the various communities intersected by their wanderings" (174). This is true of John Grady's journey to Mexico; however, in order to understand John Grady's journey to Mexico, readers must first turn their attention to his mini-quest to learn more about his mother.

Physical and emotional distance is established between John Grady and his mother's family at the start of the book foreshadowing the distance between John Grady and his mother. In providing the familial history, the reader learns "the Grady name was buried with" his grandfather (7). Despite maintaining the name Grady, the discussion of name hints at the impending tumultuous relationship between John Grady and his mother. The articulation of this severance serves both to teach the reader that John Grady is an only child, but also highlights the end to the patriarchy that defined their family in preceding centuries. The ranch, spanning eighteen thousand acres, was the property of his mother, and is real estate John Grady sought with the death of his grandfather. The death of his grandparent signifies the end of the successive reign of male dominance on the ranch. His grandfather, the oldest of eight adventure seeking males, solidifies the closure of the ranch as it had formerly been purposed.

Prior to discussing the abandonment and current location of his mother over a meal, John Grady meets his father in the lobby of St. Angelus. Born in 1185 in Jerusalem, St. Angelus is known for converting members of the Jewish community to his faith. St. Angelus is also remembered for assisting a wayward woman in finding faith and spirituality. In Licata, Italy, religious registrars discuss St. Angelus's efforts to remove a woman from an incestuous relationship with her brother, a man named Berengarus. According to the Catholic Exchange, St. Angelus is murdered after the woman is enlightened to her sins, repents, and converts to Catholicism—leaving her brother and his evil ways. Whether McCarthy's intent or not, the meeting location of St. Angelus, a saint committed to converting a misinformed woman, contains irony, as John Grady seeks out his mother, a woman whose lifestyle deviates from the societal expectations of her time.

In the Eagle Café, emotional avoidance of his mother occurs through John Grady's pithy dialogue with his father. Seated with a cup of coffee, John Grady states: "She's gone to San Antonio" (8). The use of the 'she' pronoun opposed to the word, "mama," which John Grady's father corrects, indicates both the familiarity of the topic between John Grady and his father, as well as the physical and emotional distance between John Grady and his mother. Sullivan writes that John Grady's mother betrayed him by divorcing his father and selling the ranch. Yet, John Grady is not prepared to examine a lifestyle outside the traditional one he expected on the ranch where a mother provided maternal warmth and guidance.

Ironically, when John Grady arrives in San Antonio to see his mother, he arrives at a café at 3 P.M. to be asked if he is there for the rodeo. There is a longstanding relationship between the state of Texas and the sport, rodeo, and in 1997, the Texas state legislature adopted the Rodeo as the official sport of Texas. Pecos, Texas was believed to be home to the first Rodeo in 1883. However, Mary Lou LeCompte's work, "The First American Rodeo Never Happened," details the debate of whether prior to the Pecos rodeo, a rodeo was held in Santa Fe, New Mexico, in 1847. The contrasting events occurring in San Antonio on the day of John Grady's visit—the theater performance by his mother and the rodeo—represent the tension and conflicting interests and lifestyles of John Grady and his mother.

Traditionally, women in the 1950s were encouraged to be caretakers, yet John Grady's mother deviates from the traditional gender expectations. In fact, the still popular Dixie Cup appealed to women in 1950s through print and television advertisements by sharing the Dixie Cup's ability to help maintain a clean, clutter free home ("Vintage"). When McCarthy wrote that John Grady's mother resides in San Antonio instead of the ranch, she could have been given a traditional female occupation in the 1950s like an assembly worker or secretary. According to Jarrett, John Grady and his mother represent "two versions of the contemporary Texan: the modern (the mother) who repudiates her ranching past for art, and the historicist (John Grady as son) who seeks to revive and repeat the past" (101). However, she is an actress, a profession that requires a continuous gaze from the viewer.

In 1975, Laura Mulvey's work, "Visual Pleasure and Narrative Cinema," appeared on *Screen*, which applies psychoanalysis to film. In the introduction to her work, Mulvey discusses her absorption with the Women's rights movement and her youth spent examining Hollywood cinema. The 1975 work considers, among other topics, the use of women as sexualized objects in film. She writes: "There are circumstances in which looking itself is a source of pleasure, just as, in the reverse formation, there is pleasure in being looked at" (806). The theory of male gaze is a particularly interesting theory to consider against John Grady's experience in the theater as no female patrons are discussed within the walls of the theater; unsurprisingly, only men are discussed. Outside the theater, John Grady is sold a ticket by an unnamed girl, yet once inside the theater, the only individuals John Grady comments on are men. During the intermission, John Grady rolls a cigarette under a gilded alcove, a visual that is at odds given his attire, and draws odd glances from theatergoers. This is one of the only moments in the theater that the audience members are gendered. Only during intermission does John Grady note the men who mirrored his style, "men in boots and hats," who he nodded at in an aligned sense of comradery (21). No women are mentioned, except for his mother on the stage, who enters and talks to, of course, "a woman in a chair" (21).

During his time at the play, merely feet away from his mother, John Grady searched her performance tirelessly and listened to her words seeking answers. John Grady believed "there would be something in the story itself to tell him about the way the world was or was becoming but there was not. There was nothing at all" (21). The obsolete message highlights the failure of John Grady's mother to provide the maternal guidance John Grady seeks in his life. Regarding this moment, Blair shares that John Grady fails to realize that "the answer is not in the play but in the fact that his mother has made that choice" to live in San Antonio as an actress and leave her child and the ranch behind (303).

Although critics highlight the potentially feminist vision of John Grady's mother to go off on her own to establish her life outside the home, notably absent from this scene is a sense of glamour and success. Viewed through John Grady's eyes, the theater was half empty. He notes that as the lights dimmed, patrons were able to move their seats closer to the front. When the curtain rises, the scene is amiss of detail referencing the luxury of the curtain's fabric or the excitement of the audience at his mother's entrance. Likewise, at the conclusion of the production, his mother did not receive a standing ovation. McCarthy writes that the audience rose only after the curtain closed. Without the mother's perspective on the performance, the reader is left to experience this moment through John Grady's vision, which does not depict the theater as a positive place or his mother's performance as exceptional. Ultimately, his vision highlights his failure to understand his mother's objectives, lifestyle, and success.

Although the narration limits the internal thoughts of John Grady's mother, her actions indicate her strong spirit, sense of independence, and deviation from societal expectations. On stage, the mother exhibits her independent spirit by setting herself apart from her peers and seeking personal accolades. McCarthy writes that she steps forward several times to bow, indicating her possible leading role in the play or her inflated sense of self. As an actress, the mother has not only removed herself from the privacy of the home and those accompanying responsibilities; she establishes herself as worthy of attention, worthy of gaze, worthy of standing alone. The mother, Blair writes, is a woman of "a new order whose values are not John Grady's values" (303). Seeking solace from his time in the theater and his failure to apprehend the answers to life that he sought, John Grady retreats outside where coldness awaits.

The ambiance within the theater mirrors the weather outside. The theater is void of joy, warmth, and light, and San Antonio, blanketed in snow with freezing temperatures, fails to provide John Grady with respite. In fact, the only place John Grady gains warmth is in a café, that is, of course, Mexican. There, he scans the newspaper seeking information on his mother, but is not rewarded with information. The absence of his mother's performance in the newspaper again highlights his perceived mediocrity of her career and his failure to understand the value of the life she seeks. However, the solace John Grady finds in the Mexican café prepares the reader for his need to travel beyond the United States border in search of meaning. No longer does the United States provide him answers that he seeks, although Blair writes, the United States does provide the newness that his mother yearns for. Thus, John Grady hopes the borderlands will provide an opportunity to experience life that aligns with his vision and expectations.

The differing values between mother and son come to fruition when John Grady leaves the theater, to watch his mother in her private sphere, the Menger Hotel. The Menger Hotel is not a fictitious creation within McCarthy's imagination, but a San Antonio relic steeped in history. The history of the building and its use in the text symbolizes the prestige of the mother's career that John Grady fails to comprehend while seated in the theater. The hotel's history dates back to 1859 when William and Mary Menger constructed a two-story, fifty-room hotel. Nearly twenty years later in 1881, the Mengers sold their hotel to Major J. H. Kampmann, who commissioned an addition as well as a bar, which was based on the prestigious House of Lords Club taproom in London. In 1909, the hotel was renovated by British born and esteemed architect Alfred Giles, who designed multiple buildings that obtained a coveted status on the National Register of Historic Places. In 1975, the Menger Hotel was added to the National Register of Historic Places. In 2023, the Historic Menger Hotel website boasts its prestige as the "oldest continuously operating hotel west of the Mississippi" with a "long line of honored guests" noting that at one time Theodore Roosevelt visited the Menger Bar with the Rough Riders.

The selection of the Menger Hotel, a classy hotel steeped in a tradition of prestige, architectural excellence, and luxury, symbolizes the lifestyle John Grady's mother seeks. Arriving at the hotel after walking down Broadway, a reference that serves to highlight his mother's journey, John Grady watches his mother walk through the lobby "on the arm of a man in a suit and a topcoat" and get into a cab (22). There is an irony to the moment John Grady sees his mother walk out of the Menger Hotel. In this scene, the mother remains an invisible figure and while her presence and movements in the lobby become clear, the reader sees her despite the limited description. Although his mother's clothing is absent from the description of this moment, the man she emerges with from the elevator provides evidence of her lifestyle. Not only does John Grady note that the man was impeccably dressed, but also his ability to take a cab—opposed to John Grady who hitched a ride from his hometown—indicates a wealth that departs from his own.

When John Grady learns that a Mrs. Cole is not registered at the hotel, he learns that his mother's identity is not tied to his own. Understanding his mother does not identify as a Cole, John Grady returns to his home where he immerses himself in the natural world. The glossy hotel and sleekness of her suitor contrasts the natural, rustic environment John Grady embraces in the following scene. Directly after his time at the Menger Hotel, John Grady horseback rides along a clear creek with green moss, eventually leading him past the ruins of an old ranch. The juxtaposition of place shows the contrasting identities and values of John Grady and his mother.

Ultimately, John Grady's time in San Antonio leads him to seek answers to life outside the U.S. border. With a mother who is not a source of guidance, material comfort, or security, John Grady's quest is set into action. At the estate known as the Hacienda de Nuestra Senora de la Purísima Concepcion, Dueña Alfonsa articulates the ability of individuals to be puppeteers—with an individual's actions setting into play another individual's actions—leading to a continuous cycle. Thus, an exploration into Dueña Alfonsa's words serve to better understand the relationship between John Grady's mother's actions and his decision to leave for Mexico.

Women as Puppets

With his return from prison—yet another adventure within an adventure—John Grady returns to the home of Dueña Alfonsa, where she discusses her view of, as her father put it, "the connectedness of things" (230). Dueña Alfonsa shares that she sees the world as a puppet show; but "when one looks behind the curtain and traces the strings upward he finds they terminate in the hands of yet other puppets, themselves with their own strings which trace upward in turn, and so on" (231). The analogy Dueña Alfonsa creates relates back to her own life and experiences as well as John Grady's mother. Ultimately, however, the analogy of the puppet stringing along the puppet, and so forth, is a metaphor—albeit an intimidating one—on the magnanimity of the world and the various forces at play in an individual's life.

In her story, Dueña Alfonsa refers directly to external and internal factors that fuel her actions. These factors tie into politics, love, individual choice, privilege, and gender, among others. The value of this story and this mindset teach the reader that the actions of John Grady's mother are part of a greater story. In his work *Understanding Cormac McCarthy*, Steven Fry writes that this conversation between Dueña Alfonsa and John Grady "explores the relationship between hope and the shaping reality of forces beyond the self" (106). The symbolic places, small moments, and details shared by Dueña Alfonsa shed light on the endless origins and causes at play in the life of John Grady's mother, and thus, their resulting action on his own life. Although the story of John Grady's mother occupies few pages in *All the Pretty Horses*, the implications of this story and significance of her lifestyle demonstrate the larger-than-life qualities of McCarthy's writing and characters. Woven into her narrative are the greater issues plaguing U.S. society, which bear down upon humankind and take the form of a whirling storm of puppets upon puppets upon puppets, shaping the trajectory of life.

John Grady's relationship with Dueña Alfonsa provides valuable knowledge for his self-discovery. In Stephen Tatum's Reader's Guide on *All the Pretty Horses*, Tatum explains that the events in the novel have forced John Grady to alter his view of the world from the nostalgic myth of the cowboy and deal with "what is so," which Dueña Alfonsa teaches him, takes courage (64). Her story shares that while her father's belief about the "connectedness of things" is a realistic view of the world, there are endless and often subconscious origins and causes at play impacting an individual's actions.

Dueña Alfonsa's story, then, about her childhood and desire to share her story with John Grady "because among other reasons I think we should know who our enemies are" highlights the myriad struggles oppressing individuals, the crush of human history upon an individual's current place in society, and the extensive forces at play in one's decisions (240–41). Fry writes that in Dueña Alfonsa's words, the origin and impact of individual choice become unknowns, and that "in a paradoxical sense, human beings exert a tremendous influence on the world, but they are powerless to control the process by which their actions bear fruit" (108). Despite this, one missing piece from Dueña Alfonsa's analogy is the sense of agency and intellectual capability of the individual to control their actions. Dueña Alfonsa, for example, acknowledges her perceived sense of agency and control over John Grady's time in Mexico; however, this agency and intellectuality is underscored by the history of forces that shape her story. The sheer volume of infinity that the puppet analogy creates is a breathless depiction of the challenges at play for humankind.

Although scholars and critics continue to examine the role of women in *All the Pretty Horses*, the depth and critique of women cannot be divorced from the myriad forces at play in their creation. John Grady's mother is not an invisible force in the text. Though her body remains unseen by the reader, she, like a puppet, is a visible icon on stage, residing at a hotel steeped in history, and born from a family of adventurers. The characterization of the mother symbolizes the forces at play in American society, and the resulting tension of past and present that exist in each individual's story, as humankind attempts to navigate their places in the present, moving along, influenced by puppets upon puppets upon puppets.

Works Cited

Bell, Madison Smartt. "The Man Who Understood Horses." Review of *All the Pretty Horses,* by Cormac McCarthy." *The New York Times*, 17 May 1992, p. 9, www.nytimes.com/1992/05/17/books/the-man-who-understood-horses.html.

Blair, John. "Mexico and the Borderlands in Cormac McCarthy's *All the Pretty Horses*." *Critique: Studies in Contemporary Fiction*, vol. 42, no. 3, 2001, pp. 301–07.

Bunyan, John. *The Pilgrim's Progress as Originally Published, Being a Fac-Simile Reproduction of the First Ed.* London: Elliot Stock, 1876.

Fisher-Wirth, Ann. "Abjection and 'the Feminine' in Outer Dark." *Cormac McCarthy: New Directions*. Edited by James D. Lilley. U of New Mexico P, 2002.

Frye, Steven. *Understanding Cormac McCarthy*. The U of South Carolina P, 2009.

Jarrett, Robert L. "The *Border Trilogy*: Individualism, History, and Cultural Crossings." Edited by Frank Day. Twayne, 1997.

Kaplan, Amy. "'Left Alone with America': The Absence of Empire in the Study of American Culture." *Cultures of United States Imperialism*. Edited by Amy Kaplan and E. Donald Pease. Duke UP, 1993.

Kimmel, Michael S. *The History of Men: Essays in the History of American and British Masculinities*. State U of New York P, 2005.

Ladino, Jennifer K. *Reclaiming Nostalgia: Longing for Nature in American Literature*. U of Virginia P, 2012.

Lea, Tom. "Southwest." 1956, Smithsonian American Art Museum, americanart.si.edu/artwork/southwest-71561.

LeCompte, Mary Lu. "The First American Rodeo Never Happened." *Journal of Sports History,* vol. 9, no. 2, 1982, pp. 89–96.

McCarthy, Cormac. "Cormac McCarthy's Venomous Fiction." Interview by Richard B. Woodward. *The New York Times Magazine*, 19 Apr. 1992, Section 6, p. 28, www.nytimes.com/1992/04/19/magazine/cormac-mccarthy-s-venomous-fiction.html.

__________. "Interview with Cormac McCarthy." Interview by Oprah Winfrey. *The Oprah Winfrey Show*. 5 June 2007.

Morrison, Gail Moore. "*All the Pretty Horses*: John Grady Cole's Expulsion from Paradise." Perspectives on Cormac McCarthy. Edited by Edwin T. Arnold and Dianne C. Luce. UP of Mississippi, 1999, pp. 175–94.

Mulvey, Laura. "Visual Pleasure and Narrative Cinema." *Film Theory and Criticism: Introductory Readings.* Edited by Leo Braudy and Marshall Cohen. Oxford UP, 1999, pp. 833–44.

"Our Story." The Historic Menger Hotel, www.mengerhotel.com/about-us.

Shaw, Patrick W. "Female Presence, Male Violence, and the Art of Artlessness in the *Border Trilogy*." Myth, Legend, Dust: Critical Responses to Cormac McCarthy. Edited by Rick Wallach. Manchester UP, 2000.

"St. Angelus." Catholic Exchange. catholicexchange.com/st-angelus/.

Tatum, Stephen. *Cormac McCarthy's* All the Pretty Horses. Continuum Contemporaries, 2002.

Twain, Mark. *The Adventures of Huckleberry Finn*. Dover, 1994.

"Vintage Old 1950's Dixie Paper Cups Commercial." Vintage Fanatic, 1954. *YouTube*, www.youtube.com/watch?v=48sIUgAU-pY.

Woodson, Linda. "'This Is Another Country': The Complex Feminine Presence in *All the Pretty Horses*." *Cormac McCarthy: All the Pretty Horses, No Country for Old Men, the Road*. Edited by Sara Spurgeon. Continuum, 2011.

Worthington, Leslie Harper. *Cormac McCarthy and the Ghost of Huck Finn*. McFarland, 2012.

Confronting the Capitalocene: Capitalism, Culture, and Codes in *All the Pretty Horses*

Sakti Sekhar Dash

For decades prior to the publication of *All the Pretty Horses*, Cormac McCarthy had remained a reclusive figure. A consummate artist employing figurative language, symbols, and allusions, he garnered critical acclaim for works like *The Orchard Keeper*, *Outer Dark*, *Child of God*, and *Suttree*. But the novel that established his legacy as William Faulkner's heir was *Blood Meridian* in which he seamlessly blended the history and mythology of the American West. But most readers were put off by the unremitting descriptions of violence and bloodshed with critic Harold Bloom likening it to a "United Nations report on the horrors of Kosovo in 1999" (1). The characters kill, mutilate, scalp, and eviscerate one another in every possible manner, a continual reminder of the human race's affinity for violence. After *Blood Meridian's* gory narrative, *All the Pretty Horses* feels like a whiff of fresh air. The novel's publication in 1992 coincided with Cormac McCarthy's first interview that brought the reclusive author out of the shadows of obscurity. Unlike his earlier novels that delved into deeper questions of human existence through an unflinching confrontation of violence, *All the Pretty Horses* was a romance. A sense of mellowness permeated the narrative that was in stark contrast to *Blood Meridian's* grim and brutal narrative.

The first installment in the *Border Trilogy*, *All the Pretty Horses* is a Western romance that also explores the enterprising journey of John Grady and Lacey Rawlins across the border. Their journey to Mexico is a quest to find a better life for themselves. They are cowboys and the ranching industry in America faces a threat from capitalism and industrialization. The novel is set in the year 1948 when the oil boom was transforming the American landscape. The ranch belonging to John Grady's family has been put up for sale by his mother. Though it can be read as a Western romance, it debunks the romantic notions associated with it. "We get a clue to this early on as John Grady Cole stares at a painting in the dining room of the family ranch, which is destined to be sold off to big oil interests" (Hage 22). The ranch can be viewed as a remaining symbol of the pastoral. But in the face of capitalism, John Grady Cole's mother intends to sell the ranch. She wants to sell to an oil company, which will certainly mark the end of the ranch and the ranching tradition. Much like the pastoral, a long-standing tradition will be destroyed forever. The company with oil interests will most likely exploit the land that had been closely associated with nature. In the American tradition, the ranches were seen as an embodiment of the natural way of life. Cowboys like John Grady and Lacey Rawlins preferred a life that was embodied by their association with the ranching tradition, and primarily the horses. But this tradition is on the decline, and the decay is best represented by the painting of horses present in the house. "The oil painting is a vividly dramatic rendering of horses busting through a corral, with flowing manes and 'wild' eyes. With his keen horseman and rancher's eye, Cole notices how the individual horses seem a mix and match, a Frankenstein-like patchwork of actual breeds" (Hage 22). The naturalness has been lost due to the artificiality that has encroached upon the ranch. The horses have not been represented accurately or naturally. They seem to be a mix of many different breeds. This illustrates the rootlessness of ecology. By degrees, the Americans had been losing their connection with ecology, and only a few existed who wanted to preserve the tradition.

John Grady Cole loves and respects the life he led on the ranch. Unlike his mother, he does not succumb to capitalist interests. Instead, he has a deep fondness for nature and horses in particular. McCarthy describes the curious fascination and reverence John Grady has for the horses: "What he loved in horses was what he loved in men, the blood and the heat of the blood that ran them. All his reverence and all his fondness and all the leanings of his life were for the ardenthearted and they would always be so and never be otherwise" (8).

He views the horses as living beings, who are very much equal. He does not see them as inferior beasts, reflecting the ranching tradition in which the horses played as much a part as the humans.

The thought that his mother was going to sell the ranch fills him with dread. It not only means the loss of the ranch but also the loss of his way of life. Even Franklin admits that John Grady's mother could not realize and appreciate the worth of the ranch. "Son, not everybody thinks that life on a cattle ranch in west Texas is the second-best thing to dyin and goin to heaven. She don't want to live out there, that's all. If it was a payin proposition that'd be one thing. But it aint" (20). Franklin's words reflect the degrading relationship between humans and the environment. For a long time, the ranches had stood as symbols of the interdependence between humans and nature. Cowboys and ranchers had been perceived as the custodians or guardians of the pastoral and the natural. But they fall prey to the attractions offered by booming capitalism.

The earliest settlers on the continent of America encountered a vast and terrifying wilderness. As settlements expanded, the wilderness was replaced by the pastoral. As modernization and industrialization gained pace, the pastoral gave way to a Capitalocene society. According to Jason W. Moore, "the Capitalocene signifies capitalism as a way of organizing nature—as a multispecies, situated, capitalist world-ecology" (6). Nature is perceived as a storehouse of commodities that can fuel capitalist interests. Capitalism has led to the industrialization of agriculture, prompting farmers to heavily use pesticides and chemicals for an increased crop yield. But the same chemicals and pesticides find their way into the water bodies, including the oceans. Carrying out agricultural activities on an industrial scale has led to the depletion of forest cover. Temperate forests as well as wetlands have been cleared for farming activities and human settlements. Deforestation not only results in the loss of green cover but also deprives many nonhuman life forms of their habitats. It also leads to an increase in the presence of carbon dioxide and monoxide gases in the atmosphere. It comes as no surprise that many life forms are extinct and many more are on the brink of extinction. Loss of habitat, hunting, and ecological disturbance are some of the prime factors that have led to the extinction of different life forms. In Australia, farmers saw the Tasmanian Devil as a threat to their livestock. Thus, it was hunted to extinction. In America, the loss of grasslands and hunting drove the American bison to the brink of extinction. The same thing happened with the wolves and coyotes that preyed on the cattle and livestock of the ranchers. The government sanctioned the massacre of animal species that posed a threat to capitalist interests. In Africa, trophy hunting has emerged as a capitalist venture. Rich elites pay huge sums of money to national parks and wildlife authorities to obtain permission to hunt. Wildlife reserves like Kruger National Park have emerged as popular places for trophy hunting. DeMello explains:

> Because of this emphasis on bagging a trophy at all costs, trophy hunters have evolved into a somewhat different species than the traditional American hunter. Many trophy hunters now use baiting, dogs, game farms, canned hunting ranches, guides, and technology in order to ensure a trophy at the end of the day. Over the past two hundred years, Africa has been stripped of much of its population of large game animals. (74)

Capitalism has also paved the way for the growth and rise of fashion giants like Gucci, Dior, Versace, and Armani. These fashion houses have gained popularity due to their leather and fur products. In Western countries, animals are specifically raised for harvesting their fur and hides to fuel the demands. In *Animal Liberation* Peter Singer writes about, "shooting three million kangaroos every year in the Australian outback to turn them into skins and pet food; and generally ignoring the interests of wild animals as we extend our empire of concrete and pollution over the surface of the globe" (22). All these actions resulting from the growing industrialization and capitalism have brought catastrophic consequences for the ecology. Wildlife species are disappearing at a fast pace, the green cover is getting depleted, global temperatures are rising, desertification is occurring, and an ecological crisis is staring the earth in the face.

Increasing capitalism and industrialization have destroyed the meaning of ecology. Ecology has been stripped of its holistic meaning; the only meaning it holds for the human community is in terms of material and financial gains. By rejecting the holistic meaning of ecology, humans have effectively given rise to a sixth form of nihilism—Ecological Nihilism. Donald Crosby famously outlined five different forms of nihilism; those are- political, moral, epistemological, cosmic, and existential. Crosby based his nihilistic formulations on the human relationships with politics, morality, life, and man's position in creation. What Crosby has failed to address is man's relationship with ecology and the nihilism that accompanies the relationship. According to Johan Vetlesen:

> In a capitalist culture such as ours, runaway consumer greed is not only encouraged and instilled from a person's infancy by means of the advertising so ubiquitous in our everyday life. Psychologically, consumerism is linked with a state of mind of narcissistic entitlement, one that says: "I am entitled to have and to be everything I crave as I am superior and special." (10)

The extent of damage caused by human actions has been explained by Alan Weisman; he makes it clear that nature, ecology, and the nonhuman environment can regain their former glory only in the absence of humans. Human actions, chiefly globalization, capitalism, modernization, and industrialization have contributed to the destruction of the ecology. Nature and ecology have lost their meaning as the world has made a transition into a capitalocene society.

The world has witnessed a steady shift from ecocentrism to an anthropocentric and Capitalocene society. Anthropocentrism has been responsible for promoting the supremacy of the human species; man is superior to the ecology, and this superiority has made him reject the importance of ecology and nonhuman nature. In this context, Eileen Crist writes:

> Descriptions of humanity as "rivaling the great forces of Nature," "elemental," "a geological and morphological force," "a force of nature reshaping the planet on a geological scale," and the like, are standard in the Anthropocene literature and its popular spinoffs. The veracity of this framing of humanity's impact renders it incontestable, thereby *also* enabling its awed subtext regarding human specialness to slip in and, all too predictably, carry the day. (17)

Human history, particularly anthropocentrism and capitalism rests on the dominance of nonhuman ecology. By treating nonhuman nature and ecology as the 'other,' the human community not only distances itself from the environment but also strips nonhuman nature and ecology of the holistic meaning. "Anthropocene's existential and political alliance with history and its will to secure human dominion: history has itself unfolded by silencing nonhuman others, who do not (as has been repeatedly established in the Western canon) speak, possess meanings, experience perspectives, or have a vested interest in their own destinies" (Crist 18). The capitalist demands have created a wide rift between the human community and ecology. Nature and ecology assume meaning only in terms of financial and capital gains, while holistic approaches such as sustainability and ecological conservation take a back seat. Jason W. Moore explains the manner in which capitalist forces have enslaved and exploited natural resources and Indigenous communities who are a part of the natural world. He explains:

> To register the bloody history of this Human/Nature binary is a moral protest. It is also an analytical protest. For Capitalism does not thrive on violence and inequality alone. It is a prodigiously creative and productive system too—at least until recently. The symbolic, material, and bodily violence of this audacious separation—Humanity and Nature—performed a special kind of "work" for the modern world. Backed by imperial power and capitalist rationality, it mobilized the unpaid work and energy of humans—especially women, especially the enslaved—in service to transforming landscapes with a singular purpose: the endless accumulation of capital. (79)

Anthropocentrism and the phenomenon of Capitalocene undermines the relationship between humans and ecology. Rejecting the meaning associated with ecology, they attempt to create a state of ecological nihilism, where ecology, nature, and the environment no longer matter. Ecological nihilism results in a state of apathy and indifference toward the role of nature and ecology in creation.

All the Pretty Horses narrates the loss of tradition and the destruction of livelihoods. The cowboys are cast out, no longer wanted in a society that is steadily embracing the Capitalocene. As Gail Moore Morrison says, "*All the Pretty Horses* is permeated with a sense of loss, alienation, deracination, and fragmentation" (175). The events of the novel coincide with the oil boom that was an important chapter in American capitalism. As a result of the oil boom, farmers and ranchers began to distance themselves from pastoral life. Ranches and farms were sold to oil farms, and the open spaces were taken up by oil rigs. The cowboys and ranchers suddenly found themselves without a position in a radically changed world.

The title of the novel is significant. *All the Pretty Horses* owes its origin to a lullaby. The history behind the title has been explained in detail by Kenneth Lincoln. He writes:

> The title *All the Pretty Horses* comes from a slave lullaby in a minor key, a black mammy singing a white child to sleep while her own infant "way down yonder" lies crying for his mother, bees, and butterflies around his eyes. *Hushaby, don't you cry, go to sleep my little baby. / When you wake you shall have all the pretty horses. / Dapples and grays, pintos and bays, coach and six little horses.* Something's wrong here, racially and historically and socially amiss—natural mothers in the wrong houses, fathers enslaving and splitting families, children crying out, all the pretty horses disillusional or damnably unreal. (102)

The innocent-sounding title is an illusion; the world that has been presented in *All the Pretty Horses* is anything but innocent. The few characters who retain their innocence are forced to lead the lives of outcasts. Relentlessly persecuted, they are forced to abandon their innocence and conform to social standards.

John Grady is a tragic hero. He tries to live by the morals, ethics, and codes he has gleaned from his connection with the land. But his mother fails to understand him and so do the others with the possible exception of Lacey Rawlins. Rawlins is another cowboy, who understands the importance of the ranch and the intimacy with the land. Upon the death of his grandfather, John Grady becomes aware of the loss and erosion of the past. About John Grady and his predicament, Morrison adds:

> The last of his grandfather's line with its generations-deep commitment to the land, he is certainly as powerless to protect it against foreign encroachment twentieth-century technology, and the oil interests to which his often absent actress mother sells it as was the Comanche nation he envisions as he rides out along their ancient war trail under a 'bloodred and elliptic' sun 'under the reefs of bloodred cloud' after his grandfather's funeral, 'with the sun coppering his face and the red wind blowing out of the west.' (176)

McCarthy has compared the plight of John Grady with the Comanche Indians. In earlier times, the Comanches were an integral part of the land. Their association with the land was deep and was older than anybody could tell. But the Westward expansion and mindless slaughter of the native tribes displaced the Indians from their rightful place. Something similar has happened with John Grady; due to the encroachment made by capitalism, the ranch is sold off, and he is displaced from his rightful place. "McCarthy records the dying years of the cattle-horse culture as cities swallow the plains, the archaic role of the mythic cowboy in America's history" (Lincoln 103).

John Grady and Lacey set out on a journey to find their rightful place; but they enter "into a world of passion and greed, of primal ferocity and violence" (Morrison 176). They confront the nihilistic forces that threaten their very existence. On their way, they meet Jimmy Blevins, a young lad who leads a lawless life. Blevins represents the many who are forced to abandon their position in society and seek other avenues. They are compelled by the capitalist society to give up their morals and ethical traditions owing to their alienated condition.

Blevins exemplifies the alienated individual who has chosen to lead a lawless life. He seems to share a similarity with the character of Gene Harrogate from *Suttree*. "Even though McCarthy moved his vision away from the South to the American Southwest and Mexico in *All the Pretty Horses*, the boy-man Jimmy Blevins possesses that same 'unresolved tension'—but to an even more unsettling degree"

(Hage 42). The "unresolved tension" is the result of Jimmy's failure to fit into society like Gene Harrogate and Lester Ballard. The result of this alienation is nihilism. Jimmy Blevins is a nihilist who does not hesitate to steal and commit more heinous crimes like murder. "He is a dead shot, putting a hole in the center of Rawlins's tossed billfold, and actually emerges as the real American desperado of the novel: a genuine murderer and horse thief" (Hage 43).

Despite sharing the journey with John Grady and Lacey Rawlins, Blevins, for the greater part remains a misfit. Cole and Rawlins are aware of their moral bearing built around, a "simplistic conception of good and evil" (Morrison 178). On the other hand, Jimmy Blevins is amoral and has all the makings of a dangerous sociopath. He is in his teens, yet the experiences at the hands of society have forced him to become an amoral nihilist, who would wallow in lawlessness. Initially a comical character, he steadily displays a dangerous degeneracy. "By the time that John Grady and Rawlins re-encounter Blevins in a Mexican prison, he has evolved into a truly unsettling combination of identities and become a character embodying "strong, unresolved tension and dualities characteristic of the grotesque" (Hage 43).

John Grady displays a remarkable degree of conscience and goodwill by caring for Jimmy Blevins. Lacey Rawlins was of the opinion that Blevins "had a loose wingnut." While traveling with them, Jimmy behaves in the most eccentric and ludicrous manner. But for all his eccentricities and craziness, John Grady cares for the teenager. But their association with Jimmy lands them in trouble. After stealing back his horse, they part ways. However, Jimmy's lawless ways create trouble for him. "Blevins is shackled in the jailhouse with broken feet for shooting the man who stole his pistol and wounding two *rurales* with self-same pistol, killing one of them" (Lincoln 108). Blevins follows no moral code and sticks to his own warped justice. He has no regrets about committing murder. It is certainly disturbing to note his moral depravity at such a young age.

But he becomes a victim of society. Earlier, he had been rejected as an outcast. Following that, he had become a horse thief. From a horse thief, he becomes a murderer and lands himself in prison.

In the prison, he and his fellow inmates experience the brutality of the corrupt law officials. Being the upholders of the law does not deter them from indulging in activities that can only be described as immoral. "Lacey has to bare his naked back and butt for the lascivious police" (Lincoln 108). Jimmy Blevins's legs have been broken, and he is kept in shackles. Eventually, Blevins is shot dead by the police in the woods. This is sufficient to demonstrate the brutal and violent nature of Mexican society.

John Grady had left Texas in search of pastoral paradise. Following the loss of his ranch, he traveled to Mexico, hoping to live his pastoral dream. But what he encounters is a violent, brutal, and nihilistic world. The ranch he joins is nothing more than a commercial establishment driven by capitalist interests. Don Héctor is more interested in earning profits; he is not hesitant to crossbreed the horses. For him, the horses are little more than sources of capital. He comfortably ignores the long and deep association between the humans, the horses, and the land. He displays ecological nihilism in abundance. He is willing to destroy the age-old relationship for his financial gain. Earlier, John Grady had seen an oil painting of horses. There seemed nothing natural about them; they were simply, "picture-book horses." Don Héctor wants to recreate the "picture-book horses." Nature, ecology, and nonhuman life forms have lost their meaning and remain relevant only along financial lines. The lure of capitalism compelled John Grady's mother to sell the ranch, ignoring the past association with the land. For her, the land is meaningless, as it is no longer profitable.

Through the stories of John Grady Cole and Billy Parham, McCarthy foregrounds the conflict and tension between the pastoral world and the urbanized American society. The latter is continually threatening the former, and the likes of John Grady and Billy, who represent a dying tradition, have to struggle for survival. George Guillemin outlines the pastoral structure created by McCarthy in the *Border Trilogy*. He writes:

> Moreover, the novels seem to reconceptualize literary pastoralism along post-humanist, eco-pastoral lines. Although all three of the

> novels are pastoral tales in their own right, it could be argued that taken together, they form an overarching structure composed of the three traditional pastoral motifs: escape into the pastoral realm, immersion into pastoral harmony, and purified return to urban civilization. The pastoralism thematized disagrees with literary convention insofar as wilderness is rated as the ideal pastoral space of nature, and insofar as the foregoing motifs are altered into the quest for a pastoral lifestyle (*All the Pretty Horses*), the journey through a pastoral world *(The Crossing*), and the foreclosure of the pastoral vision anywhere (*Cities of the Plain*). (95)

The protagonist, John Grady struggles against the Capitalocene that is threatening to disrupt the pastoral and ranching tradition. The story is set during the time when the United States of America was slowly becoming a capitalist economy. The growth of capitalism also coincided with oil explorations as prospectors looked for new sources of capital and financial gains. Lacey Rawlins looks at a map that shows the extent to which the oil companies had affected the American landscape:

> They reached the Devil's River by midmorning and watered the horses and stretched out in the shade of a stand of black willow and looked at the map. It was an oil company roadmap that Rawlins had picked up at the cafe and he looked at it and he looked south toward the gap in the low hills. There were roads and rivers and towns on the American side of the map as far south as the Rio Grande and beyond that all was white. (*All the Pretty Horses* 37)

Like *The Orchard Keeper, Child of God,* and *Suttree*, *All the Pretty Horses* can also be read as an elegy that laments the death of a past tradition. The tradition in question is a pastoral one, that is facing a challenge from the anthropocentric forces. Morrison writes, "*All the Pretty Horses* is permeated with a sense of loss, alienation, deracination, and fragmentation" (175). The ranches and farms that had dotted the American landscape, were being threatened by the booming oil industry and capitalist influences. It comes as no surprise that John Grady's mother cannot shrug off the anthropocentric influence; she can no longer adhere to the past and decides to sell the ranch. Her behavior and action are in stark contrast to that of Uncle Ather from *The Orchard Keeper* who takes it upon himself to keep the pastoral tradition alive, in the face of anthropocentric influences. But her son cannot accept the loss easily. He resists the change and makes a deliberate choice; he chooses to escape from the American society, where he feels out of place. Along with Lacey Rawlins, he decides to go to Mexico and work on a ranch. John Grady embodies the pastoral thinking that is slowly staring at extinction. Ranchers like John Grady's mother choose to sell their ranches and farms, preferring a more modern existence. They are willing to let go of a tradition that had been a part of their identity. Just as Cornelius Suttree's ancestral mansion stands for an old order that is dead and gone, likewise, the loss of the ranching tradition marks a sweeping change across the American landscape. Cornelius's mansion and John Grady's ranch acquire a striking similarity as symbols of a past culture that is slowly giving way to a change.

The horses are a part of their lives, and it is worth noting that the animals are treated as companions by the cowboys. John Grady viewed humans and horses as similar in more ways than one. Not only do they share the same landscape, but also share a similar fate. But the cowboys and the horses are losing their relevance in the face of increasing anthropocentrism. Due to the loss of the ranches and farmlands, the cowboys and their horses face an existential crisis. The horses are the companions of the cowboys, and thus the fate that is to befall the cowboys is most likely to befall the horses as well. The image of the horse's skull assumes significance, as it conveys a sense of loss. With the decline of the ranching tradition, the horses face the threat of being marginalized:

> There was an old horse skull in the brush and he squatted and picked it up and turned it in his hands. Frail and brittle. Bleached paper white. He squatted in the long light holding it, the comic book teeth loose in their sockets. The joints in the cranium like a ragged welding of the bone plates. The muted run of sand in the brainbox when he turned it. (*All the Pretty Horses* 8)

In an increasingly anthropocentric landscape, the very identity of the horses is facing a threat. They run the risk of losing their credibility along with the extinction of the ranching tradition. The skull belongs to a dead horse, who is a part of the past. McCarthy describes it as frail and brittle; the fate of the horses can be described as similarly frail and brittle. Without the ranch and the horses, the cowboys would be stripped of their very identity. Thus, they are willing to undertake an arduous journey across the border with their horses to preserve their own identities and the ranching tradition. During the journey, the two cowboys take utmost care of their horses. The horses aren't just animals, they are the companions of the cowboys and constitute a part of their very identity. When the cowboys cross the river, the horses aid them; the horses accompany them across the border. Thus, the horses have tied themselves to their human companions. Despite being under the control of humans, the horses are not treated as brute animals unworthy of human consideration. On the contrary, they are treated with respect as they are integral to the lives of the cowboys. The horses are their companions in the adventure, and they are treated as equals by the cowboys:

> They rode up out of the river among the willows and rode single file upstream through the shallows onto a long gravel beach where they took off their hats and turned and looked back at the country they'd left. No one spoke. Then suddenly they put their horses to a gallop up the beach and turned and came back, fanning with their hats and laughing and pulling up and patting the horses on the shoulder. (*All the Pretty Horses* 49)

This incident is sufficient to highlight the camaraderie that exists between the humans and the horses. Unlike the horses belonging to the scalp hunters in *Blood Meridian* that were typically used as instruments, the horses belonging to John Grady, Lacey, and Jimmy are treated as companions. Thus, the alienation between humans and nonhuman life forms has been negated to a large extent, particularly in the case of cowboys. This can be explained by the fact that humans and the horses are in the same boat. With the loss of the ranch, the horses will no longer be needed. Thus, they will be cast out and most likely packed off to the slaughterhouse. In the West, it was not uncommon for unwanted animals to be slaughtered. Even racehorses past their prime were slaughtered. Margo DeMello comments on the plight of animals that are no longer relevant to humans. "Thousands of horses, most of whom will never win a race, are bred each year. Most horses will see their careers end after just a season or two and will be sold at auction—sometimes to people who want them as pets, sometimes to businesses such as horseback-riding outfits, and sometimes to slaughter" (DeMello 116). Only the cowboys, who are associated with the horses, are concerned about the horses and the ranches. They also face an existential crisis like the horses; with the closure of the ranch, they will lose their identity and relevance as cowboys. They will be obsolete figures in an altered landscape.

With the loss of the ranch, they will be marginalized along with their horses. "The character of John Grady Cole is another self-sufficient savant who inhabits the beautiful and melancholy margins of society. Cole has prodigal, mythical skills with horses. He loves the animals passionately and unconditionally" (Greenwood 57). John Grady almost finds his ideal existence in Mexico, where he and Lacey are hired as helping hands on a ranch. Thus, he is able to realize his pastoral dream, by taming the wild horses. But things take a turn for the worse when John Grady and Lacey are arrested for their association with Jimmy Blevins. Thus, their dream of a stable existence comes to an abrupt end. Not only does John Grady lose his love interest Alejandra, but also the very life that had provided him with an identity. Eventually, he is released from prison and circumstances compel him to return to Texas. In the final image of the novel, John Grady and his horse make their way through a desolate desert waste:

> He touched the horse with his heels and rode on. He rode with the sun coppering his face and the red wind blowing out of the west across the evening land and the small desert birds flew chittering among the dry bracken and horse and rider and horse passed on and their long shadows passed in tandem like the shadow of a single being. Passed

> and paled into the darkening land, the world to come. (*All the Pretty Horses* 297)

But the image is heavily laden with symbolic significance. The shadows of the horse and its human rider are presented as those of a single being, highlighting the bond that exists between John Grady and his horse. But he is making his way towards a world that is unfamiliar. He and his horse are slowly fading away and fast losing their relevance in a world that has been drastically altered.

John Grady's experiences are traumatic; he is a transformed individual by the time he returns from Mexico. He witnessed violence, killed a man in self-defense, lost the girl he loved, and underwent immense suffering. From the onset, he had associated romanticism with the ranching tradition. But the harsh experiences have changed him and mellowed his romantic notions. "*All the Pretty Horses* constitutes a philosophical bildungsroman in which John Grady, his desires and ambitions chastened by the world, embraces his ethical code and demonstrates heroic action that resembles Stoic conduct" (Hillier 99). *All the Pretty Horses* is a tale about the destruction of moral values and the corruption of the innocent. Through harsh experiences, the characters come to terms with the real nature of the world. According to Kenneth Lincoln, "*All the Pretty Horses* is a lullaby for lost innocence, an elegy for a young nation of cowboys and New World breeds, a lament for first love and last chance, a love-song for a southwest border landscape of severe beauty that brings out strangeness, cruelty, and kindness in men and sorrow, compassion, and inconstancy in women" (111). *All the Pretty Horses* is a dirge that laments the rejection of the pastoral ethic and the destruction of the meaning associated with the land. It explores deep into the recesses of human nature, examining the moral choices made by individuals. The episodes of violence, lawlessness, and moral shortcomings are sufficient to justify the nihilistic position of the individuals with the exception of a few.

Works Cited

Bloom, Harold, editor. *Bloom's Modern Critical Views: Cormac McCarthy.* Infobase Publishing, 2009.

Crist, Eileen, and H. Bruce Rinker, editors. *Gaia in Turmoil Climate Change, Biodepletion and Earth Ethics in an Age of Crisis.* MIT Press, 2010.

Crosby, Donald A. *A Religion of Nature.* State U of New York P, 2002.

__________. *The Specter of the Absurd Sources and Criticisms of Modern Nihilism.* State U of New York P, 1988.

DeMello, Margo. *Animals and Society: An Introduction to Human-Animal Studies.* Columbia UP, 2012.

Greenwood, Willard P. *Reading Cormac McCarthy.* Greenwood Press, 2009.

Guillemin, George. "As of Some Site Where Life Had Not Succeeded: Sorrow, Allegory, and Pastoralism in Cormac McCarthy's *Border Trilogy*." *A Cormac McCarthy Companion: The Border Trilogy.* Edited by Edwin T. Arnold and Dianne C. Luce. U of Mississippi, 2001, pp. 92–130.

Hage, Erik. *Cormac McCarthy: A Literary Companion.* McFarland, 2010.

Hillier, Russell M. *Morality in Cormac McCarthy's Fiction: Souls at Hazard.* Palgrave Macmillan, 2017.

Lincoln, Kenneth. *Cormac McCarthy: American Canticles.* Palgrave Macmillan, 2009.

McCarthy, Cormac. *All the Pretty Horses*, 1992.

__________. *The Crossing.* Vintage, 1994.

__________. *The Orchard Keeper.* Vintage, 1965.

__________. *Outer Dark.* Vintage, 1968.

__________. *Suttree.* Vintage, 1979.

Moore, Jason W. *Capitalism in the Web of Life.* Verso, 2015.

__________, editor. *Anthropocene or Capitalocene Nature, History and the Crisis of Capitalism.* Kairos Books, 2016.

Morrison, Gail Moore. "*All the Pretty Horses*: John Grady Cole's Expulsion from Paradise." *Perspectives on Cormac McCarthy.* Edited by Edwin T. Arnold and Dianne C. Luce. UP of Mississippi, 1999, pp. 175–94.

Singer, Peter. *Animal Liberation.* Ecco, 2002.

Vetlesen, Johan Arne. *The Denial of Nature Environmental Philosophy in the Era of Global Capitalism.* Routledge, 2015.

Weisman, Alan. *The World Without Us.* Thomas Dunne Books, 2007.

RESOURCES

Chronology of Cormac McCarthy's Life*

1930	Charles Joseph McCarthy and Gladys Christina McGrail marry.
1931	Helen Jacuelyn McCarthy is born to Charles and Gladys.
1932	Charles and Gladys's second child, Barbara Ann McCarthy, is born.
1933	Charles Joseph McCarthy, Jr. [later a.k.a. Cormac McCarthy] is born on July 20, the third of six children in the McCarthy family.
1937	The McCarthy family relocates to Noelton/Cherokee Drive in Knoxville, Tennessee. Charles McCarthy, Sr. works as a lawyer for Tennessee Valley Authority.
1940	William (Bill) McCarthy is born.
1941	The McCarthy family moves to Sherrod Road and settle in a house on Martin Mill Pike in South Knoxville. Cormac McCarthy meets childhood friend, Jim Long later written as J-Bone in *Suttree.*
1942	Mary Ellen McCarthy is born.
1944	Dennis McCarthy is born.
1951	Cormac graduates from Catholic High School in Knoxville, TN, and begins attending the University of Tennessee. He majors in liberal arts.

*a.k.a. Charles Joseph McCarthy, Jr.

1953	Cormac drops out of college to join the United States Air Force where he is stationed in Alaska for two of the four years he serves. He also hosts a radio show while in Alaska.
1957	Cormac returns to the University of Tennessee and publishes two short stories in the student literary magazine, *The Phoenix*: "A Wake for Susan" and "A Drowning Incident." He publishes under the name C. J. McCarthy Jr.
1959	McCarthy wins the Ingram-Merrill Award for Creative Writing.
1960	McCarthy drops out of college once more and moves to Chicago. He works as an auto mechanic while writing his first novel. He changes his name from Charles to Cormac to avoid being confused with Edgar Bergen's dummy "Charlie McCarthy." It is also said he chose Cormac because of the ancient Gaelic king.
1961	He marries Lee Holleman. They reside in a shack in Knoxville, Tennessee, located right outside the Smoky Mountains.
1962	McCarthy and Holleman have a son, Cullen. McCarthy asks his wife to care for the baby while he gets another job. She moves to Wyoming, files for divorce, and becomes a teacher.
1965	McCarthy receives a fellowship from the American Academy of Arts and Letters and travels on the Sylvania to Blarney Castle, built by King Cormac McCarthy. *The Orchard Keeper* is published by Random House.

1966	McCarthy wins the William Faulkner Foundation Award for notable first novel. McCarthy marries English singer/dancer, Anne DeLisle, in England. The couple tour southern England, Switzerland, France, Italy, and Spain. McCarthy and Anne briefly settle in Ibiza. McCarthy receives a grant from the Rockefeller Foundation (1966–1968).
1967	The McCarthys return to America and rent a home in Rockford, Tennessee. McCarthy's parents, Charles McCarthy and Gladys McGrail McCarthy, relocate to Washington DC.
1968	*Outer Dark* is published by Random House.
1969	McCarthy receives the Guggenheim Fellowship for Creative Writing. McCarthy and Anne move into a barn in Louisville, Tennessee. McCarthy renovates the barn, doing stonework himself and using bricks from James Agee's childhood home to construct his fireplace.
1973	*Child of God* is published.
1974	McCarthy begins writing *The Gardener's Son: A Screenplay* for PBS. McCarthy travels with Richard Pearce for a year to research industrialization in the South.
1976	Anne DeLisle and Cormac McCarthy separate. McCarthy moves to El Paso, Texas.
1977	*The Gardener's Son: A Screenplay* premieres, directed by Richard Pearce. The episode, *Visions*, is nominated for two primetime Emmy awards.

1979	*Suttree* (semi-autobiographical) is published.
1981	McCarthy is awarded a $236,000 MacArthur Fellowship ("Genius Grant"). He travels Southwest. DeLisle and McCarthy divorce.
1984	He begins work at the Sante Fe Institute after the encouragement of friend and founder Murray Gell-Mann.
1985	*Blood Meridian* is published.
1987	Albert Erskine, McCarthy's editor at Random House, retires. McCarthy moves to Alfred A. Knopf, and a new editor, Gary Fisketjon. He relocates to Tesuque, New Mexico.
1992	McCarthy has his first interview ever with *The New York Times Magazine*. *All the Pretty Horses* is published. He wins the National Book Award and the National Critics Circle Award. McCarthy buys a new pickup truck with his award money.
1994	*The Stonemason* is published. (Play) *The Crossing* is published.
1995	*The Stonemason* is performed.
1996	*The Gardener's Son: A Screenplay* is published (Ecco Press).
1997	McCarthy marries Jennifer Winkley.

1998	*Cities of the Plain* is published.
1999	John Francis McCarthy is born to Cormac and Jennifer.
2003	Harold Bloom's influential *The Western Canon* names McCarthy's *Child of God, Suttree*, and *Blood Meridian* as three works that would endure as canonical. Bloom calls the latter novel "the greatest single book since Faulkner's *As I Lay Dying*." He also names McCarthy as one of the four best living writers in English.
2005	*No Country for Old Men* is published.
2006	*The Road* is published. *The Sunset Limited: A Novel in Dramatic Form* is published, premiering in May. (Play) Winkley and McCarthy divorce.
2007	*No Country for Old Men* is adapted into a film, directed by Coen Bros. (2007); Paramount (2008). McCarthy is awarded the Pulitzer Prize for *The Road*. Among other honors this year, McCarthy is awarded the James Tate Black Memorial Prize. McCarthy attends his first television interview on *The Oprah Winfrey Show* in June.
2009	*The Road* is adapted into a film, directed by John Hillcoat (2009); 2929 Entertainment (2010). The now-vacant McCarthy family home on Martin Mill Pike burns down.
2011	*The Sunset Limited: A Novel in Dramatic Form* is adapted into a screenplay for a film, directed by Tommy Lee Jones (2011); HBO Films (2012).
2013	McCarthy sells his screenplay, *The Counselor*, and it is adapted into a film.

2015	McCarthy announces drafting for a new novel, *The Passenger,* at multimedia events in Santa Fe.
2016	Helen Jacquelyn ("Jackie") McCarthy Hickey passes away.
2017	McCarthy publishes "The Kekule Problem."
2022	*The Passenger* is published. *Stella Maris* is published.
2023	Cormac McCarthy dies on June 13, 2023, at his home in Santa Fe, New Mexico.

Works by Cormac McCarthy

Fiction

"Wake for Susan." *The Phoenix* 1959.

"A Drowning Incident." *The Phoenix* 1960.

The Orchard Keeper. Random House 1965.

Outer Dark. Random House 1968.

Child of God. Random House 1973.

Suttree. Random House 1979.

Blood Meridian. Random House 1985.

All the Pretty Horses. Knopf 1992.

The Crossing. Knopf 1994.

Cities of the Plain. Knopf 1998.

No Country for Old Men. Knopf 2005.

The Road. Knopf 2006.

The Passenger. Knopf 2022.

Stella Maris. Knopf 2022.

Drama

The Stonemason: A Play in Five Acts. Ecco Press 1994.

The Sunset Limited: A Novel in Dramatic Form. Dramatists Play Service Inc. 2006.

Nonfiction

"The Kekulé Problem." *Nautilus*, 2017.

"Cormac McCarthy Returns to the Kekulé Problem." *Nautilus*, 2017.

Screenplays (published)

The Gardener's Son: A Screenplay. Ecco Press 1996.

The Counselor: A Screenplay. Knopf Doubleday Publishing Group 2013.

No Country for Old Men (movie). Dir. Coen Brothers. 2007. Paramount, 2008.

The Road (movie). Dir. John Hillcoat. 2009. 2929 Entertainment, 2010.

Sunset Limited (movie). Dir. Tommy Lee Jones. 2011. HBO Films, 2012.

Screenplays (unpublished)

Whales and Men. ca.1982.

Cities of the Plain. 1984.

No Country for Old Men (original screenplay draft). 1984.

Bibliography

"About the Cormac McCarthy Society." The Official Web Site of the Cormac McCarthy Society, www.cormacmccarthy.com/about-the-society/.

Arnold, Edwin T. "Review: The Achievement of Cormac McCarthy." *Appalachian Journal*, vol. 16, no. 3, 1989, pp. 262–64.

__________. "The American Western and the Postmodern: Cormac McCarthy's *All the Pretty Horses*." *Studies in American Fiction*, vol. 24, no. 2, 1996, pp. 211–21.

__________. "McCarthy's *All the Pretty Horses*." *Explicator*, vol. 54, no. 3, 1996, pp. 169–71.

__________, and Dianne C. Luce. *Perspectives on Cormac McCarthy*. UP of Mississippi, 1999.

Bell, Madison Smartt. "The Man Who Understood Horses." Review of *All the Pretty Horses* by Cormac McCarthy. *The New York Times*, 17 May 1992, p. 9, www.nytimes.com/1992/05/17/books/all-the-pretty-horses.html.

Bell, Vereen M. *The Achievement of Cormac McCarthy*. Louisiana State UP, 1988.

Benson, Josef. "A Hero by Default: John Grady Cole as Hypermasculine Heroic Failure in *All the Pretty Horses*." *Hypermasculinities in the Contemporary Novel: Cormac McCarthy, Toni Morrison, and James Baldwin*. Lanham, 2014, pp. 25–54.

Berry, Allen. "The Cross-Border Relationship Pastiche in Cormac McCarthy's *All the Pretty Horses*." *Journal of the American Studies Association of Texas*, Nov. 2014, pp. 27–40.

Blair, John. "Mexico and the Borderlands in Cormac McCarthy's *All the Pretty Horses*." *Critique: Studies in Contemporary Fiction*, vol. 42, no. 3, 2001, pp. 301–07.

Bloom, Harold, editor. *Cormac McCarthy's All the Pretty Horses*. Chelsea House Publishers, 2000.

__________, editor. *Bloom's Modern Critical Views Cormac McCarthy*. Infobase Publishing, 2009.

Brewton, Vince. "The Changing Landscape of Violence in Cormac McCarthy's Early Novels and the *Border Trilogy*." *The Southern Literary Journal*, vol. 37, no. 1, 2004, pp. 121–43. *JSTOR*, www.jstor.org/stable/20078400.

Burnett, John. "After 16 Years, Author Cormac McCarthy Gifts Two New Novels to Readers." *NPR*, 22 Oct. 2022, www.wfae.org/2022-10-22/after-16-years-author-cormac-mccarthy-gifts-two-new-novels-to-readers.

Caldwell, Gail. "Cormac McCarthy's High Frontier: The Novelist's Unmistakable Voice Brings Majesty to the Badlands: [City Edition]." *The Boston Globe*, 3 May 1992, p. B41.

Campbell, Neil. *The Cultures of the American New West*. Fitzroy Dearborn, 2000.

Cooper, Lydia R. *Cormac McCarthy: A Complexity Theory of Literature*. Manchester UP, 2021. *EBSCOhost,* search.ebscohost.com/login.aspx?direct=true&db=mlf&AN=202122515163&site=eds-live.

"Cormac McCarthy on Writing." *Oprah.com*, www.oprah.com/oprahsbookclub/cormac mccarthy-on-writing.

Cremean, David N. "On Cormac McCarthy." *Cormac McCarthy*. Edited by David N. Cremean, Salem Press, 2012, pp. 3–17.

Crews, Michael Lynn. "The Crossing." *Books Are Made Out of Books: A Guide to Cormac McCarthy's Literary Influences*, U of Texas P, 2017, pp. 232–35. *JSTOR*, www.jstor.org/stable/10.7560/313480.13.

Cronon, William. "The Trouble with Wilderness, or, Getting Back to the Wrong Nature." *Uncommon Ground: Toward Reinventing Nature*. Edited by William Cronon. Norton, 1995, pp. 69–90.

__________, et al. *Under an Open Sky: Rethinking America's Western Past*. W. W. Norton, 1992.

Cutchins, Dennis. "All the Pretty Horses: Cormac McCarthy's Reading of 'For Whom the Bell Tolls.'" *Western American Literature*, vol. 41, no. 3, 2006, pp. 266–99. *JSTOR*, jstor.org/stable/43022482.

Doyle, Martin. "The 100 Best Novels in English? Irish Writers and Critics Have Their Say." *The Irish Times*, 20 Aug. 2015, www.irishtimes.com/culture/books/the-100-best-novels-in-english-irish-writers-and-critics-have-their-say-1.2322884.

Dudley, John. "McCarthy's Heroes: Revisiting Masculinity." *The Cambridge Companion to Cormac McCarthy*. Edited by Steven Frye. Cambridge UP, pp. 175–88.

Duvall, John N. "The End of the Frontier: History, Myth, and Memory in Cormac McCarthy's *Border Trilogy*." *Arizona Quarterly: A Journal of American Literature, Culture, and Theory*, vol. 60, no. 2, 2004, pp. 109–34.

Dyer, Geoff. "Books: *All the Pretty Horses* by Cormac McCarthy." *The Guardian,* 6 Apr. 1993.

Eckstein, Lars. "Cowboys, Literature, and the 'Crimes' of the Frontier: The Case of Cormac McCarthy." *Western American Literature,* vol. 46, no. 4, 2012, pp. 382–97.

Eder, Richard. "John's Passion: *All the Pretty Horses*." *Los Angeles Times*, 17 May 1992, p. 3, www.latimes.com/archives/la-xpm-1992-05-17-bk-562-story.html.

Ellis, Jay. *No Place for Home: Spatial Constraint and Character Flight in the Novels of Cormac McCarthy.* Routledge, 2006.

Estes, Andrew Keller. *Cormac McCarthy and the Writing of American Spaces*. Rodopi, 2013.

Fehrenbach, T. R. *Fire and Blood: A History of Mexico*. Macmillan, 1973.

Feldman, James. *A Storied Wilderness*. U of Washington P, 2011.

Foote, Jennifer. "Trying to Take Back the Planet." *Newsweek*, 5 Feb. 1990, pp. 24–25.

Frye, Steven. *Understanding Cormac McCarthy*. The U of South Carolina P, 2009.

__________, editor. *The Cambridge Companion to Cormac McCarthy*. Cambridge UP, 2013.

Giemza, Bryan. "Cormac McCarthy, An Irish Southerner Among the Heresiarchs." *Irish Catholic Writers and the Invention of the American South*. Louisiana State UP, 2013.

Greenwood, Willard P. *Reading Cormac McCarthy.* Greenwood P, 2009.

Guillemin, George. "As of Some Site Where Life Had Not Succeeded: Sorrow, Allegory, and Pastoralism in Cormac McCarthy's *Border Trilogy*." *A Cormac McCarthy Companion:* The *Border Trilogy*.

Edited by Edwin T. Arnold and Dianne C. Luce. UP of Mississippi, 2001, pp. 92–130.

Hage, Erik. *Cormac McCarthy A Literary Companion.* McFarland, 2010.

Hall, Wade, and Rick Wallach. *Sacred Violence: A Reader's Companion to Cormac McCarthy: Selected Essays from the First McCarthy Conference, Bellarmine College, Louisville, Kentucky, October 15–17, 1993.* U of Texas at El Paso, 1995.

Hamilton, Patrick L. "Recuperation and Re-Imagination: Frontier Space in Cormac McCarthy's 'All the Pretty Horses' and Alfredo Véa's 'The Silver Cloud Café.'" *Interdisciplinary Literary Studies*, vol. 9, no. 2, 2008, pp. 29–44. *JSTOR*, jstor.org/stable/41210293.

Heinen, Tom. *Cormac McCarthy: A Western Perspective.* U of New Mexico P, 2001.

Herlihy-Mera, Jeffrey. "Mojado-Reverso" or, A Reverse Wetback: On John Grady Cole's Mexican Ancestry in Cormac McCarthy's *All the Pretty Horses*. *Modern Fiction Studies*, vol. 61, no. 1, pp. 469–92.

Hillier, Russel M. *Morality in Cormac McCarthy's Fiction: Souls at Hazard.* Palgrave Macmillan, 2017.

Hoberek, Andrew. "Cormac McCarthy and the Aesthetics of Exhaustion." *American Literary History*, vol. 23, no. 3, 2011, pp. 483–99.

Holloway, David. "Modernism, Nature, and Utopia: Another Look at 'Optical Democracy' in Cormac McCarthy's Western Quartet." *Southern Quarterly*, vol. 38, no. 3, Spring 2000, pp. 186–205.

Jarrett, Robert L. "The *Border Trilogy*: Individualism, History, and Cultural Crossings." Edited by Frank Day. Twayne, 1997.

__________. *Cormac McCarthy*. Twayne, 1997.

Jones, Jr., M. "Literary Lion in the Desert." *Newsweek*, vol. 119, no. 20, 18 May 1992, p. 68, www.newsweek.com/literary-lion-desert-199164.

Kimmel, Michael S. *The History of Men: Essays in the History of American and British Masculinities*. State U of New York P, 2005.

King, Meg. "'Where Is Your Country?': Locating White Masculinity in *All the Pretty Horses*." *The Cormac McCarthy Journal*, vol. 12, 2014, pp. 69–88. *JSTOR*, www.jstor.org/stable/10.5325/cormmccaj.12.69.

Klyza, Christopher McGrory, editor. *Wilderness Comes Home: Rewilding the Northeast.* UP of New England, 2001.

Kreml, Nancy. "Stylistic Variation and Cognitive Constraint in *All the Pretty Horses.*" *Sacred Violence: Cormac McCarthy's Western Novels*. Edited by Wade Hall and Rich Wallach, vol. 2, Texas Western P, 2002, pp. 37–49.

Ladino, Jennifer K. *Reclaiming Nostalgia: Longing for Nature in American Literature*. U of Virginia P, 2012.

LeCompte, Mary Lu. "The First American Rodeo Never Happened." *Journal of Sports History,* vol. 9, no. 2, 1982, pp. 89–96.

Lilley, James D. *Cormac McCarthy: New Directions*. U of New Mexico P, 2002.

Lilley, James D. "Of Whales and Men: The Dynamics of Cormac McCarthy's Environmental Imagination." *The Southern Quarterly: A Journal of the Arts in the South*, vol. 38, no. 2, 2000, pp. 111–22. EBSCOhost, search.ebscohost.com/login.aspx?direct=true&db=mlf&AN=2001530052&site=eds-live.

Lincoln, Kenneth. *Cormac McCarthy American Canticles.* Palgrave Macmillan, 2009.

Luce, Dianne C. *Embracing Vocation: Cormac McCarthy's Writing Life, 1959–1974*. U South Carolina P, 2023.

__________. "Remarks on the State of Cormac McCarthy Scholarship." *The Cormac McCarthy Journal*, vol. 1, no. 1, 2001, pp. 7–11.

__________. *Reading the World: Cormac McCarthy's Tennessee Period.* U of South Carolina P, 2009.

__________, and Zachary Turpin. "Cormac McCarthy Interviews in Tennessee and Kentucky, 1968–1980." *The Cormac McCarthy Journal*, vol. 20, no. 2, 2022, pp. 108–35.

Mayne, Natasha. "As Far as the Eye Could See: Cormac McCarthy, Myth and Masculine Visions in the 'New' American West." *Australasian Journal of American Studies*, vol. 20, no. 2, 2001, pp. 1–12. *JSTOR*, www.jstor.org/stable/41053864.

McCarthy, Cormac. *All the Pretty Horses.* Vintage, 1992.

__________. *Blood Meridian*. Random House, 1985.

__________. *Cities of the Plain*. Knopf Doubleday, 1998.

__________. *Child of God*. Random House, 1973.

__________. "Cormac Country." Interview by Richard B. Woodward. *Vanity Fair,* 1 Aug. 2005, www.vanityfair.com/culture/2005/08/cormac-mccarthy-interview.

__________. *The Crossing*. Alfred A. Knopf, 1994.

__________. "Interview with Cormac McCarthy" Interview by Oprah Winfrey. The Oprah Winfrey Show, 5 June 2007.

__________. *No Country for Old Men*, Knopf Doubleday, 2005.

__________. *The Orchard Keeper*. Random House, 1965.

__________. *Outer Dark*. Random House, 1974.

__________. *The Passenger*. Knopf Doubleday, 2022.

__________. "Rare Thoughts on Writing from Cormac McCarthy in This Unlikely Interview." Interview by Murray Carpenter. *Literary Hub*, 15 Mar. 2022, lithub.com/rare-thoughts-on-writing-from-cormac-mccarthy-in-this-unlikely-interview/.

__________. *The Road*. Knopf Doubleday, 2006.

__________. *Stella Maris*, Knopf Doubleday, 2022.

__________. *Suttree*. Random House, 1979.

McCrum, Robert. "The 100 Best Novels Written in English: The Full List." *The Guardian*, 17 Aug. 2015, www.theguardian.com/books/2015/aug/17/the-100-best-novels-written-in-english-the-full-list.

McGilchrist, Megan Riley. *The Western Landscape in Cormac McCarthy and Wallace Stegner: Myths of the Frontier*. Routledge, 2010.

McPhee, John. *Basin and Range* (*Annals of the Former World*). Farrar, Straus and Giroux, 2000, pp. 25–143.

Mitchell, Lee Clark. "A Man Being Beaten." *Westerns: Making the Man in Fiction and Film*. U of Chicago P, 1996, pp. 150–87.

Mitgang, Herbert. "Books of the Times; Boys on Horseback, Loose in Mexico." *The New York Times*, 27 May 1992, p. 18, www.nytimes.com/1992/05/27/books/books-of-the-times boys-on-horseback-loose-in-mexico.html.

Monk, Nicholas. "*All the Pretty Horses*, the Border, and Ethnic Encounter." *The Cambridge Companion to Cormac McCarthy*. Edited by Steven Frye, Cambridge UP, 2013, pp. 121–32.

Morrison, Gail Moore. "*All the Pretty Horses*: John Grady Cole's Expulsion from Paradise." *Perspectives on Cormac McCarthy.* Edited by Edwin T. Arnold and Dianne C. Luce. UP of Mississippi, 1999, pp. 175–94.

Morton, Adam David. "The Warp of the World: Geographies of Space and Time in the *Border Trilogy* by Cormac McCarthy." *Environment and Planning: D. Society and Space*, vol. 33, no. 5, Oct. 2015, pp. 831–49.

Nash, Roderick Frazier. *Wilderness and the American Mind.* 4th edition, Yale UP, 2001.

Pearce, Richard. *Cormac McCarthy: American Canticles.* Continuum, 2009.

Pilkington, Tom. "Fate and Free Will on the American Frontier: Cormac McCarthy's Western Fiction." *Western American Literature*, vol. 27, no. 4, 1993, pp. 311–22. *JSTOR*, www.jstor.org/stable/43021039.

Priola, Marty. "Review of *All the Pretty Horses*, the film." Directed by Billy Bob Thornton. *The Cormac McCarthy Journal*, vol. 1, no. 1, 2001, pp. 69–71.

Raigadas, David Rio. "Cormac McCarthy's Borderlands: A Challenge to a Mythic Construct of the American West." *ES*, no.25, 2003–04, pp. 193–202, 1library.co/document/4yrg138q-cormac-mccarthy-borderlands-challenge-mythic-construct-american-west.html.

Reimer, Jennifer. "All the Pretty Mexican Girls: Whiteness and Racial Desire in Cormac McCarthy's *All the Pretty Horses* and *Cities of the Plain*." *Western American Literature*, vol. 48, no. 4, winter 2014, pp. 422–42.

Russo, John Paul. *The Future without a Past: The Humanities in a Technological Society.* U of Missouri P, 2005.

Scoones, Jacqueline. "The World on Fire: Ethics and Evolution in Cormac McCarthy's *Border Trilogy*." *Southern Quarterly*, vol. 38, no. 3, Spring 2000, p. 99. EBSCOhost, search.ebscohost.com/login.aspx?direct=true&db=hlh&AN=9984693&site=eds-live.

Shaw, Patrick W. "Female Presence, Male Violence, and the Art of Artlessness in the *Border Trilogy*." *Myth, Legend, Dust: Critical Responses to Cormac McCarthy*. Edited by Rick Wallach, Manchester UP, 2000.

Slotkin, Richard. *Gunfighter Nation: The Myth of the Frontier in Twentieth-Century America*. Macmillan, 1992.

__________. *Regeneration Through Violence: The Mythology of the American Frontier, 1600–1860.* 1st edition, Wesleyan UP, 1973.

Smith, Henry Nash. *Virgin Land: The American West as Symbol and Myth.* Harvard UP, 1950.

Snyder, Phillip A., and Delys W. Snyder. "Modernism, Postmodernism, and Language: McCarthy's Style." *The Cambridge Companion to Cormac McCarthy*. Edited by Steven Frye. Cambridge UP, 2013, pp. 7–40.

Spurgeon, Sara L. "'Pledged in Blood': Truth and Redemption in Cormac McCarthy's 'All the Pretty Horses.'" *Western American Literature*, vol. 34, no. 1, 1999, pp. 24–44. *JSTOR*, jstor.org/stable/43024973.

Stegner, Wallace. *The American West as Living Space*. The U of Michigan P, 1987.

Sugg, Katherine. "Multicultural Masculinities and the Border Romance in John Sayles's Lone Star and Cormac McCarthy's Border Trilogy." *CR: The New Centennial Review*, vol. 1, no. 3, 2001, pp. 117–54. *JSTOR*, www.jstor.org/stable/41949296.

Tatum, Stephen. *Cormac McCarthy's* All the Pretty Horses*: A Reader's Guide*. Continuum Contemporaries, 2002.

"Texas State Acquires McCarthy Archives." *Daily Freeman*. 24 Jan. 2008, www.dailyfreeman.com/2008/01/24/texas-state-acquires-mccarthy-archives/.

Tompkins, Jane P. *West of Everything: The Inner Life of Westerns.* Oxford UP, 1992.

__________. "Women and the Language of Men." *West of Everything: The Inner Life of Westerns*. Oxford UP, 1992, pp. 47–67.

Tracy, Kathleen. Imus: *America's Cowboy*. Carroll and Graf, 1999.

Turner, Frederick Jackson. "The Significance of the Frontier in American History." *The Frontier in American History.* 1893/1920. *Project Gutenberg,* gutenberg.org/files/22994/22994-h/22994-h.htm.

Vieth, Ronja. "Cormac McCarthy's Critical Reception." *Critical Insights: Cormac McCarthy*. Edited by David N. Cremean. Salem Press, 2012.

Wallach, Rick. "Don Imus, RIP." The Official Web Site of the Cormac McCarthy Society. 27 Dec. 2019, www.cormacmccarthy.com/topic/don-imus-rip/.

__________. "Cormac McCarthy's *All the Pretty Horses*: A Reader's Guide by Stephen Tatum." *The Cormac McCarthy Journal*, vol. 2, no. 1, 2002, pp. 61–63.

Wegner, John. "Editor's Page." *The Cormac McCarthy Journal*, vol. 1, no. 1, 2001, pp. 4–6.

White, Christopher T. "Dreaming the *Border Trilogy*: Cormac McCarthy and Narrative Creativity." *The Cormac McCarthy Journal*, vol. 13, no. 1, Sept. 2015, pp. 121–42. EBSCOhost, doi-org.ezproxy.ferrum.edu/10.5325/cormmccaj.13.1.0121.

White, Richard. "*It's Your Misfortune and None of My Own*": *A History of the American West*. U of Oklahoma P, 1991.

Woodson, Linda. "McCarthy's Heroes and the Will to Truth." *The Cambridge Companion to Cormac McCarthy*. Edited by Steven Frye. Cambridge UP, pp. 15–26.

__________. "'This Is Another Country': The Complex Feminine Presence in *All the Pretty Horses*." *Cormac McCarthy: All the Pretty Horses, No Country for Old Men, The Road.* Edited by Sara L. Spurgeon, Continuum, 2011, pp. 25–42.

Woodward, Richard B. "Cormac McCarthy's Venomous Fiction." *The New York Times Magazine*, 19 Apr. 1992, www.nytimes.com/1992/04/19/magazine/cormac-mccarthy-s-venomous-fiction.html.

__________. "'Whatever I was going to be I wanted to be really good' Cormac McCarthy's Life in Writing." *The Guardian*, 22 Oct. 2022, theguardian.com/books/2022/oct/22/cormac-mccarthy-life-in-writing-books-the- passenger.

Woolmer, J. Howard "Woolmer to McCarthy." 24 Mar. 1994, Texas State University, Woolmer Collection of Cormac McCarthy 1969–2006, www.thewittliffcollections.txst.edu/research/a-z/woolmer.html.

Worster, Donald. *Under Western Skies: Nature and History in the American West*. Oxford UP, 1994.

Worthington, Leslie Harper. *Cormac McCarthy and the Ghost of Huck Finn*. McFarland, 2012.

Zenowich, Christopher. "Coming of Age." *Chicago Tribune*, 10 May 1992, www.chicagotribune.com/news/ct-xpm-1992-05-10-9202110419-story.html.

About the Editors

Laura Nicosia, PhD, earned her doctorate at New York University and is Professor of English at Montclair State University, New Jersey, where she teaches American literature, Young Adult literature, and genre literatures. She is a New Jersey Council for the Humanities Public Scholar, serves as the New Jersey State Ambassador to the Assembly on Literature of Adolescents and is the author of *Educators Online: Preparing Today's Educators for Tomorrow's Digital Literacies.* She and her husband, James F. Nicosia, have co-edited six collections for Salem/Grey House: *Digital Literacy: Skills & Strategies*; *Critical Insights: Catch-22*; *Notable Writers of the American West & the Native American Experience*; *Notable American Women Writers*, vols. 1 & 2; *Critical Insights: John Steinbeck's* The Pearl; and *Critical Insights: Virginia Woolf.* The duo has also co-edited *Examining Images of Urban Life: Resources for Teachers of Young Adult Literature* (Myers Education Press). Nicosia has also co-edited *Through a Distorted Lens: Media as Curricula and Pedagogy in the 21st Century* (Sense).

James F. Nicosia, PhD, earned his doctorate at New York University, where he worked with Harold Bloom on his studies of Poet Laureate Mark Strand. Bloom would later write the introduction to Nicosia's book, *Reading Mark Strand* (Palgrave Macmillan). Nicosia teaches children's literature, Young Adult Literature, Grammars of English, varied courses in the Honors Program, and all periods of American literature at Montclair State University in New Jersey. He is a children's literacy advocate and has reviewed works for various national publications; he also publishes the BoyBookoftheMonth.com website for reluctant readers. He regularly speaks to teachers and young readers about invigorating their reading lives. His latest work includes editing, with his son, Jake D. Nicosia, *Principles of Forestry & Conservation* and the upcoming *Principles of Probability & Statistics*, both with Salem Press.

Contributors

Aaron A. Cloyd is an associate professor at the University of Jamestown (North Dakota). His scholarship and teaching engage with images and interpretations of wilderness in contemporary literature. His work has been published in *Geoforum, disClosure*, *International Journal of Comic Art*, and *Journal of the Fantastic in the Arts*.

Stephen Daly received a master's degree in twentieth-century literature from the University of Edinburgh and is currently a PhD candidate at the Chinese University of Hong Kong. His research interests include nineteen and twentieth-century American literature, the gothic and modernism, but he is also interested in the intersection between visual and literary art forms.

Sakti Sekhar Dash is a fellow of the Social Science Research Council (SSRC), Open Association of Research Society, USA. He holds a PhD from Ravenshaw University, India. With a profound interest in literature, history, and culture, he has extensively studied the myths, legends, and folklore of ancient Greece, Egypt, Rome, and India. As a researcher he loves to revisit and re-examine ancient texts from multiple perspectives. An experienced educator and honorary member of the Illinois Medieval Association, he has served as the editor in chief of its international peer-reviewed journal. He has extensively written and published on a diverse range of topics, including, modernism, Greek drama, environmental studies, Theatre of the Absurd, and Shakespearean drama.

Seth Forrest is a professor at Coppin State University, a small HBCU in Baltimore. He received his PhD from the University of California, Davis, studying poetry and poetics, American literature, and ecological literary theory. His primary area of academic expertise is poetry and poetics, and he has written on McCarthy, as well as on poetic and literary style, often in connection with environmental and ecological literary studies.

Elissa Greenwald, PhD has taught literature at the high school and college levels. She has written a book, *Realism and the Romance: Hawthorne, Henry James, and American Fiction* (UMI Press, 1989), and articles on Woolf, Heller, Adrienne Rich, and other English and American writers. She reviews books for the *New York Journal of Books* and teaches adults through the Open University of Wellfleet (Cape Cod).

Allison Harl serves as associate professor of English at Ferrum College where she teaches American literature surveys, Literature and Film of the American Frontier, and Literature and the Environment. Her master's thesis (1997) focused on language theory in Cormac McCarthy's early novels, and her doctoral dissertation (2008) on American frontier literature. Dr. Harl has presented at conferences all over the country and has published in journals, book collections, as well as high school and college textbooks.

Melinda Knight is professor of English and the founding director of the Center for Writing Excellence at Montclair State University. She teaches undergraduate and graduate courses on nineteenth- and twentieth-century American literature, with a focus on realism and naturalism, African American writers, the Lost Generation, and the Harlem Renaissance. She earned a PhD in American civilization at New York University, and her research interests include the intersections of class, gender, identity, and race in American culture. Recent publications include articles on Willa Cather, Joseph Heller, John Steinbeck, and Edith Wharton. She was the Principal Investigator for a year-long project funded by the National Endowment for the Humanities entitled "Rediscovering American Democracy: Teaching the Humanities in the Time of COVID."

Amy Leshinsky received her EdD from Northeastern University, where she wrote her dissertation on the experiences of secondary English distance educators using Intelligent Agents to target student engagement in asynchronous classrooms. During the height of the pandemic in 2020, Leshinsky provided professional development to school districts on best practices in distance education. She received an MA in English from Boston College and an MAT from Tufts University. She has been a guest lecturer on human rights violations in literature at many universities including Notre Dame and the University of Connecticut, Storrs. Her work has been published in various books, newspapers, and journals. Leshinsky spent nearly 20 years teaching English and is currently an assistant professor of education at Curry College.

Rosa Parker is a PhD researcher, seminar leader at the University of Southampton, and a private tutor for students with SEN in English. Her research focuses on the impact of film on 1930s–40s literature, reflected in her current thesis: "Of Novel and Noir: 1920s German Expressionism and Constructions of Los Angeles in Film and Literature." Most recently, she spoke on the impact of production code on Wilder's *Double Indemnity* at the 2022 PAMLA conference.

J. Gavin Paul teaches English literature at Kwantlen Polytechnic University and at the University of British Columbia. He is the author of *Shakespeare and the Imprints of Performance* (Palgrave, 2014). His work on the intersections of editorial practice, textual theory, and performance history has appeared in *The Review of English Studies*, *Shakespeare: The Journal of the British Shakespeare Association*, *The Bulletin for the Society of Renaissance Studies*, *Comitatus*, *The Upstart Crow*, and *Literature Compass* (where he is the three-time winner of Blackwell Publishing's Essay Prize). He contributed numerous biographical entries to the *Encyclopedia of Comic Books and Graphic Novels* (Greenwood, 2010) and *Comics Through Time* (Greenwood, 2014).

Shubham Singh currently is an assistant professor of American literature at the Department of English and Modern European Languages, University of Allahabad. His doctoral research is rooted in contemporary American drama for which he participated in the Mellon School of Theater and Performance Research at Harvard University to share his work with the academic fraternity and to receive critical inputs. He has interests in trauma studies and postmodern literatures. Dr. Singh has contributed articles to reputed journals and anthologies and has been a resource person in several conferences and workshops.

Jericho Williams is an assistant professor of English at the University of Fairbanks, Alaska. He previously served as professor of English at Spartanburg Methodist College, South Carolina. His research interests include American literature, African American literature, and film. He has previously published articles in *The James Fenimore Cooper Society Journal, The New Centennial Review, Studies in American Naturalism, South Atlantic Review*, and *Supernatural Studies*.

Amanda Zastrow is a PhD candidate at Marquette University in Milwaukee, Wisconsin. Currently, she is studying the American West, specifically female pioneer narratives including the works of Laura Ingalls Wilder and Willa Cather. She is interested in the existence of a uniquely female pioneer narrative within a historically masculine genre.

Index